Economic Women

Economic Women

Essays on Desire and Dispossession in
Nineteenth-Century British Culture

EDITED BY

LANA L. DALLEY
AND **JILL RAPPOPORT**

THE OHIO STATE UNIVERSITY PRESS
COLUMBUS

Copyright © 2013 by The Ohio State University.
All rights reserved.

Library of Congress Cataloging-in-Publication Data
Economic women : essays on desire and dispossession in nineteenth-century British culture / Edited by Lana L. Dalley and Jill Rappoport.
    p. cm.
  Includes bibliographical references and index.
  ISBN-13: 978-0-8142-1236-3 (cloth : alk. paper)
  ISBN-10: 0-8142-1236-0 (cloth : alk. paper)
  ISBN-13: 978-0-8142-9338-6 (cd-rom)
  ISBN-10: 0-8142-9338-7 (cd-rom)
 1. English fiction—19th century—History and criticism. 2. Women and literature—Great Britain—History—19th century. 3. Women—Great Britain—Economic conditions—19th century. 4. Women in literature. 5. Economics in literature. I. Dalley, Lana L. II. Rappoport, Jill.
  PR868.W6E27 2013
  823'.8093522—dc23
                        2013023713

Cover design by Mary Ann Smith
Text design by Juliet Williams
Type set in Adobe Granjon

∞ The paper used in this publication meets the minimum requirements of the American National Standard for Information Sciences—Permanence of Paper for Printed Library Materials. ANSI Z39.48–1992.

9 8 7 6 5 4 3 2 1

CONTENTS

List of Illustrations vii

Acknowledgments ix

Introducing Economic Women
LANA L. DALLEY AND JILL RAPPOPORT 1

PART I • THE ETHICS OF EXCHANGE

1 Gentry, Gender, and the Moral Economy during the Revolutionary and Napoleonic Wars in Provincial England
   KATHRYN GLEADLE 25

2 Women, Free Trade, and Harriet Martineau's *Dawn Island* at the 1845 Anti-Corn Law League Bazaar
   LESLEE THORNE-MURPHY 41

3 Sacrificial Value: Beyond the Cash Nexus in George Eliot's *Romola*
   ILANA M. BLUMBERG 60

PART II • POLITICAL ECONOMY

4 Florence Nightingale's Contributions to Economics
   MARY POOVEY 77

5 The Cost of Everything in *Middlemarch*
   GORDON BIGELOW 97

6 Demand and Desire in *Dracula*
   DEANNA K. KREISEL 110

CONTENTS

PART III · FINANCING THE FAMILY

7 "A *pauper* every wife is": Lady Westmeath, Money, Marriage, and Divorce in Early Nineteenth-Century England
   JANETTE RUTTERFORD   127

8 Marriage, Celibacy, or Emigration? Debating the Costs of Family Life in Mid-Victorian England
   ERIKA RAPPAPORT   143

9 "Absolutely Miss Fairlie's own": Emasculating Economics in *The Woman in White*
   ESTHER GODFREY   162

PART IV · WOMEN'S BUSINESS

10 "She'd give her two ears to know": The Gossip Economy in Ellen Wood's *St. Martin's Eve*
    TARA MacDONALD   179

11 Charlotte Riddell: Novelist of "the City"
    NANCY HENRY   193

12 A "Formidable" Business: British Women Travelers in the Colonial Medical Market
    NARIN HASSAN   206

Afterword — and Forward
Economic Women in Their Time, Our Time, and the Future
    REGENIA GAGNIER   219

Contributors   225
Index   229

ILLUSTRATIONS

FIGURE 2.1	Free Trade Bazaar at Covent Garden Theater	42
FIGURE 2.2	Stall at the Free Trade Bazaar	44
FIGURE 2.3	The Leeds stall, using the space of a theater box, with a table set up below	47
FIGURE 2.4	The frontispiece of *Dawn Island,* drawn and etched by J. Stephenson	53
FIGURE 4.1	Nightingale's Diagram of the Causes of Mortality in the Army of the East. *Left*: April 1855–March 1856. *Right*: April 1854–March 1855.	80
FIGURE 4.2	Nightingale's Diagrams of the Mortality in the Army of the East. *Left*: April 1855–March 1856. *Right*: April 1 1854–March 1855.	81

ACKNOWLEDGMENTS

The scholars who contributed their work to this volume did so long before we could guarantee publication; we thank them for their enthusiasm, their generosity, and their patience. Sandy Crooms at The Ohio State University Press supported the project when it was still in its infancy, and we are very grateful to have had her encouragement throughout the process. We also thank the (then anonymous) reviewers from The Ohio State University Press, Claudia Klaver and Talia Schaffer, who offered such valuable advice at a critical stage of the work, and Michael Genovese, Sarah Hagelin, and Ellen Malenas Ledoux, whose sharp eyes and keen insights improved the volume as well.

We are grateful for support from the University of Kentucky, California State University, Fullerton, and Villanova University; research assistance from Benjamin Raymond, Afton Woodward, Lauren Bailey, and Andrea Holliger; and additional help from Cindy Brightenburg at Brigham Young University's Harold B. Lee Library and Florence Gillich at Yale University's Cushing and Whitney Medical Historical Library.

ACKNOWLEDGMENTS

FROM L. D.:

I'd like to thank Jill for what began as a brief chat over coffee at NAVSA but developed into a lovely friendship and a productive collaboration. My portion of this volume is dedicated to my mom, Lannette Huelson, who provided my earliest and finest lessons on what it means to be an economic woman; my three children—Elijah Grey, Finley Sofia, and Sawyer August—who fill every day (even the long ones) with laughter and with joy; and, of course, to Tristan, whose patience, generosity, and love are assets of immeasurable value.

FROM J. R.:

With many thanks to Lana for the pleasure of collaboration, and to Mike for a partnership that exceeds words, I'd like to dedicate my portion of this volume to my parents, whose lives continue to teach me about the power of gifts and the purpose of exchange—Ann L. Rappoport and Paul Rappoport—in honor of the future that they've helped to shape for my children, Isaac Edward Genovese and Max Asher Genovese.

Introducing Economic Women

LANA L. DALLEY
AND JILL RAPPOPORT

*I*n Karl Marx's critique of capitalism, Robinson Crusoe is the prototype of "Homo Economicus."[1] King of his island, living (with the help of some scavenged English tools and materials) off of his own labor and that of Friday, Daniel Defoe's shipwrecked hero exemplifies the traits of prudence, production, and power that made him the model of economic individualism. Despite Marx's recognition that such extreme isolationism is a fantasy of fiction,[2] nineteenth- and even twentieth-century economic philosophers looked, like Defoe, for the new spaces of production and trade that would characterize Economic Man. But where, in this fiction, is Economic Woman? Marx, who considered the family's division of labor to be a "spontaneously developed system,"[3] didn't bother to look for her, and, for the most part, neither did his contemporaries. Although recent discussions of Economic Man by economists and cultural historians of the period have richly complicated his isolated productive stance, his analogue, Economic Woman, remains at best a liminal figure.

---

[1] "Capital," in *The Marx–Engels Reader,* ed. Robert C. Tucker (1978), 324–25.
[2] Jacques Derrida, *The Beast and the Sovereign,* vol. 2 (2011), 26.
[3] "Capital," 326.

By telling Economic Woman's story, this volume builds on the wealth of interdisciplinary economic criticism published in the last twenty years and also intervenes in its larger narratives of economic subjectivity and the prevailing behaviors that attend it. Crusoe's economic tale—from his rejection of a middling rank to his claims to sovereignty over a Caribbean island—ignores women almost entirely, and no corresponding female character has personified economic individualism within the popular imagination. Indeed, for much of the nineteenth century, "individualism" itself was a concept at odds with dominant notions of women's place within domestic ideology. Consigned to the "private" sphere by such conduct-book writers as Sarah Stickney Ellis and fiction writers as Charles Dickens, considered a "relative" creature whose aims were to serve her family rather than herself, she was an unlikely character to showcase the self-interest so crucial to political economy.[4] Even such economically significant efforts as her household management and reproduction were most frequently detached from the market and characterized as modes of service that privileged the needs of others over the individual economic agent. Writing the history of nineteenth-century Economic Woman requires new modes of conceptualization that take into account her carefully circumscribed socioeconomic position and the behavior it elicited; she cannot simply be modeled on Economic Man.

Whereas the familiar fiction of Economic Man posits "a conscious, knowing, unified, and rational subject,"[5] this volume argues that more wide-ranging popular representations of Economic Women throw both characters into question. Instead of seeking one solitary, self-serving figure to mirror Economic Man, we do better to recognize the complex and exciting set of economic options that were available to a diverse range of nineteenth-century mothers, daughters, wives, and "surplus" women during a period when many women were fighting for economic opportunities. The nineteenth century saw significant changes in economic thought and practice: production and then consumption replaced household management as the focus of economics, various forms of labor were increasingly professionalized and regulated, and consumer markets drastically expanded at home

---

[4] Of course, in practice women were entering the public sphere and, according to some scholars, even "feminizing" it through their participation. See, for example, Anne K. Mellor, *Mothers of the Nation* (2000).

[5] Susan Feiner, "A Portrait of *Homo Economicus*" (1999), 193. For more on women's relationship to Economic Man, see Anne Laurence, Josephine Maltby, and Janette Rutterford, eds., *Women and Their Money* (2009), 1–2; Edith Kniper and Jolande Sap, eds., *Out of the Margin* (1995); Marianne Ferber and Julie A. Nelson, eds., *Beyond Economic Man* (1983); and Catherine Gallagher, *The Body Economic* (2008), chapters 5 and 6.

and abroad. The real and fictional women discussed in this volume were part of this well-known economic trajectory, but they also challenged it and in some cases embodied the anxieties it produced. Our emphasis on gender suggests how, and with what social costs, the familiar story of Economic Man was written. It also allows us to recover and explore the lesser-known stories of Economic Women. These women were not simply marginalized by Economic Man. Nor did they achieve uniform liberation in the markets of Victorian Britain. In their various roles as domestic employees, middle-class women contemplating the costs of marriage, and upper-class ladies pursued for their wealth, the women discussed in the following essays were givers and takers, producers and consumers. Some staked out a share in colonial markets, while others negotiated investments and business back home. And, as we will see, some succeeded in their economic efforts, while others revealed the steep opportunity costs of their attempts.

Many of these Economic Women were also fictions, characters produced and consumed by an avid reading public. Literature allowed both men and women to consider the economic dilemmas they faced, to spell out their real or imagined consequences, and to envision solutions.[6] And although writing was sometimes a private affair, publication offered financial security for many of the women discussed here, allowing their work to have economic significance in both practical and theoretical ways. In order to demonstrate how facts and fantasies about Economic Women coexisted with and informed one another, this volume places essays on novels and short stories alongside essays on historical actors, and emphasizes private as well as public records: our contributors have consulted archives of diaries, letters, and ledgers in addition to more widely circulated fiction, periodicals, travel writing, and essays.

Within these wide-ranging texts, Economic Women enact many roles. Some of their stories have received more critical attention than others, typically as specific subsets of economic activity.[7] Rather than rehearse the most obvious examples of women's labor (prostitution, factory work), this collection focuses on other, less easily classified practices. Our aim is not to catalogue every economic role that women might have had during the long

---

[6] See Susan Zlotnick, *Women, Writing, and the Industrial Revolution* (1998); for a discussion of the generic relationship between literature and economics in the nineteenth century see Mary Poovey, *Genres of the Credit Economy* (2008).

[7] For instance, Nancy Henry and Cannon Schmitt, eds., *Victorian Investments* (2008); Linda H. Peterson, *Becoming a Woman of Letters* (2009); Patricia Johnson, *Hidden Hands* (2001); Judith Walkowitz, *Prostitution and Victorian Society* (1980); and Elsie B. Michie, *The Vulgar Question of Money* (2011).

nineteenth century. Instead, we propose a broad understanding of what this topic might include and, to that end, showcase a wide sampling of current critical approaches to the subject by many of the best-known and emerging scholars in the field. Since traditional categories do not fully account for Economic Women, the four sections of this volume offer exciting ways of conceptualizing how nineteenth-century women not only mediated existing economic theories and practices but also negotiated new ones. Yet the "economic" aspects of each section overlap and refuse single categorization. For instance, Janette Rutterford's exploration of marital property is also a story about investment, while Leslee Thorne-Murphy's history of a charitable bazaar is also a narrative about free trade. Similarly, Nancy Henry's account of women's business practices, when read in the context of domestic finance and political economy, helps us to see "business" itself as one of many arenas for female economic activity, rather than privileging it as the sole acceptable—or even most desirable—model. We encourage students and scholars of the period to read across sections, forge their own connections between essays, and engage in the fuller, richer picture our contributors paint of Economic Women in nineteenth-century British culture.

I. THE ETHICS OF EXCHANGE

When Marx positioned himself against the individualist ethos of Economic Man, he gave less thought to already extant forms of economic behavior that depended on more communal ideals: the feelings of obligation and mutuality implicit in traditional notions of an elite, paternalistic economy; the charitable efforts of a rising middle class; the increasing interest in philosophies of altruism and sacrifice.[8] Marx was not alone in leaving such practices—and the Economic Women engaged in them—at the margins of economic thought. In histories of the Victorian turn away from *œconomy* and toward political economy, the gift practices associated with community care typically give way to less interpersonal notions of independent contract and self-help.[9] The infamous New Poor Law of 1834, which rejected

---

[8] See Susan F. Feiner, "Reading Neoclassical Economics" (1995); Martha Vicinus, *Independent Women* (1985); F. K. Prochaska, *Women and Philanthropy* (1980); Dorice Williams Elliott, *The Angel Out of the House* (2002); Seth Koven, *Slumming* (2006); Beth Fowkes Tobin, *Superintending the Poor* (1993); Jill Rappoport, *Giving Women* (2012); and Ilana Blumberg, *Victorian Sacrifice* (2013).

[9] For example, Feiner, "A Portrait," 193; Nancy Folbre and Heidi Hartman, "The Rheto-

traditional ideas of a parish's responsibility for its able-bodied destitute, is perhaps the best-known example of this shift in economic attitudes. Yet the rupture between old and new was never as clearly cut in practice as it was in theory.

The nineteenth-century women featured in this section highlight the varied and contested economies that persisted alongside the more familiar activities of Economic Man. Essays by Kathryn Gleadle, Leslee Thorne-Murphy, and Ilana Blumberg reveal the complexity of economic activity that not only deviated from prevailing legal efforts and social trends but also depended on particular configurations of gender, class, religion, and politics. The stories they detail are not always triumphant. Women's alternative economic practices were often ridiculed as ladies' work, they frequently emerged out of suffering, and they occasionally even destroyed the women who practiced them. At the same time, however, the Economic Women who emerge in these studies push beyond the limits set out for them by social expectations or legal restrictions. In personal correspondence, works of fiction, and widely publicized social action, they insist on their right and ability to take wide-ranging economic action on behalf of others, and, by doing so, they effect important changes in their local and larger communities. The essays in this section chart women's rich and sometimes troubling efforts to both articulate and enact forms of mutually beneficial, ethical exchange.

Drastic food shortages and the consequent economic crises of the 1790s blurred the lines between political and moral economies by emphasizing how the fiscal management of a household mirrored and also shaped the economics of the nation.[10] At a time when political economy was presumably replacing earlier models for economic action, traditional moral economy rooted in paternalist ideas of mutual obligation continued to undergird the outlook of female elites, according to Kathryn Gleadle's essay in this volume. Drawing on extensive private manuscripts to demonstrate how Katherine Plymley, an extremely well-connected member of the Shropshire gentry, adhered to the class-based system of paternalism rather than exclusively gendered patterns of behavior or benevolence, Gleadle challenges straightforward narratives of both radical reform and feminine philanthropy. She argues that women's charitable action should be seen as an informed response to contemporary economic issues as much

---

ric of Self-Interest: Ideology and Gender in Economic Theory" (1988), 187, 196. In contrast, Margot Finn stresses the coexistence of gift and market practices; see *The Character of Credit* (2003).

[10] See, for example, Edward Copeland, *Women Writing about Money* (1995).

as an outgrowth of developing social consciousness or religious conviction. Attempting to balance her radical political sympathies with her commitment to the hierarchical relationships of the elite, Plymley exemplifies how women's economic stances were shaped by identity markers beyond gender—in her case, those of social class and religion in particular.

The Plymley archive testifies to women's awareness of and engagement in contemporary economic thought at the turn of the century not only through Katherine Plymley's careful documentation and private criticism of current affairs but also through her tragic account of her niece, Jane. As the family responded to local shortages through projects of dietary economy, gendered patterns emerged. Plymley's brother the Archdeacon experimented with recipes to conserve grain and provide the poor with the means to prepare cheap food. This practice, with its emphasis on self-help, exemplifies a more general movement away from paternalism and destabilizes gendered associations of who should be in the kitchen. At the same time, the women of the family took to extreme and eventually deadly degrees the household's effort to restrict its own consumption in order to make basic food available to the poor. Fourteen-year-old Jane Plymley, whose severe dietary abstinence proved fatal, emerges in Katherine Plymley's diaries not as a fading flower of femininity but as an ethical (if misguided) economic agent. Understanding Jane's private, bodily actions as part of the gentry's wider emphasis on restricted consumption and moral economy, Plymley associates her starvation with Jane's thwarted desire for the larger sphere of public economic action available to her father but not to her.

If Jane, in 1801, ultimately found it impossible to reconcile private economic efforts with her larger public ambitions, other women would assume increasingly visible roles in political debates about economic affairs. For instance, by the hungry forties, women's charitable labor had begun to serve the economic and political function of endorsing free trade. Women took center stage as the organizers, producers, and staff of the 1845 Anti-Corn Law League fund-raising bazaar that would make a stunning financial contribution to the campaign for free trade. Ironically, as Leslee Thorne-Murphy's essay indicates, it did so through methods that appeared to contradict the League's avowed economic aim, because the bazaar itself relied on the creation of an artificially inflated market. In an attempt to resolve these disparate economic practices, the League aligned women's charitable contributions to the bazaar with the contemporary shift away from outdoor relief for the poor, claiming that the women's efforts, by working toward free trade, would replace handouts with political reform and fair prices. Again, as in Gleadle's essay, charity emerged out of and on behalf of economic concerns at least as much as out of sentimental consciousness. Yet, as Thorne-Murphy reveals through her exploration of League publications and other press coverage, the two market systems of the bazaar came into conflict, and that conflict was emphatically gendered. Women's needlework productions were associated with the higher prices and superficial fancywork of a "ladies' fair," while items of masculine manufacture also on display were advertised at wholesale rates in promotion of industry. These disparities prompted debate about the relative value of these items and demonstrated the extent to which valuation itself depended on extramarket forces.

One contribution to the bazaar explicitly took up this question of gendered labor and attempted to show how a reevaluation of women's work might support both the moral imperatives of charitable economics and the political purposes of free trade. Harriet Martineau—best known for her popular tales of political economy—also supported ladies' fund-raising fairs and wrote a fable of colonial free trade for the League bazaar. In *Dawn Island* (1845), the expansion of free trade improves native women's marginal status, thanks to its new valuation of their productive and reproductive labor as integral to the marketplace. By making women central to commerce, the tale also suggests that "feminine" morality, domesticity, and religion—along with women's previously undervalued labor—are inseparable from the successful operations of free trade.

While Martineau worked to merge "feminine" and "masculine" economies on behalf of free trade, George Eliot in the 1860s struggled instead to construct a realm of ethical economic activity for women, independent of the cash nexus and hoarding she associated with men's marketplace exchange. In her novel *Romola* (1862–63), according to Ilana Blumberg's essay in this volume, female self-sacrifice is a trenchant commentary on Victorian gender politics, ethics, and economics. Understanding sacrifice not as the "self-lacerating and inhibiting forms of repression we have been used to associate with Victorian female experience" but as a transaction that exchanges painful loss for even greater profit, Blumberg argues that *Romola*'s emphasis on sacrificial value refuses a basic principle of fungible currency. Eliot, according to this essay, insists that not all forms of value are equal despite their seeming equivalence in transactions.

For Eliot, masculine economies pose gendered threats to women, who are often exchanged as objects or hoarded as prized possessions. Whereas Martineau finds a healthy balance in Dawn Island's merger of male and female economies, Eliot points to the inherent dangers of the former, which fails to differentiate between objects and people as both circulate to men's advantage and women's detriment. In its place, she establishes a mode of ethical exchange for her heroine that uses female self-sacrifice to look beyond the narrow, egotistical values of male market dealings in favor of a wider sense of sympathy and shared debt. When Romola redeems her husband Tito's treacherously earned money by using it to feed the bodies of his extralegal wife and illegitimate child, she chooses physical absorption by others over the more personal or permanent glory of procuring material memorials. Romola's sacrifice dissolves the lines between self and other that have previously divided ethical from economic practice. Unlike Jane Plymley's tragic efforts to offer up her own body for the greater good, though, George Eliot's fictional portrayal allows her to imagine ways in which ethical economics might effectively inform everyday exchange.

In their shared interest in alternatives to traditional market practices, Gleadle, Thorne-Murphy, and Blumberg find particular value in women's bodies and bodily acts. Whether through their own restricted diet or their nourishment of others, their manual labor or reproduction, their exchanges are largely material, concrete, embodied. The significance of food itself in these three essays further suggests that women's economic activity began most readily with private economies and concerns appropriate to the traditional dictates of Victorian domestic femininity. Yet food takes on political and even national significance here, and bodies—fed or unfed, busy at fancywork or in childbirth—exist alongside women's more abstract reflections on moral, political, or sympathetic economies. Together, these essays not only demonstrate the variety of extracommercial exchanges that Economic Women were pursuing during the nineteenth century but, in their intersections, also challenge contemporary associations of women with extravagant consumption[11] by suggesting just how economical their regulation of bodies—their own as well as those of others—could be.

II. POLITICAL ECONOMY

Moral economy presented a seemingly logical space for women to occupy, even though, as we have seen, their participation in it was never straightforward. In contrast, scholars typically encounter real problems trying to place women within and relative to the rise of nineteenth-century political

---

[11] See Erika Rappaport, *Shopping for Pleasure* (2000), 52; and Krista Lysack, *Come Buy, Come Buy* (2008).

economy, primarily because of women's near invisibility within the theory itself.[12] From its late eighteenth-century emergence through its dissociation from household management (*œconomy*) and then moral economy, to its establishment as a full-fledged mathematical science, political economy failed to address Economic Woman.[13] Not until John Stuart Mill's *Principles of Political Economy* (1848) were women treated in discussions of work, division of labor, and fair wages, and even here the references are still few and far between. Complicating the matter further is that few women were writing economic treatises and even fewer were considered to be economists. When women such as Jane Marcet, Harriet Martineau, and Millicent Garrett Fawcett did write explicitly about economic theory in the nineteenth century, they were viewed as "popularizers" of the science rather than as "economists."[14] Yet by featuring women as economic actors and domestic practices as critical to the operation of larger-scale economics, their popular didactic tales attempted to redress the uneven picture offered by economists, even as the commercial success of such writing allowed these women to enact some of the theoretical principles they espoused.[15]

As the essays in this section show, women also contributed to the discourse of political economy in other important and highly visible ways: they formulated new models for understanding economic data; they weighed in on debates about value; they were deeply implicated in economists' configurations of consumption and desire. In this section, Mary Poovey, Gordon Bigelow, and Deanna Kreisel reveal the extent to which women were instrumental to the formation of nineteenth-century economic thought. Although political economists may not have conceptualized women as economic actors, women affected and were affected by the value of objects and labor, the supply and demand of commodities, the economics of reproduction, and the fiscal principles of household management. Whether as statisticians proposing new ways to present and understand data, as novelists complicating the economic understanding of value, or as embodiments of

---

[12] See Peter Groenewegen, ed., *Feminism and Political Economy in Victorian England* (1994), chapters 1 and 2; Michelle Pujol, *Feminism and Anti-Feminism in Early Economic Thought* (1992), 1–23; and Jane Rendall, "Virtue and Commerce: Women in the Making of Adam Smith's Political Economy" (1987).

[13] For a useful overview of the transition from classical political economy to neo-classical economics, and the history of Economic Man, see Regenia Gagnier, *The Insatiability of Human Wants* (2000), 1–5 and chapter 1.

[14] See Lana L. Dalley, "Domesticating Political Economy: Language, Gender, and Economics in *Illustrations of Political Economy*" (2010); and Elaine Freedgood, *Victorian Writing About Risk* (2000), chapter 1.

[15] See Ella Dzelzainis, "Feminism, Speculation, and Agency in Harriet Martineau's *Illustrations of Political Economy*" (2010); and Claudia Klaver *A/Moral Economics* (2003), 118–37.

cultural anxieties about unrestricted consumption, women claimed a stake in nineteenth-century political economy.

Although critics have generally assumed that women were most concerned with the moral aspects of midcentury political economy, Mary Poovey's essay in this volume suggests that Florence Nightingale helped advance the mathematical "science" of late-century economics. Nightingale is, of course, best known for her efforts to reform nursing during the Crimean War, but, according to Poovey, she also deserves to be known for her innovations in descriptive statistics. Her early attempts to present complex information graphically helped render authoritative such simplifying, selective modes of presentation. Facing criticism of the mortality rates she documented, Nightingale turned to statistics in *Notes on Matters Affecting the Health of the British Army* (1858), where she used a combination of polar-area diagrams, fictional accounts, and editorial commentary to argue for sanitary reform. For Nightingale, statistics widened the scope of sympathetic response by "link[ing] individuals to the collective." More concerned with saving lives than saving money, Nightingale was, nonetheless, also arguing for greater fiscal responsibility in hospitals. As Poovey demonstrates, the economic dimensions of Nightingale's work are brought into sharp focus in Harriet Martineau's *England and Her Soldiers* (1859), a work that—like Martineau's earlier *Illustrations of Political Economy* (1832–34)—aimed to clarify and popularize Nightingale's theories.

Acknowledging Nightingale's important contributions to economics draws attention to the ways in which women were instrumental to the formation of the discipline, and the ways in which their efforts may be obscured in the historical record. Poovey's essay also reminds us that discourses we now perceive as separate—religion and mathematics, morality and economics—were often not so distinct in their practitioners' minds. Nightingale put forth her statistical models in the heyday of classical political economy, yet these models provided the foundation for what would become the primary representational system for rendering economic factors in the early twentieth century. As the premises of classical political economy were swept aside by the subjectivist method advocated in England by W. S. Jevons, the religious grounding of Nightingale's work (she referred to statistics as "a religious service") was increasingly eclipsed by the utility of her statistical models.

George Eliot's novel *Middlemarch* (1871–72) appeared just at this pivot point of nineteenth-century economic thought. Despite recent critical efforts to link Eliot to the emerging neoclassical economic model that privileged consumption and demand over labor and production, Gordon Bigelow argues that Eliot develops a view of economic behavior that is radically at odds with this subjectivist model, in its understanding both of subjective perception and of moral consumer choice. Just as Nightingale made sense of sanitation by highlighting the collective, Eliot's ruminations on cost and consumer desire challenge the individualist premises of existing economic models by shifting focus to the complex social construction of value. In *Middlemarch,* Bigelow argues, desire for valuable things is not shaped by private wants and needs, as it appears to be, but rather by social contexts;[16] for Jevons, market prices are a response to human desire, but according to Eliot, "desire follows price." Even the pursuit of pleasure is not clearly distinguishable from pain in *Middlemarch,* as characters' patterns of consumption frequently bring them suffering rather than the satisfaction of fulfilled personal desire. The psychological texture of Eliot's late fiction and its continuing emphasis on the radical distinctiveness of individual experience ultimately insist not on subjectivity but on intersubjectivity; the evident thrust of her work is toward sympathetic connection, even as she offers detailed analyses of what warps and obstructs it.

In the early 1870s the new marginal revolution was highly contested, but by the 1890s it held firmer cultural footing, and so did the new theory of value that emphasized the necessity of unceasing and ever-expanding consumption. In her essay on Bram Stoker's *Dracula* (1897), Deanna Kreisel further explores women's vexed relationship to Jevons at the fin-de-siècle by arguing that the women of the novel embody the unconscious cultural anxieties attendant upon this model of consumption. Examining the figure of the female vampire, Kreisel argues that bodily fluids such as blood and breast milk are particularly cogent emblems of economic operations: they are the only "products" that are "manufactured" solely in response to demand. The women of *Dracula* thus literally embody the spectacular fears attendant upon the neoclassical theory of value that emphasized the necessity of unceasing and ever-expanding consumption—a consumption that comes to be seen as the special purview of the bourgeois woman over the course of the nineteenth century. The ultimate irony of *Dracula,* Kreisel argues, is that the model of vampirism, in which consumption actually brings new products into being, is the perfect resolution to the anxiety generated by a demand theory of value, but one that—like female

---

[16] For the larger significance of things themselves in Victorian culture, see Elaine Freedgood, *The Ideas in Things* (2006).

vampires—is inadmissible to middle-class Victorian values because of its improper, gendered consumption.

III. FINANCING THE FAMILY

Whether women were represented as preying upon blood or consuming extravagantly in general, their presumed failure to manage their households with restraint was seen as threatening the stability of the bourgeois family. The familiar story of nineteenth-century economics echoes this sense of women as domestic liabilities: since women were disadvantaged from birth by the common-law doctrine of primogeniture, reliant on fathers and brothers while unmarried, and frequently compelled to marry for financial stability, their role was one of dependence and obligation.[17] This section, however, challenges these longstanding assumptions about gendered contributions to the Victorian household and demonstrates women's important contributions to family finances.

Our contributors don't minimize the suffering that many women experienced as a result of imbalanced economic laws and unfair social perceptions of women's financial roles, but they don't limit themselves to those tales of victimhood, either. By giving Economic Women a fuller place in the story, chapters by Janette Rutterford, Esther Godfrey, and Erika Rappaport offer much more nuanced accounts of real and imagined Victorian families. Acknowledging the precarious situation of women at a time when they had little control over the material conditions of marriage, these scholars nevertheless reveal how women mediated existing legal frameworks,[18] claimed agency in their economic lives, contributed to the financial well-being of their households, and even established independent livelihoods through their own efforts and through networks outside of their families. Furthermore, their essays undermine the privileged place that men have held in the familiar narrative, showing how—whether single, married,

---

[17] Even as a wife, she could not claim property in her own name until the Married Women's Property Acts of 1870 and 1882. See Ruth Perry, *Novel Relations* (2004); Mary Lyndon Shanley, *Feminism, Marriage, and the Law in Victorian England* (1989); Susan Staves, *Married Women's Separate Property in England, 1660–1833* (1990); and Lee Holcombe, *Wives And Property* (1983). For exceptions to this uniformly bleak portrait, see Amanda Vickery, "Golden Age to Separate Spheres?" (1993), 405; and Amy Louise Erickson, *Women and Property in Early Modern England* (1993), 26, 78, 224.

[18] See also Margot Finn, "Women, Consumption and Coverture" (1996), 706, 707; and Joanne Bailey, "Favoured or Oppressed? Married Women, Property, and 'Coverture' in England, 1660–1800" (2002).

or separated—men frequently found themselves nearly as dependent on women for their economic stability as women were on men. Whether marrying for money, driven to desperation by their wealthier wives' economic autonomy, or compelled to pay alimony to their estranged wives, the men described by Rutterford, Godfrey, and Rappaport do not appear to benefit from the imbalance of economic laws as much as existing scholarship suggests they do.

Real, imagined, or self-imposed, the strains on men's finances emerge to a remarkable extent in midcentury print culture. For Esther Godfrey, this increasing focus on men's precarious relation to wealth is in part an anxious response to new efforts to secure married women's property. Godfrey's discussion of *The Woman in White* (1859–60) argues that the sensationalism of Wilkie Collins's novel derives less from recounting the familiar narrative of a woman's economic disadvantage than from destabilizing that narrative. The heroine's wealth makes her both a coveted wife and an heiress beyond reach for the two men vying for her, and she weighs the advantages of her approaching marriage with open eyes before choosing to marry without love. In place of a wife's dependence on her new husband, Collins depicts men whose own economic agency is threatened by that of a woman whose wealth has been secured to her as her own "separate estate" and who is consequently able to make her own legal decisions even after her marriage. When, ultimately, his heroine does become the victim of her husband's plotting, her plight highlights the desperate ends to which men might be driven by women's increasing economic autonomy instead of identifying a woman's legal situation as necessarily one of disadvantage or dispossession. The heightened anxiety produced by women's increasing economic agency coupled with the ideological loss of men's financial foothold threatened the very genre that described these relationships, as the sensational techniques they require ultimately upend the conventional marriage plot of Victorian fiction. Showcasing the dramatic stakes of male disempowerment in the nineteenth-century novel, Godfrey suggests that only the imprisonment and infantilization of Economic Woman, the (temporary) loss of her wealth, and its restoration in the hands of a male heir can restore the fragile state of family affairs introduced by the imagined consequences of women's economic autonomy.

The cost of family itself becomes grounds for debate in the three hundred letters published by the *Daily Telegraph* during the summer of 1868, as Erika Rappaport's chapter in this volume discusses. Whereas male correspondents relied on familiar tropes of women's rampant consumerism and extravagant consumption to bemoan the expensive tastes of middle-class women and to frame marriage as a luxury beyond their financial means, the female correspondents Rappaport discusses refused to accept these charges. Rather than allowing themselves to be seen as liabilities in marriage, they uniquely rendered visible their domestic labor in order to show the significance of their housekeeping to family budgets. By their accounts, wives' mending, cooking, cleaning, and child care offered important economic counterpoints to husbands' financial earnings, though such domestic work typically went unseen in the bourgeois home. Moreover, they argued, men were as much to blame as women for the excessive spending that kept marriage increasingly out of reach for many. If marriage sometimes granted women greater access to consumerism than was available to single women, that was only part of the story. Men's own expensive tastes also shaped the marriage market. If they continued to court only the most fashionable women, one correspondent wondered, how could they expect to gain anything but expensive wives? Yet men remained bachelors as much to indulge their own desire for luxury items as out of any concern about a future wife's spending. Bachelors, according to these letters, were choosing cigars, theater-going, gambling, prostitution, and fine clothing instead of investing in family life.

The extent of this debate suggests that the economics of middle-class family life at midcentury were more complicated and highly contested than typical accounts of parasitic women allow. Women's responses to men's accusations in the *Daily Telegraph* series reveal both the strength of their own economic contributions and the fallacy of associating shopping only or even primarily with women. Indeed, within couples of the lower or middle classes hoping to establish or maintain the appearance of a respectable bourgeois identity, men and women were at least equally driven to match the social expectations that attended their (would-be) status. So, for instance, as Gordon Bigelow remarks in his contribution to Part II of this volume, *Middlemarch*'s Rosamond Vincy—educated at an expensive boarding school and well attuned to the details of dress—initially admires the town's new doctor, Lydgate, for his ease at wearing the "right clothes" (267). Yet if her own class aspirations are depicted as both shallow and gendered—in a financial pinch, she is hardly a helpmeet—they also match Lydgate's own, as he lunges into debt "without any notion of being extravagant" (348). The essays in this volume call into question Victorian depictions of consuming wives as a financial burden for budget-conscious husbands and of hardworking husbands as the sole providers for the family. In the case that Bigelow describes, as in the wide-ranging testimonies documented by Erika Rappaport's essay, men (both single and married) were as likely to live beyond their means as women, and women were as likely as men to contribute in diverse ways to the household economy.

Whether they could afford marriage was less problematic for some men than whether they could afford its dissolution. Janette Rutterford's essay on Lady Emily Westmeath's marriage and divorce proceedings—which spanned the period 1812–37—not only undermines the premise that marriage offered women financial stability but also demonstrates the innovative ways in which women could secure independent wealth. Rutterford further shows how, despite the common-law doctrine that gave husbands rights to their wives' wealth when it was unprotected by settlements, husbands could still be held legally responsible for taking advantage of their wives' property and compelled to support them after a separation.

Drawing on an extensive archive of personal correspondence, legal documents, and financial transactions for her case study, Rutterford explores the difficulties of a wife's position in marriage. Notwithstanding her high class standing, Lady Westmeath was subjected to financial threats, denied her pin money, stripped of gifts and inheritances received after her marriage, and denied the jointure that had presumably been settled on her. These circumstances, along with her husband's custody of their children and the steep cost of obtaining a divorce before the 1857 Act, made her situation precarious. Yet Lady Westmeath was no victim. Separating herself physically from her husband before she was granted a legal separation, she documented his adultery, his cruelty, and his financial abuses and used them against him in their ongoing legal battle. Even more striking were the bold, creative approaches that this Economic Woman took toward achieving an independent lifestyle. From running up debts that her husband would be forced to pay to exploiting a vast network of wealthy connections outside of marriage, Lady Westmeath procured an extensive income through unconventional means. The most notable of these was her investment in high-risk stocks and bonds; her investment portfolio not only challenges the well-established notion that women's investments, rare in and of themselves, were generally conservative, but also undermines the idea that a woman's economic life necessarily depended on her male kin. Lady Westmeath's investment strategies benefited from the advice and connections of a single female friend.

Together, Rutterford, Rappaport, and Godfrey show how women did more (and men sometimes less) toward financing their families than previous studies have acknowledged. Just as significantly, their essays suggest how even the forms a family could take depended on women's economic status and self-positioning during the nineteenth century.

IV. WOMEN'S BUSINESS

Despite these signs of women's financial contributions, during the nineteenth century professions increasingly operated in spaces outside of the home and in gendered spheres that domestic ideology labeled masculine.[19] As the 1851 census made clear, women's options were limited not only by gender but also by class; very few women could pursue the kind of economic opportunities that Emily Westmeath enjoyed through speculation and investment. Yet Economic Women were innovative, playing with market options rather than conforming to their constraints, exploring alternative economies as well as conventional ones. Accruing both financial benefit and professional status, women cultivated profitable relationships through creative business practices that capitalized on their access to and circulation of information.

In the final section of this volume, our contributors show how creative forms of exchange redefined the business of Victorian women so that it comprised much more than the nursing, teaching, or retail positions frequently thought of as "women's work" during the period. Without downplaying the significance of those earlier and ongoing efforts or presenting these newer forms of exchange as the culmination of economic activity for women, Narin Hassan, Nancy Henry, and Tara MacDonald explore how women adopted lucrative roles as "doctresses," businesswomen, and even purveyors of gossip. As nineteenth-century women wrote about their experiences in these roles, they crafted economic identities by carefully mediating between their public and domestic selves and, in so doing, challenged popular notions of what constituted women's business. These essays show how the expansion of women's commercial reach was contingent upon the careful dissemination of information; as new markets opened in the nineteenth century, women increasingly depended on print culture to legitimate their participation in them. The expansion of print culture in the nineteenth century created a rewarding—though sometimes volatile—knowledge economy, in which women acted as both producers and consumers.[20]

Reading against dominant paradigms of patriarchal inheritance and women's marginalized financial status in Ellen Wood's *St. Martin's Eve* (1866), Tara MacDonald's essay demonstrates how gossip in the novel constitutes its own economy, wherein private information functions as treasured currency for certain female characters and even the novelist herself.

---

[19] See Mary Poovey, *Uneven Developments* (1988).
[20] See Linda H. Peterson, *Becoming a Woman of Letters: Myths of Authorship and Facts of the Victorian Market* (2009); and Kate Flint, *The Woman Reader, 1837–1914* (1993).

Arguing that for many nineteenth-century readers the circulation of novels was akin to the circulation of gossip, MacDonald shows how Wood adopted the role of "gossipy, feminine amateur" in order to reconcile her public role as a writer with her domestic role as a wife and, as a consequence, to achieve financial success. While gossip had long been considered the purview of women, Wood reimagines it as an economic practice. Within *St. Martin's Eve,* MacDonald argues, women are both objects and agents in the gossip economy; bad gossip can "drive one's 'price' down"—a fact that is especially pertinent to the marriage market—while good gossip can garner money, respect, and connections. In the novel, the everyday exchange of information is an economic act with far-reaching and, at times, devastating implications. As MacDonald shows, it is an economy that both feeds upon and is especially driven by women. It is also one that appears to privilege servants, offering them unusual financial opportunities at a time when working-class women were generally unable to eke out more than subsistence in domestic service or factory work.[21]

Whereas the gossip economy identified by MacDonald is dominated by women, Nancy Henry takes up women's participation in an economy long considered the province of Economic Man. Henry's essay explores the writing of Mrs. J. H. (Charlotte) Riddell, who defended everyday business practices and business people as valid literary subjects. Riddell believed that representing everyday aspects of business, trade, and finance offered a more complete and inclusive picture of Victorian attitudes toward business life than novels focusing on dramatic financial events such as bubbles, swindles, and bankruptcies. The sympathetic and capable businesswoman in Riddell's financial fiction refutes the popular conception that women were unfit for the financial sphere, and Riddell's own command of business knowledge within her fiction challenged the scope of what was deemed appropriate material for women writers. Like Wood, Riddell regarded writing as a lucrative business and one that she used to support her family after her husband declared bankruptcy. By writing novels that engage with the mundane technicalities of "the City" and insisting that business matters require a new form of storytelling, Riddell also argues that the economics of "the City" are women's business.

Away from the financial center of London, the expansion of Western medicine was a successful entrepreneurial enterprise for English women in the colonies. According to Narin Hassan's essay in this volume, access

---

[21] For two seminal accounts of Victorian working women, see Wanda Neff, *Victorian Working Women* (1929); and Ivy Pinchbeck, *Women Workers and the Industrial Revolution, 1750–1850* (1930).

to portable medical kits and new discourses of family medicine allowed British women in India and the Middle East to carve out roles as female doctors to natives. Travel narratives by Lucie Duff Gordon and Isabel Burton detail the ways in which their interactions with native populations allowed them to build informal medical practices that were both profitable and professionally rewarding. Like both Riddell and Wood, these women travelers carefully negotiated their public and private identities, in this case by characterizing their doctoring as simultaneously scientific, charitable, and remunerative. Hesitant to define their work solely as economic ventures, they nonetheless make it clear that they are running businesses. Although they sometimes received monetary returns, they were also compensated through barters and gift exchanges. Hassan shows how such travel narratives offered compelling evidence of successful female entrepreneurs, as well as authoritative advice to readers who might want to join their ranks. Here, as in many of this volume's essays, Economic Women found that self-interested gain and mutual cooperation could be compatible; even as they pursued their own livelihoods, they also provided models for other women to emulate their methods.

As the range of activity featured in this volume suggests, locating Economic Women requires us to broaden our understanding of what constitutes economics itself. These chapters thus enrich our comprehension of both nineteenth-century economics and nineteenth-century women. Our contributors tell multiple stories that reveal ambivalence as well as achievement, setbacks as well as forward motion. The lines drawn by class, race, religion, and education in these essays also remind us of the divisions we face whenever attempting to speak of such a diverse group as women, for whom economics has always constituted various forms of management and discipline, labor and consumption, desire and dispossession.

WORKS CITED

Bailey, Joanne. "Favoured or Oppressed? Married Women, Property, and 'Coverture' in England, 1660–1800." *Continuity and Change* 17.3 (2002): 351–72.

Blumberg, Ilana. *Victorian Sacrifice: Ethics and Economics in Mid-Century Novels*. Columbus: The Ohio State University Press, 2013.

"Capital, Volume One." In *The Marx-Engels Reader,* 2nd ed., ed. Robert C. Tucker. New York: Norton, 1978. 294–438.

Copeland, Edward. *Women Writing about Money: Women's Fiction in England, 1790–1820*. Cambridge: Cambridge University Press, 1995.

Dalley, Lana L. "Domesticating Political Economy: Language, Gender, and Economics in *Illustrations of Political Economy.*" In *Harriet Martineau: Authorship, Society and Empire,* ed. Ella Dzelzainis and Cora Kaplan. Manchester: Manchester University Press, 2010. 103–17.

Derrida, Jacques. *The Beast and the Sovereign,* vol. 2. ed. Michel Lisse, Marie-Louise Mallet, and Ginette Michaud. Trans. Geoffrey Bennington. Chicago: University of Chicago Press, 2011.

Dzelzainis, Ella. "Feminism, Speculation, and Agency in Harriet Martineau's *Illustrations of Political Economy.*" In *Harriet Martineau: Authorship, Society and Empire,* ed. Ella Dzelzainis and Cora Kaplan. Manchester: Manchester University Press, 2010. 118–37.

Elliott, Dorice Williams. *The Angel Out of the House: Philanthropy and Gender in Nineteenth-Century England.* Charlottesville: University of Virginia Press, 2002.

Erickson, Amy Louise. *Women and Property in Early Modern England.* London: Routledge, 1993.

Feiner, Susan F. "A Portrait of Homo Economicus as a Young Man." In *The New Economic Criticism: Studies at the Intersection of Literature and Economics,* ed. Martha Woodmansee and Mark Osteen. New York: Routledge, 1999. 193–209.

———. "Reading Neoclassical Economics: Toward an Erotic Economy of Sharing." In *Out of the Margins: Feminist Perspectives on Economics,* ed. Edith Kuiper and Jolande Sap. London: Routledge, 1995. 151–66.

Ferber, Marianne, and Julie A. Nelson, eds. *Beyond Economic Man: Feminist Theory and Economics.* Chicago: University of Chicago Press, 1983.

Finn, Margot C. *The Character of Credit: Personal Debt in English Culture, 1740–1914.* Cambridge: Cambridge University Press, 2003.

———. "Women, Consumption and Coverture in England, c. 1760–1860." *The Historical Journal* 39.3 (September 1996): 703–22.

Flint, Kate. *The Woman Reader, 1837–1914.* Oxford: Oxford University Press, 1993.

Folbre, Nancy, and Heidi Hartman. "The Rhetoric of Self-Interest: Ideology and Gender in Economic Theory." In *The Consequences of Economic Rhetoric,* ed. Arjo Klamer, Donald N. McCloskey, Robert M. Solow. Cambridge: Cambridge University Press, 1988. 184–203.

Freedgood, Elaine. *The Ideas in Things: Fugitive Meaning in the Victorian Novel.* Chicago: University of Chicago Press, 2006.

———. *Victorian Writing about Risk: Imagining a Safe England in a Dangerous World.* Cambridge: Cambridge University Press, 2000.

Gallagher, Catherine. *The Body Economic: Life, Death, and Sensation in Political Economy and the Victorian Novel.* Princeton, NJ: Princeton University Press, 2008.

Gagnier, Regenia. *The Insatiability of Human Wants: Economics and Aesthetics in Market Society.* Chicago: University of Chicago Press, 2000.

Groenewegen, Peter, ed. *Feminism and Political Economy in Victorian England.* Aldershot, England: Edward Elgar, 1994.

Henry, Nancy, and Cannon Schmitt, eds. *Victorian Investments: New Perspectives on Finance and Culture.* Bloomington: Indiana University Press, 2008.

Holcombe, Lee. *Wives And Property: Reform of the Married Women's Property Law in Nineteenth-Century England.* Toronto: University of Toronto Press, 1983.

Johnson, Patricia. *Hidden Hands: Working Class Women and Victorian Social Problem Fiction.* Athens: Ohio University Press, 2001.

Klaver, Claudia. *A/Moral Economics: Classical Political Economy and Cultural Authority in Nineteenth-Century England*. Columbus: The Ohio State University Press, 2003.

Kuiper, Edith, and Jolande Sap, eds. *Out of the Margin: Feminist Perspectives on Economics*. London: Routledge, 1995.

Koven, Seth. *Slumming: Sexual and Social Politics in Victorian London*. Princeton, NJ: Princeton University Press, 2006.

Laurence, Anne, Josephine Maltby, and Janette Rutterford, eds. *Women and Their Money, 1700–1950: Essays on Women and Finance*. New York: Routledge, 2009.

Lysack, Krista. *Come Buy, Come Buy: Shopping and the Culture of Consumption in Victorian Women's Writing*. Athens: Ohio University Press, 2008.

Mellor, Anne. *Mothers of the Nation: Women's Political Writing in England, 1780–1830*. Bloomington: Indiana University Press, 2000.

Michie, Elsie B. *The Vulgar Question of Money: Heiresses, Materialism, and the Novel of Manners from Jane Austen to Henry James*. Baltimore, MD: The Johns Hopkins University Press, 2011.

Neff, Wanda. *Victorian Working Women: An Historical and Literary Study of Women in British Industries and Professions, 1832–1850*. London: George Allen and Unwin, 1929.

Perry, Ruth. *Novel Relations: The Transformation of Kinship in English Literature and Culture, 1748–1818*. Cambridge: Cambridge University Press, 2004.

Peterson, Linda H. *Becoming a Woman of Letters: Myths of Authorship and Facts of the Victorian Market*. Princeton, NJ: Princeton University Press, 2009.

Pinchbeck, Ivy. *Women Workers and the Industrial Revolution, 1750–1850*. London: Routledge, 1930.

Poovey, Mary. *Genres of the Credit Economy: Mediating Value in Eighteenth- and Nineteenth-Century Britain*. Chicago: University of Chicago Press, 2008.

———. *Uneven Developments: The Ideological Work of Gender in Mid-Victorian England*. Chicago: University of Chicago Press, 1988.

Prochaska, F. K. *Women and Philanthropy in Nineteenth-Century England*. Oxford: Oxford University Press, 1980.

Pujol, Michele. *Feminism and Anti-Feminism in Early Economic Thought*. Brookfield, Vermont: Edward Elgar, 1992.

Rappaport, Erika Diane. *Shopping for Pleasure: Women in the Making of London's West End*. Princeton, NJ: Princeton University Press, 2000.

Rappaport, Jill. *Giving Women: Alliance and Exchange in Victorian Culture*. Oxford: Oxford University Press, 2012.

Rendall, Jane. "Virtue and Commerce: Women in the Making of Adam Smith's Political Economy." In *Women in Western Political Philosophy, Kant to Nietzsche*, ed. Ellen Kennedy and Susan Mendus. Brighton, England: Wheatsheaf Books, 1987. 44–77.

Shanley, Mary Lyndon. *Feminism, Marriage, and the Law in Victorian England*. Princeton, NJ: Princeton University Press, 1989.

Staves, Susan. *Married Women's Separate Property in England, 1660–1833*. Cambridge, MA: Harvard University Press, 1990.

Tobin, Beth Fowkes. *Superintending the Poor: Charitable Ladies and Paternal Landlords in British Fiction, 1770–1860*. New Haven, CT: Yale University Press, 1993.

Vicinus, Martha. *Independent Women: Work and Community for Single Women, 1850–1920*. Chicago: University of Chicago Press, 1985.

Vickery, Amanda. "Golden Age to Separate Spheres? A Review of the Categories and Chronology of English Women's History." *The Historical Journal* 36.2 (June 1993): 383–414.

Walkowitz, Judith. *Prostitution and Victorian Society: Women, Class, and the State.* Cambridge: Cambridge University Press, 1980.

Woodmansee, Martha, and Mark Osteen, eds. *The New Economic Criticism: Studies at the Intersection of Literature and Economics.* London: Routledge, 1999.

PART I

The Ethics of Exchange

CHAPTER 1

Gentry, Gender, and the Moral Economy during the Revolutionary and Napoleonic Wars in Provincial England

KATHRYN GLEADLE

*I*n recent years, scholars have challenged the narratives that long shaped our perceptions of middling women and their relationship to the emerging industrial economy of the late eighteenth and early nineteenth centuries. In contrast to the picture painted by Leonore Davidoff and Catherine Hall, who assumed a gradual, if complicated, decline in women's capacity to function as active economic agents,[1] a new generation of historians has noted the continuing (and sometimes widening) economic opportunities provided for women in the expanding urban economies of the late eighteenth century, particularly in the retail and service industries.[2] At the same time, research has shown how women of the middling and gentry classes were able to intervene in wider civic life too, through their

---

[1] Leonore Davidoff and Catherine Hall, *Family Fortunes: Men and Women of the English Middle Class, 1780–1850* (London: Hutchinson, 1987).

[2] See, for example, Anne Laurence, Josephine Maltby, and Janette Rutterford, eds., *Women and their Money, 1700–1950* (London: Routledge, 2009); Hannah Barker, *The Business of Women: Female Enterprise and Urban Development in Northern England, 1760–1830* (Oxford: Oxford University Press, 2006); and Penelope Lane, "Women, Property and Inheritance: Wealth Creation and Income Generation in Small English Towns, 1750–1853," in Jon Stobart and Alastair Owens, eds., *Urban Fortunes: Property and Inheritance in the Town, 1700–1900* (Aldershot: Ashgate, 2000), 172–94.

contributions to philanthropic organizations and local charitable ventures.[3] However, as I argue in this chapter, we derive a more nuanced story of women's unfolding relationship to the new imperatives of the industrial nation by exploring how women were implicated in the functioning of the traditional "moral economy." The gradual breakdown of this customary view of the market was a critical component in the period's shifting socio-economic relationships, but one that has not hitherto been explored in the context of women of the middle and gentry classes. This essay provides a case study of one such woman and her family at the turn of the century.

In contrast to the "political economy" that emerged at the end of the eighteenth century and that advocated free-market relations, the moral economy, as defined by E. P. Thompson, was a concept rooted in paternalistic notions of the social order. Whereas the new political economy was to privilege the values of independence and self-help, the moral economy was enmeshed in older ideals of mutuality. It supposed that the market should be regulated so as to ensure the appropriate circulation of goods (particularly grain) at a just price in the local market without the interference of "middlemen." As a result, medieval legislation was often enacted during times of food shortage, such as setting the assize of bread (an agreed-upon price and quality of loaf), and prosecuting trading practices such as "engrossing" (the hoarding of grain in an attempt to enhance its market price). Higher food prices, seen as transgressions against the moral economy, often led to food riots. As such, food riots should not be seen as undisciplined, violent outbursts but were rather expressions of a sense of injustice when accepted norms of pricing and market management were contravened.[4]

By the end of the eighteenth century, the moral economy was faltering as free-trade arguments gained intellectual credence. The older notion of *œconomy,* with its sense of the stewardship of resources based on the model of household financial management, was starting to lose its currency, and the modern concept of the "economy"—as a "self-contained and self-regulating system of the production and distribution of commodities"—was

---

[3] K. Gleadle, *Borderline Citizens: Women, Gender and Political Culture in Britain, 1815–1867* (Oxford: Oxford University Press and British Academy, 2009); and F. K. Prochaska, *Women and Philanthropy in Nineteenth-Century England* (Oxford: Clarendon Press, 1980).

[4] E. P. Thompson, "The Moral Economy of the English Crowd in the Eighteenth Century," *Past and Present* 50 (1971): 76–136. For discussion see John Stevenson, "The 'Moral Economy' of the English Crowd: Myth and Reality," in Anthony J. Fletcher and John Stevenson, eds., *Order and Disorder in Early Modern England* (Cambridge: Cambridge University Press, 1985), 218–38.

beginning to emerge.⁵ Malthusian claims concerning the deleterious consequences of assisting the poor acted as further solvents on the traditional assumptions that had shaped market relations.⁶ Nonetheless, during the periods 1794–96 and 1799–1801 terrible weather conditions led to appalling harvests. The rocketing food prices precipitated desperate conditions among large sections of the laboring poor. During these years of dearth, the outbreak of numerous food riots illustrated the continuing adherence to the notion of a moral economy among the poor.⁷ The responses of the elites demonstrated that many in this stratum also concurred with the values of the moral economy. As historians of the poor laws have argued, the assumption that the parish had a duty to provide relief for the poor had long been enmeshed in the broader set of ideas that encompassed the moral economy.⁸ In addition, the rash of subscription societies and projects of dietary reform (such as abstaining from the consumption of wheat and corn to preserve them for the poor) appear to provide evidence of what one historian has described as a "new form of moral economy" in which local people responded to crisis conditions through recourse to further non-conflictual strategies.⁹ Thus, despite a backdrop in which new modes of economic discourse and socioeconomic relations were gaining ascendancy, these are crucial years in understanding the contested and uneven emergence of modern notions of economic practice and behavior. This essay will suggest that these developments were also implicated in broader shifts in gender relations.

Scholarly literature on the moral economy has considered at length the extent to which food riots were distinguished by a gendered profile. The assumption that women were typically responsible for the provision

---

⁵ Margaret Schabas, *The Natural Origins of Economics* (London and Chicago: University of Chicago Press, 2005), 5; Ann Firth, "From Oeconomy to 'The Economy': Population and Self-Interest in Discourses on Government," *History of the Human Sciences* 11.3 (1998): 19–35, 21.

⁶ Andrew Charlesworth, "From the Moral Economy of Devon to the Political Economy of Manchester, 1790–1812," *Social History* 18 (1993): 205–17; E. P. Thompson, "The Moral Economy Reviewed," in E. P. Thompson, *Customs in Common* (London: Merlin Press, 1991), 259–351.

⁷ For full details see Roger Wells, *Wretched Faces: Famine in Wartime England, 1793–1801* (Gloucester: Alan Sutton, 1988).

⁸ Lynn Hollen Lees, *The Solidarities of Strangers: The English Poor Laws and the People, 1700–1948* (Cambridge: Cambridge University Press, 1998), 79.

⁹ Joshua Bamfield, "Consumer-Owned Community Flour and Bread Societies in the Eighteenth and Early Nineteenth Centuries," *Business History* 40.4 (1998): 16–36, 22. See also Wells, *Wretched Faces,* chap. 12, 202–18; Walter M. Stern, "The Bread Crisis in Britain, 1795–6," *Economica* 31.122 (1964): 168–87; and John Stevenson, "Social Control and the Prevention of Riots in England, 1789–1829," in A. P. Donajgrodski, ed., *Social Control in Nineteenth-Century Britain* (London: Croom Helm, 1977), 27–50, 42–43.

of food within individual families has been seen as a key factor in their apparent prominence in food riots.[10] However, there has been no discussion of whether gender was an equally significant factor in the moral economy of the elites. Indeed, given the extent of attention paid to female philanthropy in this period, it is surprising that women's activities have not hitherto been seen in this light. As we shall see, contextualizing women's charitable ventures through their engagement with contemporary notions of the moral economy reveals their activities to be a more faltering phenomenon than is suggested in the assessments of historians such as F. K. Prochaska. It was a series of practices in which ideas about female community assistance were refracted through a range of gendered subjectivities, including individual sensitivities to local status and age.

This essay explores this theme through a case study of the extensive diaries kept by Katherine Plymley (1758–1829), sister of the Archdeacon of Salop, Joseph Plymley. During the period with which we are concerned she and her sister Ann lived with Joseph, assisting in the upbringing of three children from his first marriage: Josepha, Panton, and Jane (his wife had died giving birth to the latter). The family lived in the small village of Longnor, just a few miles from Shrewsbury, the provincial capital of the western county of Shropshire. As well as functioning at the center of a nexus of regional markets, Shrewsbury had flourished during the urban renaissance to emerge as a fashionable and lively venue for cultural and commercial exchange.[11] The Plymleys' eclectic social network embraced Shropshire ironmasters, local Anglican clergy, and radical dissenting ministers, as well as experimental scientists and doctors living in the environs of the town. In addition, the Plymleys moved on the peripheries of bluestocking circles, and their wider associates included leading figures in the anti-slavery campaign, most notably William Wilberforce, Josiah Wedgwood, and Thomas Clarkson. A number of their coterie (such as Theophilus Houlbrooke, a member of the Scottish Convention) were at the vanguard of revolutionary politics. While Katherine Plymley herself was a radical Whig who believed the government should defuse popular unrest by introducing measures of constitutional reform, her identity as a

---

[10] For debate see John Bohstedt, "Gender, Household and Community Politics: Women in English Riots, 1790–1810," *Past and Present* 120 (1988): 88–122; Thompson, "The Moral Economy"; and Malcolm I. Thomis and Jennifer Grimmett, *Women in Protest: 1800–1850* (London: Croom Helm, 1982), chap. 2, 28–46.

[11] Peter Borsay, *The English Urban Renaissance: Culture and Society in the Provincial Town 1660–1770* (Oxford: Clarendon Press, 1989); Angus McInnes, "The Emergence of a Leisure Town: Shrewsbury, 1660–1760," *Past and Present* 120 (1988): 53–87; Barrie Trinder, *The Industrial Revolution in Shropshire* (1973; London and Chichester: Phillimore and Co., 1981 ed.).

member of the local gentry in her Longnor parish was also of considerable importance to her.¹² This complex amalgam of influences had significant implications for her response to social and economic issues.

Considerable attention has been paid to women's involvement in political debates during the revolutionary period,¹³ but less explored is the fact that for many this was entwined with a keen interest in related economic questions. Indeed, I will suggest here that at the local level an awareness of these issues could be a compelling reason for women to participate in public affairs. It is a sensitivity of which Hannah More, for one, was clearly acutely aware. For example, her famous song *The Riot; or Half a Loaf Is Better than No Bread* sought to convince the working classes that food riots were futile and misjudged, arguing that the government could not be held responsible for poor harvests; and the Quaker preacher Catharine Phillips issued a lengthy disquisition—*Considerations on the Causes of the High Price of Grain, and Other Articles of Provision*—that was an extended consideration of the economic, political, and agricultural factors underlying high food costs.¹⁴ In contrast, Plymley's written engagement remained within the private medium of manuscript notebooks, where she recorded in detail current events and her family's responses to them. Plymley was acutely conscious of her brother's superior political and social standing in relation to her own, and large sections of the notebooks are dominated by her transcriptions of his letters to well-known political figures or accounts of his opinions. She followed her brother in noting the deleterious impact of war on British commerce, and was alert to the ways in which the consequent "credit crunch" was leading to high rates of bankruptcy, with ill effects for the local iron trade.¹⁵ Pitt's fiscal response to the extraordinary

---

¹² For further discussion see Kathryn Gleadle, "'Opinions Deliver'd in Conversation': Conversation, Politics, and Gender in the Late Eighteenth Century," in Jose Harris, ed., *Civil Society in British History: Ideas, Identities, Institutions* (Oxford: Oxford University Press, 2003), 61–78.

¹³ From a wide literature, see, for example, G. Kelly, *Women, Writing, and Revolution, 1790–1827* (Oxford: Clarendon Press, 1993); A. Craciun and K. Lokke, eds., *Rebellious Hearts: British Women Writers and the French Revolution* (Albany: State University of New York Press, 2001); and K. Gleadle, "British Radical Women and the Late Nonconformist Enlightenment," in A. Vickery, ed., *Women, Privilege and Power: British Politics, 1750 to the Present* (Stanford, CA: Stanford University Press, 2001).

¹⁴ Hannah More, *The Riot; or Half a Loaf Is Better than No Bread* (Perth: R. Morison, 1800); Catharine Phillips, *Considerations on the Causes of the High Price of Grain, and Other Articles of Provision, for a Number of Years Back; and Propositions for Reducing Them* (London: James Phillips, 1792).

¹⁵ This included frequent increases in the taxes on spirits, tea, and sugar; on house-building materials (1794); on horses used for industry, tobacco, the wearing of wigs and hair powder, collateral successions to personal property (1795); on houses, servants, glass, paper, timekeep-

costs of the war with France included regular, steep tax increases. Plymley frequently alluded to the harmful impact of "the enormous increases of taxes" occasioned by what she and her brother perceived as an iniquitous and unnecessary war.[16] Yet her sense of engagement in these issues was not purely dependent upon her brother's views. It is clear that she was highly well-informed herself—in 1793 she commented on the many excellent pamphlets she had read regarding the commercial situation.[17] At other times it is possible to detect subtle dissension from aspects of her brother's views. By the early nineteenth century her output included notebooks that attempted a more retrospective analysis of family events. This included a narrative of the life and death of her niece, Jane. Jane's self-imposed fast and subsequent illness formed a critical theme in the family's response to the dearth of 1800–1801. These events prompted Plymley to articulate a highly self-conscious analysis of the relationship between young female identities and public economic discussion, as well as a defense of her own attempts to negotiate with Jane over her self-harming behavior. The various ways in which Plymley articulated women's engagement in economic issues thus suggests how intricately layered the construction of female subjectivity could be.

Plymley's understanding of her family's responsibilities during the years of economic crisis was rooted in the older ideals of community welfare and patrician responsibility that continued to structure public interactions in the rural parish sphere. For Plymley, as for other women in her circle, her desire to assist the poor must be seen in this light, rather than deriving from a feminized notion of womanly benevolence. During the critical years of 1794–96 and 1800–1801 it became evident that Plymley's democratic politics were complicated—and sometimes paradoxically reinforced—by the enduring resonance these traditional hierarchical relationships held for her. Plymley exhibited a firm commitment to the maintenance of cross-class interactions. She wrote on one occasion that "subordination being however an evil, though a necessary one, all good people will endeavour to lessen it by kindness to those within their reach."[18] Such views had significant consequences for the family's response to economic issues. Their position as paternalistic members of the gentry class

---

ers, armorial bearings (1797 onwards), and income tax. See Stephen Dowell, *A History of Taxation and Taxes in England from the Earliest Times to the Present Day,* vol. ii (London: Longmans Green, 1884), 202–17.

[16] Shropshire Record Office, Plymley Notebooks (hereafter SRO), 1066 / 13.

[17] SRO, 1066 / 18.

[18] SRO, 1066 / 28.

depended on the cultivation of an appearance of wealth. Katherine Plymley clearly felt the strains of such a situation and was relieved to discover of her close friend, Fred Iremonger, that "his situation in life has much resemblance to our own; both of us obliged to strict economy to support the appearance necessary to our situation."[19] The family's self-positioning as consumers was thus complex. It was thought necessary to retrench some of their expenditure so that they could continue to display a certain level of financial well-being in other regards. This gave them authority and status within the community, but it was also important to Plymley that the family demonstrate an interventionist approach in responding to the needs of others. As Plymley recorded, Shropshire, due to its good corn-growing conditions, was less affected than some areas by the food shortages of 1794–95 and 1800–1801. Nonetheless, the local poor were hit significantly by the huge rise in food prices—the details of which she recorded carefully in her diary, noting in 1795 the "very high price of every necessary of life." This, plus the "increase in taxes," imposed a duty, she wrote, "on all who had the power to contribute to the relief of the poor."[20]

Sandra Sherman has observed that during the 1790s a number of commentators, including Edmund Burke and Arthur Young, adopted a harsh and extreme interpretation of Adam Smith's conception of the market as a self-regulating machine. This led them to reject current poor-relief practices.[21] Some in Plymley's circle, such as her friend Archibald Alison, were certainly articulating what was to become the dominant voice of political economy: that the "morals" of the English poor were corrupted by the current system of poor relief.[22] However, Plymley herself was most impressed by those, such as Mr. Matthews of Shelderton, who practiced generosity toward those in need and remained committed to the principle of poor relief.[23] She wrote of the patience and worthiness of the poor, referring warmly to those "noblest institutions for the relief of those under the pressure of any accidental distress," and arguing that those requiring charity should be treated with generosity and respect.[24] Many in the community clearly agreed. In Shrewsbury the "principal farmers, millers and others"

---

[19] SRO, 1066 / 61.

[20] SRO, 1066 / 32–33, 35.

[21] Sandra Sherman, "*The Wealth of Nations* in the 1790s," *Studies in Eighteenth-Century Culture* 34 (2005): 81–96.

[22] SRO, 1066 / 22, 37–38, 55. Disquiet over the social implications of parochial poor relief was eventually to lead, of course, to the draconian enactments of the 1834 Poor Law Amendment Act, which aimed to abolish outdoor relief to the able-bodied.

[23] SRO, 1066 / 37.

[24] SRO, 1066 / 13, 37, and 42.

entered into an agreement that they would bind themselves to fix grain prices in an attempt to assist the poor.[25] Individual actions were also vital. In 1795 Plymley detailed the actions of a local woman, Mrs. King, who, when faced during her husband's absence with a crowd of hostile colliers demanding that she provide them with grain, successfully negotiated with the protesters and arranged for corn to be distributed to them at a reduced price.[26] As recent research has shown, it was high economic standing, rather than feminine cultural capital, that appears to have provided women with the most direct means to act as dynamic agents within their community.[27] This seems to have applied equally to women's participation in the moral economy.

Supporting the culture of the moral economy was not an uncontested process. As Plymley carefully chronicled, some local gentry feared that price-fixing merely exacerbated the panic, others that farmers took advantage of subscriptions for the purchase of grains to raise their prices even higher. Moreover, there was considerable discussion about whether the food shortages had been aggravated or even caused by the practices of wealthy farmers and millers who were accused of preventing the just circulation of grain. "It is now much suspected that the scarcity was artificial," wrote Plymley in 1795.[28] The detailed economic calculations of Plymley's brother indicated a significant, actual shortfall in grain production, but Plymley clearly believed that many were hoarding their goods: "there is plenty in their granaries, they create this want, they grow rich by it," she fumed in 1795.[29] Therefore, whereas Joseph Plymley was increasingly interested in economic diagnoses that analyzed the economy in terms of its functioning as a macro phenomenon, Katherine Plymley remained heavily invested in a more traditional approach that privileged the importance of individual relationships and behavior.

At this point in Shrewsbury, as elsewhere, the wealthier inhabitants also began to uphold the moral economy through projects of dietary economy to free up foodstuffs for the poor. While this immediately turned the focus toward practices of household consumption, it did not provide a simple conduit for greater female participation, as one might assume. The gendered responses to these projects reveal the complex constitution of mas-

---

[25] *Shrewsbury Chronicle,* 11 June 1795.
[26] SRO, 1066 / 35.
[27] See Gleadle, *Borderline Citizens,* chaps. 4 and 6.
[28] SRO, 1066 / 35.
[29] SRO, 1066 / 33. See also SRO, 1066 / 35 and Plymley's brother's assessment reported in SRO, 1066 / 39.

culine and feminine identities within the day-to-day practices of the moral economy. "In many places," wrote Plymley, "the inhabitants agreed to use only brown bread [and] to abstain from the use of puddings [and] pastry."[30] Plymley further recorded how attempts to limit the consumption of grain by eating more meat, rice, and vegetables were "very much acted upon and very many families limitted [sic] the allowance of bread to their servants and to themselves," while "many forbore the use of bread at every meal but breakfast."[31] The Plymley household itself experimented with a new recipe for bread, substituting one-third of the wheat with potatoes. However, in representing attempts at dietary reform as a household decision, Plymley tended to subtly reinforce a sense of male domestic authority. This potato bread (a recipe for which was published in the *Shrewsbury Chronicle*) was soon adopted by other "gentlemen's families," as Plymley described them.[32] Despite women's close association with the practices of household consumption, the practice of alimentary economy did not necessarily result in greater female agency. "Associations are forming among the gentlemen in many places to use one third barley to two of wheat in their bread," she noted in the autumn of 1795.[33] Plymley presented this as a male-led activity, and one that was rooted as much in the public as in the private sphere.

Consumption and cooking were, in this context, gendered as masculine concerns, related to the male-dominated worlds of high politics and public duties. The privy council and both houses of Parliament issued pledges committing themselves to dietary abstinence; a Home Office circular exhorting people to attempt to reduce their consumption of wheat by a third achieved wide publicity through being announced by local clergy; and bills on wheaten bread, and debates on the price of corn, were fervently discussed in Parliament during 1795–1796.[34] As David Eastwood notes, magistrates attempted to encourage "the more fortunate in the virtues of self-sacrifice and restraint" as a means of assuaging the mounting food crisis.[35] Joseph Plymley exemplified this pattern. He actively encouraged the Board of Agriculture, of which he was a member, to institute voluntary associations among the elites to refrain from eating pastry or

---

[30] SRO, 1066 / 35.

[31] SRO, 1066 / 35 and 60.

[32] SRO, 1066 / 35 and 37, *Shrewsbury Chronicle,* 8 May 1795.

[33] SRO, 1066 / 37.

[34] For details, see J. R. Poynter, *Society and Pauperism: English Ideas on Poor Relief, 1795–1834* (London: Routledge and Kegan Paul, 1969); Beatrice and Sidney Webb, "The Assize of Bread," *Economic Journal* 14.54 (1904): 196–218, 208.

[35] David Eastwood, *Governing Rural England: Tradition and Transformation in Local Government, 1780–1840* (Oxford: Clarendon Press, 1994), 116.

puddings made with wheat flour, and further suggested the desirability of agreements "among the more opulent not to give formal dinners."[36] Joseph also took the lead in his household's consumption decisions, his domestic authority presumably bolstered by his masculine identities as a magistrate and an agricultural expert. "My brother," wrote Katherine Plymley, "from a liberality of mind, has an utter repugnance to limit his servants in the articles of meat and drink, but as far as our own example went we spared bread as much as we easily could."[37] In addition, Joseph Plymley's responses indicate his preparedness to experiment with newer, more extensive schemes. He prepared detailed advice concerning the preparation of cheap broth, including the proportions required, and possible means of cheaply flavoring it.[38] As Sherman has suggested, such ambitious ideas to provide the poor with soup from the mid-1790s onwards formed part of a broader shift away from traditional paternalism in favor of efficient, universalizing schemes.[39]

The nature of women's contributions to such projects varied. When a meeting was held at Shrewsbury Guildhall in 1795 to set up a fund to assist the poor and to discourage elite consumption of wheat, women—presumably those of independent economic means—formed nearly twenty percent of subscribers. The names of Joseph Plymley's female kin did not appear among them, however.[40] Joseph Plymley was a prominent local figure, and the Plymley women seem to have looked upon him as their public representative. They exercised charity not through associational activity but through personal philanthropy in their parish. Regarding the particular agenda of food consumption, they preferred to make their contribution through domestic efforts. Indeed, if the family's practices of tightened consumption were largely carried out under Joseph's directions, his female relatives were especially zealous in their execution. This phenomenon requires some careful unpacking, however—the gendered imperatives at work were far from straightforward. For Katherine, the implications of the moral economy for personal consumption accorded well with the amalgamation of Evangelicalism and radical politics that already typified her views. In 1792 her personal notes on the Scriptures included a disquisition

---

[36] SRO, 1066 / 38, 54; *Shrewsbury Chronicle*, 2 August 1792.

[37] SRO, 1066 / 60. The Plymley household was one of many that boycotted Caribbean sugar as a means of economic protest. Similarly, Plymley did not present the campaign as a peculiarly female phenomenon; for example, SRO 1066 / 31.

[38] SRO, 1066 / 57.

[39] Sandra Sherman, *Imagining Poverty: Quantification and the Decline of Paternalism* (Columbus: The Ohio State University Press, 2001), chap. 6, 177–215.

[40] *Shrewsbury Chronicle*, 17 July 1795.

on what she perceived to be the shocking waste of food in elite households, noting that "those whose fortune enables them to keep such a table" should realize it is "an encroachment on the rights of the poor."[41] In 1799 she suggested that in the oppressive political climate of the day, in which the concept of liberty was so sensitive, it was possible only to express a religiously inspired liberty. Taking inspiration from 2 Corinthians 3, she wrote of "the truest liberty, freedom from the dominion of the passions."[42] Her aversion to the rule of the passions accorded with her respect for the work of William Paley, who insisted, in his *Principles of Moral and Political Philosophy* (1785), that the poor had a right to basic levels of subsistence, and that the rich had a duty to limit their diet so as to provide for them.[43] Katherine Plymley was particularly struck by his ideas on virtuous self-restraint—views she sought to instill in her nephew and nieces—and was appalled to hear stories of Paley's apparent gluttony.[44] Katherine and her young charges were also careful students of Joseph Butler, often reading aloud his *Analogy of Religion* (1736), which asserted there to be a hierarchy of human behaviors in which visceral passions and needs held the lowest place.[45] As this indicates, Plymley did not construct her understandings of "virtue" purely in terms of its gendered resonances; rather, the Plymley women sought to establish their economic actions with reference to a specific Anglican intellectual canon.[46]

However, in the execution of these ideals a distinct pattern of gendered behavior swiftly emerged within the household—one that especially affected Katherine's fourteen-year-old niece, Jane. For Jane, the practice of moral economy was refracted through a series of other notions of appropriate femininity. These involved sensibilities deriving from her experience of a gendered body, her age, and an awareness of the lack of other opportunities for action available to her. Jane had already been suffering from an undiagnosed illness that led to a loss of appetite when, in 1801, she began to deliberately limit her diet. It was soon apparent that Jane, contriving to

---

[41] K. Plymley, "Thoughts written at Lyth" (1792), SRO, 567 / 5 / 5 / 1 / 33.

[42] K. Plymley, "Thoughts written at Longnor" (1799), SRO, 567 / 5 / 5 / 1 / 34.

[43] See T. A. Horne, "'The Poor Have a Claim Founded in the Law of Nature': William Paley and the Rights of the Poor," *Journal of the History of Philosophy* 23 (1985): 51–70.

[44] SRO, 1066 / 58 and 55.

[45] For a discussion of Butler and Evangelicalism, see Boyd Hilton, *The Age of Atonement: The Influence of Evangelicalism on Social and Economic Thought, 1785–1865* (Oxford: Clarendon Press, 1988), 170–83.

[46] Jane's asceticism also derived from the influence of Quaker mores, according to J. K. L. Dahn, "A Construction of Taste with Special Reference to Katherine Plymley, 1758–1829," PhD thesis, University of Wales, 2001.

eat alone where possible, was abstaining from both breakfast and lunch, and would take only the plainest food at dinner and supper. Jane's strict regimen reached a peak in 1801, but she continued to live by an extremely ascetic dietary code. In 1802 her aunt reported that Jane "scarcely could be more emaciated."[47] Until her death six years later, Jane experienced many of the physical side effects now associated with anorexia nervosa: abdominal pain, lethargy, weakness, heart problems, and poor circulation.

By the time of Jane's illness, the tone of Plymley's notebooks had shifted considerably. There was still a marked tendency for Katherine to recount her narratives in terms of a collective family identity, but a much more emphatic register becomes evident at this point, perhaps because of the emotional factors involved. She was anxious to convey the family's attempts to reason with Jane, remembering with anguish that "we argued with her, entreated her . . . And in vain urged everything we could think of that was likely to produce any effect. She heard us but we had the mortification to see that we failed to convince."[48] Nonetheless, she also wished Jane's behavior to be remembered as an ethical (if misguided) decision. She understood Jane's actions in the context of the wider efforts of dietary abstinence being practiced within their community: "in the latter end of 1800 and spring of 1801, it was thought by many . . . an advisable measure that those who could afford to purchase flesh meat should live much upon that and garden stuff, rice etc that as much corn may remain for the consumption of the poor as could be contrived." Jane's food denial, according to her aunt, thus "began from the purest the most charitable, the most conscientious motives." For Plymley this was consistent with Jane's character. She presented her as an intensely religious young woman who desisted from the reading of plays and novels, and who lived a quiet life of contemplation and study.[49]

Nonetheless, just as the sugar boycott provided a way for women and children to intervene in public political debates,[50] dietary abstinence appears to have formed a means for Jane to register an engagement with the economic crisis unfolding around her. "Her idea," Plymley explained, "was that the poor were obliged to live upon very little, yet they not only did live but work'd. She believed herself undeserving of more than wou'd support nature in health, and she thought from the example of the lower

---

[47] SRO, 567 / 5 / 5 / 1 / 20.
[48] SRO, 1066 / 60.
[49] SRO, 1066 / 56.
[50] See Clare Midgley, "Slave Sugar Boycotts, Female Activism and the Domestic Base of British Anti-slavery Culture," *Slavery and Abolition* 17 (1996): 137–62.

orders that a very little would do that."⁵¹ Jane, recorded her aunt, "thought very highly of the general character of the poor and very lowly of herself."⁵²

Plymley chose to cast Jane's character within highly gendered terms. "She loves all the useful works that belong to women," claimed Plymley, "and is very industrious in them."⁵³ However, in a retrospective account she revealed that a female domain of virtuous conduct was constructed at considerable psychological cost. She remembered that Jane's great intelligence led her to entertain "more extensive ideas of usefulness than could be performed by one of her age and in her situation." Plymley explained that Jane had repeated "reveries" concerning the kinds of activities she might enact, but "she hoped in future not to give way to it, but to direct her thoughts to duties she could perform in her situation." Katherine recorded Jane's prayer that she might "learn to be content in insignificancy and perform to the best of my ability the passive duties of my confined sphere of action."⁵⁴ Although the family were prepared to consider women having public economic influence (they discussed with the anti-slavery campaigner Thomas Clarkson his plans for female shareholders to be able to exercise a vote in the running of the Sierra Leone company),⁵⁵ these were not opportunities that the teenaged Jane felt were available to her, and she articulated a need to suppress her wider public ambitions.

While Plymley seemed rather unruffled by the alcoholic excesses and adultery of some of her friends,⁵⁶ the ideal citizen, for her, combined both private and public virtue. That is to say, domestic virtue was not configured as simply "feminine" within this family. She praised Wilberforce for his abstemious habit of eating at his desk: "how much private care and comfort public men, who are really conscientious, give up to the discharge of their duty," she mused.⁵⁷ Similarly, in eulogizing her brother she emphasized that in addition to his exemplary public character, he was "not less estimable for the virtues of private life."⁵⁸ These were values that Jane clearly shared, but of course as an adolescent female she was unable to fulfill the other half of Katherine's formula for the model citizen: public duty. Jane therefore turned her life into a mission to excel in the practice of private virtue—seemingly to counteract the fact that she was deprived of the opportuni-

---

⁵¹ SRO, 1066 / 60.
⁵² SRO, 1066 / 60.
⁵³ SRO, 1066 / 56.
⁵⁴ SRO, 1066 / 147.
⁵⁵ SRO, 1066 / 16.
⁵⁶ SRO, 1066 / 49, 108.
⁵⁷ SRO, 1066 / 67.
⁵⁸ SRO, 1066 / 140.

ties for public excellence. This required repressing her fantasies of greater public exertion. In the process, her sense of virtue seems to have become entwined in broader cultural discourses concerning the female body. Fasting, of course, is not simply a feminine behavior.[59] In Georgian Britain, public fasts were still announced at times of national crisis as a means of focusing the country's worship. Yet there was a long tradition associating female piety with fasting, and cultural constructs of femininity contributed to such a pattern.[60] The widespread involvement of women in the thriving consumerism of the late eighteenth-century economy was accompanied by ubiquitous criticisms of the corrupting and corruptible female consumer. As a result, the female body became the site of considerable cultural contestation. To affect the mien of model female gentility required peculiar strategies of discipline.[61] The nature of female eating was often held up to scrutiny by contemporary commentators. John Gregory's widely read *A Father's Legacy to His Daughters* (1774) dwelled much on the horrors of female gluttony. The "luxury of eating," Gregory insisted, "is a despicable selfish vice in men; but in your sex it is beyond expression indelicate and disgusting."[62] Gregory's work would surely have been well-known to Jane Plymley (she was very friendly with Gregory's own daughter, Dorothy Alison). Jane's abhorrence of food, forged in the economic crisis of 1800–1801, appears to have merged customary models of the moral economy with the emergent, wider cultural constructions of appropriate female conduct—and to tragic ends. The moral economy was a set of practices and assumptions rooted in the hierarchies of status, not gender. However, the example of Jane Plymley suggests that it encouraged behaviors that intersected with discrete, gendered discourses to produce complicated female subjectivities.

Arguably, the older, pre-industrial understanding of *œconomy*, which was based on the household model of the guardianship of resources, had the potential to validate female skills and culture to a greater degree than the newer notion of the economy as a self-regulating entity. The former might

---

[59] See R. M. Griffith, "Apostles of Abstinence: Fasting and Masculinity during the Progressive Era," *American Quarterly* 52.4 (2000): 599–638.

[60] Phyllis Mack, *Visionary Women: Ecstatic Prophecy in Seventeenth-Century England* (Berkeley: University of California Press, 1992); see also Karen Hollis, "Fasting Women: Bodily Claims and Narrative Crises in Eighteenth-Century Science," *Eighteenth-Century Studies* 34.4 (2001): 523–38.

[61] Elizabeth Kowaleski-Wallace, *Consuming Subjects: Women, Shopping, and Business in the Eighteenth Century* (New York: Columbia University Press, 1997); John Brewer, "'The Most Polite Age and the Most Vicious': Attitudes Towards Culture as a Commodity, 1660–1800," in Ann Bermingham and John Brewer, eds., *The Consumption of Culture, 1600–1800: Image, Object, Text* (London: Routledge, 1995), 341–61, 355.

[62] John Gregory, *A Father's Legacy to His Daughters* (London: W. Strahan, 1774), 39.

CHAPTER 1. GLEADLE, "GENTRY, GENDER, AND THE MORAL ECONOMY"

have had special resonance for married women of gentry status, especially those who were either childless or at a mature stage in their life cycle, and who had the requisite personal and monetary resources for such financial stewardship. Joseph Plymley's second wife, whom he married in 1790, is rarely mentioned by Katherine. She was very young and by 1795 had three small children. In contrast, Plymley recorded that her ideal of "the true housewife and eoconomist [sic]" was her friend Mrs. Bache, a woman of more mature years and described by Plymley as "accessable [sic] to, and ready to help all who are in want."[63] In contrast, for those women whose position in the life cycle or lack of independent means restricted their activities, engaging in the culture of the moral economy might involve enacting its values through conduits of behavior that had more problematic consequences. For Jane, unlike the older figure of Mrs Bache, it was bodily abnegation that provided the most accessible means to participate in the moral economy.

The complicated makeup of the Plymley women's subjectivities is a testament to the conflicting intellectual and sociocultural practices that were fracturing dominant economic discourses in this transitional period. Recent scholars have demonstrated that it is unhelpful to present the traditional moral economy and the new imperatives of political economy as sharp dichotomies, and it is clear that notions of the former persisted well into the nineteenth century.[64] The Plymley archive supports such a conclusion, while also pointing to the complex gendered patterns this involved. Female empowerment in both the traditional moral economy and also the emergent industrial economy was highly contingent, often depending on regional or personal circumstances, such as an individual's financial or marital position. Married women may still have had more room for independent engagement in the moral economy than was often the case with dependent, unmarried females, although as we have seen, family consumer decisions were not simply gendered in this way.

Traditionally, the increasing philanthropic energy of women from the middling sorts has been interpreted in the light of social and political narratives, such as the emergence of Evangelicalism, the development of middle-class consciousness, and the challenges occasioned by the French Revolution. I have argued here that women's activities need also

---

[63] SRO, 1066 / 44.
[64] For example, Susan E. Brown, "'A Just and Profitable Commerce': Moral Economy and the Middle Classes in Eighteenth-Century London," *Journal of British Studies* 32.4 (1993): 305–32; and Peter Jones, "Swing, Speenhamland and Rural Social Relations: The 'Moral Economy' of the English Crowd in the Nineteenth Century," *Social History* 32.3 (2007): 271–90.

to be viewed as an informed response to contemporary economic issues. The challenge to the traditional norms of the moral economy that emerged starkly in the 1790s led to a reactive reassertion of paternalism in some local contexts—a process in which women clearly played an important role. However, as we have seen, individuals negotiated these activities through the prism of other discourses and practices, and these were often more sharply gendered. During the harsh economic climate of the 1790s and early 1800s, the practical implications of deprivation meant that the body itself became a site for the articulation of economic effects. As Kowaleski-Wallace suggests, "It is important to incorporate 'the role of the human body' in the processes of 'social formation.'"[65] The philanthropic impulse that historians have noted as central to the burgeoning civic involvement of women had complicated social and cultural roots and was not necessarily experienced as an indicator of female public advancement. Women could feel engaged in economic debate and practice in a multitude of ways. The testimony of Katherine Plymley suggests that varying, and even contradictory, conceptions of the economy and the distribution and regulation of resources could overlap and be enmeshed in the day-to-day lives and thoughts of contemporaries. This was a process in which gender was critical—but in subtle and sometimes unpredictable ways.

---

[65] Kowaleski-Wallace, *Consuming Subjects,* 11.

CHAPTER 2

Women, Free Trade, and Harriet Martineau's *Dawn Island* at the 1845 Anti-Corn Law League Bazaar

LESLEE THORNE-MURPHY

On May 8, 1845, the Anti-Corn Law League opened its grand London bazaar. The League staged its bazaar in Covent Garden Theater, completely transforming the theater itself into a replica of a Norman Gothic hall. The rows of chairs were removed. The orchestra pit was boarded over. A false ceiling and columns created the look of a stone hall with illuminated stained-glass windows, and rows of tables piled with goods for sale lined the sides and center of the hall. The theater in its entirety had become a stage, so that as patrons mounted the stairwell to enter, they were presented with an immense scene laid out before them. As the *Illustrated London News* reported, "the visitor . . . [can] take in the whole at the first glance, and hence the effect of the *coup d'oeil* is most striking and imposing" (see figure 2.1).[1]

---

[1] "Opening of the Anti-Corn-Law League Bazaar," *Illustrated London News,* 10 May 1845, 295. In *Bazaars and Fair Ladies: The History of the American Fundraising Fair,* Beverly Gordon examines American bazaars that attempted to create similarly thematic and grandiose scenery for bazaars, beginning with the sanitary fairs during the American Civil War (Knoxville: University of Tennessee Press, 1998). As several historians have noted, and as many Victorians themselves observed, the League bazaar was a precursor to the Great Exhibition of 1851. See, in particular, Archibald Prentice, *History of the Anti-Corn-Law League (1853),* 2nd ed., vol. 2 (New York: Augustus M. Kelley, 1968), 327; Peter J. Gurney, "'The Sublime of the Bazaar': A

Figure 2.1
Free Trade Bazaar at Covent Garden Theater.
From the *Illustrated London News*, 10 May 1845, p. 296

CHAPTER 2. THORNE-MURPHY, "WOMEN, FREE TRADE, *DAWN ISLAND*"

Thousands of visitors flocked to the bazaar on each of the seventeen days it ran, specially scheduled trains brought visitors from various regions of England, specially scheduled steamboats brought visitors from Scotland, eventually admission prices had to be raised in order to keep the number of patrons down, the major newspapers (whatever their political stance) covered the event, and hundreds of people worked throughout the weeks to keep the stalls stocked and staffed (see figures 2.2 and 2.3). The stage hosted a restaurant, and a daily newspaper published on-site gave consumers an overview of the plentiful goods available. In short, the bazaar was a stunning success. By the time it closed, the bazaar had raised £25,000 for the Anti-Corn Law League's massive £100,000 fund-raising campaign.[2] Perhaps as important, the League saw the bazaar as a moral victory, an indication that public opinion was shifting to favor its cause.[3] As a champion of free trade, specifically lobbying for the repeal of tariffs on foreign grain, the League boasted that because of the bazaar, "London is penetrated, possessed, conquered by Free-Trade opinion."[4]

According to League publications, this imposing affair was originally proposed by "the earnest entreaty of a number of ladies."[5] One would expect a bazaar to have been the suggestion of ladies; after all, Victorian bazaars were often known as ladies' sales. Women typically organized bazaars, made the goods sold at them, and staffed the stalls. As F. K. Prochaska remarks, "The bazaar . . . was pre-eminently a female affair."[6] As a

---

Moment in the Making of a Consumer Culture in Mid-Nineteenth Century England," *Journal of Social History* 40.2 (Winter 2006): 385–405; and Tammy Whitlock, *Crime, Gender, and Consumer Culture in Nineteenth-Century England* (Burlington, VT, and Aldershot, England: Ashgate, 2005), 57. Several newspapers called for a larger, government-sponsored exhibition as they commented on the bazaar, most notably the *The Art-Union: Monthly Journal of the Fine Arts, the Arts Decorative and Ornamental* (hereafter *The Art-Union*) and the *League.*

[2] Norman McCord, *The Anti-Corn Law League, 1838–1846* (London: Allen and Unwin, 1958), 161.

[3] See, for example, "The Bazaar," *League*, 15 March 1845, 385–86; "The Bazaar—Its Moral Results," *League*, 24 May 1845, 545; and "Retrospect," *League*, 5 July 1845, 642.

[4] "The Bazaar—Its Moral Results," *League*, 24 May 1845, 545.

[5] "The Bazaar," *League*, 16 November 1844, 115.

[6] F. K. Prochaska, *Women and Philanthropy in Nineteenth-Century England* (Oxford: Clarendon Press, 1980), 57. Prochaska's chapter on bazaars (47–72) offers the most comprehensive overview of English bazaars. Gordon's *Bazaars and Fair Ladies* gives a detailed study of American fundraising fairs. See also Whitlock, *Crime, Gender, and Consumer Culture*, chapter 2: "Vanity Fairs: The Growth of Bazaars and Fancy Fairs," 41–69; and Gary Dyer, "The 'Vanity Fair' of Nineteenth-Century England: Commerce, Women, and the East in the Ladies' Bazaar," *Nineteenth-Century Literature* 46.2 (September 1991): 196–222. Ironically, though the bazaar may have been undertaken at the suggestion of League ladies, it was George Wilson, the Chairman of the Council, who spearheaded the preparations for the bazaar.

PART I. THE ETHICS OF EXCHANGE

Figure 2.2
Stall at the Free Trade Bazaar.
From the *Illustrated London News*, 17 May 1845, p. 309

cultural phenomenon specifically associated with middle- and upper-class women, the Victorian fund-raising bazaar offers a fertile field for exploring their involvement with a female-oriented marketplace. Since these women's marketplaces existed outside the workaday world of commerce, women could manipulate the variables of a typical marketplace to accomplish their purposes, and one of the most consistent and notorious rules of these temporary markets was the dictum to overcharge. After all, goods were supposed to be priced exorbitantly at a fund-raising fair; the idea was to create an artificially inflated market in order to raise as much money as possible for a good cause. Everyone knew this; most bazaars flaunted the fact with satirical stories of fair ladies wheedling money from duped men who would find themselves leaving with an armful of overpriced and useless items. Many lyrics played with the notion of the women selling themselves as much as their goods—flirtation was a staple element of bazaars. Usually this was part of the fun, part of the entertainment one expected. Fund-raising fairs walked a thin line between the moral earnestness of charitably donating to a good cause and the carnivalesque appeal of playfully inverting the logic of capitalism.

The irony of the Anti-Corn Law bazaar was that a political organization whose sole reason for existence was the promotion of free trade would adopt a fund-raising and public relations technique self-consciously identified as an artificially inflated market. Not surprisingly, the two market systems came into conflict within the League bazaar itself. As the print matter generated for the bazaar reveals, this conflict was heavily gendered—the internal market logic of the ladies' fair in conflict with the masculinized manufacturing marketplace. In this essay, I trace the conflict as it plays out in the League's publications and in press coverage of the bazaar. I then examine a publication that negotiated the gendered implications of the conflicting marketplace ideologies—Harriet Martineau's *Dawn Island* (1845). As a renowned author who had made her reputation as an exponent of political economy, and also as a woman who regularly contributed needlework to fund-raising fairs, Martineau was in a unique position to enter gendered discussions of market theory and practice. She wrote *Dawn Island* specifically to be sold at the Anti-Corn Law League bazaar, and within its pages she wove a subtle argument responding to the gendered rhetoric of the bazaar by insisting on the value of women's work to the healthy functioning of free trade.

I. THE ANTI-CORN LAW LEAGUE BAZAAR

When the League's official weekly newspaper announced the bazaar in November 1844, it suggested that local League offices organize committees to prepare and gather items to be sold at the bazaar.[7] Both Ladies' committees and Gentlemen's committees were to be formed; the ladies to make "fancy" goods, solicit contributions, and staff the stalls; the gentlemen to canvass for donated goods for the ladies to use in their handicrafts. The paper also introduced an element atypical of bazaars, one that would take this fund-raising fair far beyond the realm of the typical ladies' sale: it suggested that the committees attempt to gather items representing the staple manufactures of their respective locales.[8] Four months later, this mere suggestion formed a major component of the plans:

> Unlike ordinary Bazaars, that which the League is about to open will, to a great extent, assume the character of a National Exposition of the Products

---

[7] "The Bazaar," *League*, 16 November 1844, 115.
[8] Ibid.

PART I. THE ETHICS OF EXCHANGE

of British Skill and Industry. The Council are already informed that several of the great marts of industry intend sending specimens of all the staple manufactures of their districts.

As an exposition, the Bazaar will be more perfect and complete than was at first anticipated.[9]

The League had found a way for a ladies' sale to contribute to its free-trade ideology. By introducing elements of an industrial exposition, the bazaar would illustrate the power of manufacturing and the necessity of allowing industry to thrive in an open market.

Given the combination of ladies' fair and industrial exhibition, both League members and the press puzzled over the term "bazaar" itself. An article promoting the bazaar in the *League* confessed:

We have always regretted being obliged to content ourselves with an old word for a perfectly new thing; but, as the dictionary affords us no latitude of choice, we must be satisfied to continue using the old term "Bazaar," under protest, however, that it is calculated to give a partially erroneous and altogether inadequate idea of the spectacle which London and the world will next month witness.[10]

Other writers attempted to find more adequate words, including a "museum of British manufactures," a "great national exhibition," a "British Museum of arts and manufactures," an "exhibition of manufactures," a "national Free-Trade jubilee," and "a National Exposition of the Products of British Skill and Industry."[11] Note that all these terms attempted

---

[9] George Wilson, "National Anti-Corn-Law Bazaar, to Be Held in the Theatre Royal, Covent Garden, London, May, 1845," 18 March 1845, circular (Manchester: J. Gadsby, 1845), 1, *The Making of the Modern World: The Goldsmiths'-Kress Library of Economic Literature*, Gale Cengage, http://primofe1.byu.edu/primo_library/libweb/action/getItAction.do?indx= 1&ct=getit&doc=dedupmrg14686345&fctV=&fctN=&frbg=&dum=true&vid=byu-PC&vl(17 3474579UI1)=all_items&vl(173474578UI0)=any&srt=rank&indx=1&dstmp=1285877155695 &tab=search&ct=search&scp.scps=scope%3A(LEE)%2Cscope%3A(BYU)%2Cscope%3A(by ugle)%2Cscope%3A(Unicorn_online)%2Cscope%3A(CONTENTdm)%2Cscope%3A(JUV) %2Cscope%3A(SPEC)%2Cscope%3A(INTERNET)%2Cscope%3A(SWKT)%2Cscope%3A (SLC)%2Cscope%3A(LEELRC)%2Cscope%3A(MUSIC)%2Cscope%3A(saskia)%2Cscope% 3A(CONTENTdm2)%2Cprimo_central_multiple_fe&vl(freeText0)=National Anti-Corn-Law Bazaar%2C to Be Held in the Theatre Royal%2C Covent Garden%2C London%2C May%2C 1845&fn=search&mode=Basic&dscnt=0.

[10] "The Bazaar," *League*, 12 April 1845, 449.

[11] *London Times*, 9 May 1845, 6; *Bazaar Gazette*, 1, 1; *Taits Edinburgh Magazine*, July 1845, 475; *League*, 22 March 1845, 407; *League*, 19 April 1845, 465; and Wilson, "National Anti-Corn-Law Bazaar," 1.

Figure 2.3
The Leeds stall, using the space of a theater box, with a table set up below.
From *The Art-Union: Monthly Journal of the Fine Arts, the Arts Decorative and Ornamental*, July 1845, p. 212

PART I. THE ETHICS OF EXCHANGE

to ignore the fact that the bazaar had originated as a ladies' sale. Indeed, if writers wanted to praise the bazaar, they overplayed the industrial exhibition element of the bazaar; if they wanted to disparage the bazaar, they did so by terming it a mere ladies' sale.[12] The *Morning Chronicle*'s position was typical of League supporters: "From day to day the Bazaar has increasingly assumed its higher and more interesting character, as a display of the resources and capabilities of British industry."[13]

The *Bazaar Gazette,* the daily newspaper published at the bazaar, itself reflected this perspective. Each day it highlighted certain stalls, listing notable items for sale and giving an overview of the various goods displayed. The items it mentioned fell into three general categories: manufactured goods, ladies' fancy items, and curiosities such as collections of minerals or signatures of celebrities. Calculating how many items are listed in each of these categories gives us an interesting perspective on what the editor thought worthy of mention. Manufactured goods made up seventy-two percent of the items, ladies' work was listed twenty percent of the time, and eight percent of the items were curiosities.[14] Obviously the highlight of the bazaar for the editor was its function as an exhibition of manufactured goods. It is noteworthy that the *Morning Herald* (unsympathetic to the League) estimated that three-fourths of the goods for sale were ladies' items, while the *Bazaar Gazette* mentioned manufactured goods nearly three-fourths of the time.[15]

If the League and its sympathizers actually wanted an industrial exhibition, why would they have taken the trouble to organize a bazaar? Aside from the money the bazaar would raise, the answer draws upon the moral and religious overtones of ladies' sales. As Paul Pickering and Alex Tyrrell argue, the League went to great lengths to depict itself as a philanthropic cause, and part of this effort involved soliciting women's participation, for "the support of women could transform debatable policy proposals into religious and moral imperatives that allowed no legiti-

---

[12] See, for example: *Bazaar Gazette,* 16, 3; "The Mercantile Value of the Fine Arts," *The Art-Union,* 1 July 1845, 209–28, 209; and *Morning Herald,* quoted in *League,* 10 May 1845, 516–17, 517.

[13] Quoted in *Bazaar Gazette,* 16, 3.

[14] I suspect that the editor and writer of the *Bazaar Gazette* was Samuel Carter Hall, editor of *The Art-Union. The Art-Union* published a feature article on the bazaar in July 1845, and there are many similarities between the coverage of the bazaar in this article and the coverage in the *Gazette.* Whoever he or she was, the editor was a proponent of the industrial aspects of the bazaar. The percentages I calculate do not indicate the number of goods listed, for at times the editor simply mentioned "printed cashmeres" or "embroidered articles," but they do indicate the percentages of times he or she chose to mention certain types of items.

[15] Quoted in *League,* 10 May 1845, 516–17, 517.

mate counter-argument."[16] This logic was used to great effect by W. J. Fox, one of the League's speakers, who advised women to contribute to and participate in the bazaar because it was a charitable endeavor to help the needy afford bread, a humane effort to counter the "inhuman" rationale of "monopolies."[17] Unlike charitable efforts based on "the selfishness of sentimental benevolence,"[18] the efforts of League women would avoid merely giving handouts of food and clothing; instead, they would "procure for . . . [the poor], daily and permanently, a supply of all these—to procure the abolition of the cruel monopolies which make all these things dear, and work scarce and wages low."[19] In essence, sponsoring a ladies' sale contributed to the League's efforts to depict itself as a proponent of what it saw as the best type of charity—free trade. As another League speaker, Robert Moore, phrased it, "while the Bazaar would be memorable and unexampled for its specimens of the industry and ingenuity of the British manufacturer, the League was especially desirous that the amount of ladies' work should show that the question had become a home question."[20] If women were unabashedly involved, then the fight for repeal of the corn laws must be a moral and religious cause worthy of involving women's domestic interests and labor in overt political action.

Since the League wanted the bazaar to be both ladies' sale and industrial exhibition, it was forced to negotiate aspects of the two markets that were inherently opposed, specifically the bazaar dictum to overcharge for goods. League publications attempted to settle this problem beforehand by instructing donors on how to price their own goods: "It is respectfully requested that, wherever practicable, the contributors themselves will affix their own prices to the articles according to the known cost of the raw materials, and the additional value given by the labour subsequently expended upon them."[21] As a simplified statement of Adam Smith's labor theory of value, this pricing technique appears straightforward and unproblematic.[22]

---

[16] Paul A. Pickering and Alex Tyrrell, *The People's Bread: A History of the Anti-Corn Law League* (London and New York: Leicester University Press, 2000), 127.

[17] "Letters on the Corn Laws, No. VIII. To the Women of Great Britain," *League*, 23 November 1844, 136.

[18] *League*, 14 December 1844, 185.

[19] "A Letter on the Duties of Englishwomen to One Another," *League*, 19 April 1845, 469.

[20] "Edinburgh," *League*, 5 April 1845, 436.

[21] "National Anti-Corn-Law Bazaar," *League*, 5 April 1845, 440. This same announcement was posted in each issue of the *League* until the bazaar opened.

[22] Adam Smith, *Inquiry into the Nature and Causes of the Wealth of Nations*, ed. R. H. Campbell and A. S. Skinner, 2 vols. (1776; rpt. Indianapolis, IN: Liberty Classics, 1976). Smith argues that labor is the standard on which "real price" is based (1:51). The components of labor that result in any given commodity's market price are wages, rent, and profit, tempered

When it came to thousands of different individuals assigning prices to their separate items, however, complexities arose. In their report on the opening of the bazaar, the *London Times* correspondent complained that the goods at the bazaar were absurdly overpriced and pointed out the irony of the League bewailing high bread prices while inflating the price of goods they offered for sale.[23] Hypocrisy was not an accusation the League wished to merit, especially when it came to issues of pricing. Duly, the first page of the *Bazaar Gazette* the next day reported, "Complaints having been made that some articles were too highly priced, the ladies' secretaries have gone round and recommended a reduction in all the charges that could be regarded as exorbitant."[24] These secretaries were specifically targeting the handmade fancy goods contributed by the Leagues' women, for "at the stalls for manufactured goods, all . . . are being sold at wholesale prices."[25] The ladies' goods, on the other hand, were priced according to the conventions of a typical fancy fair. This did not defy the League's advice on pricing, it simply interpreted that advice differently, for, as the *Bazaar Gazette* admitted, "Fancy articles have, it is true, a higher conventional value than ordinary goods, on account of the fair hands by which they have been wrought."[26] In other words, when calculating the price of raw materials plus labor, the makers of the handmade items claimed a much higher value for their labor. Their labor was infused with the intangible value of moral worth associated with charity, religion, and the connections of family and home.

II. HARRIET MARTINEAU'S *DAWN ISLAND* AND WOMEN'S LABOR

The value of women's labor was exactly the issue Martineau placed at the heart of her tale written for the bazaar. Martineau was a long-time sup-

---

by supply and demand (1:67–68). The League asks its contributors to calculate the price of their donations according to the cost of their supplies (resulting from the costs of wages, rent, and profit) and their own labor, donating all the proceeds as profit. The League's simplified version of pricing and value does not take into account the complexities addressed by Smith and other early political economists, particularly David Ricardo in *On the Principles of Political Economy and Taxation* (1817).

[23] "The National Free Trade Bazaar at Covent-Garden Theatre," *London Times*, 9 May 1845, 6.
[24] *Bazaar Gazette*, 3, 1.
[25] *Bazaar Gazette*, 3, 1.
[26] *Bazaar Gazette*, 3, 1.

porter of the League. Having made her literary reputation with the best-selling series *Illustrations of Political Economy* (1832–34), she was well versed in the ideology of free trade. Indeed, the nineteenth tale in her *Illustrations* series, titled "Sowers Not Reapers" (1834), specifically advocated repeal of the corn laws. As a self-proclaimed popularizer of the tenets of political economy, Martineau staked her professional success on her ability to present complex political and economic ideas clearly, succinctly, and logically, as Mary Poovey's contribution to this volume demonstrates. For her this was not merely a matter of political expediency—it was a moral quest to educate all members of her society in the basic economic tenets that she believed would improve their well-being.

For Martineau, contributing to the bazaar was another means of accomplishing her purposes. Since she was an invalid when the bazaar was first announced, Martineau intended to donate copies of her books or pieces of her own fancywork.[27] By the time the bazaar was held, however, Martineau had regained her health and decided to write a new book as her contribution: "I have now to write a tale,—a little book for our great League Bazaar,—being too well and busy to do the fancy-work I had intended to send."[28] The fancywork she "had intended to send" was a common pastime for Martineau, and she often donated it to benefit a good cause, particularly to American anti-slavery bazaars.[29] Deborah Anna Logan discusses this aspect of Martineau's work, detailing the parallels between needlework and penwork in Martineau's professional and philanthropic efforts. As Logan explains, "Martineau was proud of her needleworking skill and regarded needles and pens as complementary, not antithetical, means of expression."[30] Replacing her intended fancywork with a newly composed tale, then, was a natural substitution for Martineau. She indicates in turn that her fancywork would have been a more laborious, but equally important, contribution. As a woman who regularly contributed to bazaars and as a best-selling author who crafted her reputation as an advocate of the free trade demanded by England's industrial interests, Martineau strad-

---

[27] Martineau to William Johnson Fox, 23 April 1844, *The Collected Letters of Harriet Martineau*, 5 vols., vol. 2, ed. Deborah Anna Logan, The Pickering Masters (London: Pickering and Chatto, 2007), 284–86, 285.

[28] Martineau to Mrs. Henry G. Chapman, 15 March 1845, *Memorials of Harriet Martineau*, by Maria Weston Chapman (Boston and New York: Houghton, Mifflin and Company, 1877), 361. See also Martineau to Miss Pease, 18 March 1845, *Collected Letters*, vol. 3, 6–7; and Deborah Anna Logan, *The Hour and the Woman: Harriet Martineau's "Somewhat Remarkable" Life* (Dekalb: Northern Illinois University Press, 2002), 78.

[29] Chapman, *Memorials*, 363. See also Logan, *The Hour and the Woman*, 39–77.

[30] Logan, *The Hour and the Woman*, 30.

dled the gendered divide of the bazaar, valuing it as a ladies' sale to which she could donate needlework as well as an industrial exhibition where her writings on political economy would be perfectly at home.

Martineau's tale for the bazaar, *Dawn Island,* participates in the rhetoric regarding the dual nature of the bazaar. It addresses the value of women's labor, though the tale is a deceptively simple fable of colonial free trade. Drawing upon accounts of European explorers' contact with the peoples of the Pacific islands, specifically of Tahiti, Martineau depicts a small, seemingly idyllic island.[31] All is not right, however, on Dawn Island. Continual warfare, human sacrifice, and the ritual infanticide of the first three children born to each woman are resulting in a significant population decline, so that the priest Miava dreads the realization of an ancient prophecy: "the forest-tree shall grow; the coral shall spread and branch out; but man shall cease" (22).[32] As the moral center of the tale, Miava and his adopted daughter Idya lament many of their own cultural practices, though they feel themselves bound to follow the precepts of their society. When an English trading ship arrives at the island, with a Captain who preaches the doctrine of free trade, the islanders are converted to principles of commerce. The Captain convinces them to stop all human sacrifice, and Miava foresees a peaceful future in which the various villages of the island will trade goods with one another and with the seagoing vessels.

Given *Dawn Island*'s setting, it is no surprise that most recent critics have discussed it from the perspective of postcolonial studies. They focus on its relationship to other writing of the British Empire, elucidating Martineau's place within imperial ideology.[33] Notably, however, the narrative

---

[31] Rod Edmond refers to Martineau drawing upon accounts of Tahiti by the missionary William Ellis in *Polynesian Researches* (1829) (*Representing the South Pacific: Colonial Discourse from Cook to Gauguin* [Cambridge: Cambridge University Press, 1997], 136). Martineau's depictions of Dawn Island also appear to be indebted to published accounts of Captain Cook's voyages, such as *An Account of the Voyages Undertaken by the Order of His Present Majesty for Making Discoveries in the Southern Hemisphere: and Successively Performed by Commodore Byron, Captain Wallis, Captain Carteret, and Captain Cook, in the Dolphin, the Swallow, and the Endeavour: Drawn up from the Journals Which Were Kept by the Several Commanders, and from the Papers of Joseph Banks, Esq.* (1773).

[32] Harriet Martineau, *Dawn Island, A Tale* (Manchester: J. Gadsby, 1845). Subsequent references to this text are cited parenthetically in the text. In a review of Melville's *Omoo*, the *Dublin Review* attributes this prophecy to a Tahitian High Priest named Tecarmoar (23 [September and December 1847], 341–63, 363). See also Logan, *Harriet Martineau, Victorian Imperialism, and the Civilizing Mission* (Farnham, Surrey, and Burlington, VT: Ashgate, 2010), 103.

[33] See, for example, Logan, *Civilizing Mission,* 99–105; Edmond, *Representing the South Pacific,* 130–42; Patrick Brantlinger, *Rule of Darkness: British Literature and Imperialism, 1830–1914* (Ithaca, NY, and London: Cornell University Press, 1988), 30–32; Brantlinger, "'Dying Races': Rationalizing Genocide in the Nineteenth Century," in *The Decolonization of*

Figure 2.4
The frontispiece of *Dawn Island*, drawn and etched by J. Stephenson

avoids much of the typical rhetoric of British colonial expansion—the claiming of territory, the possibility of British settlers, and the religious conversion of the native population. Instead, the tale focuses specifically on the moral import of trade. As Logan explains, "In its depiction of the confrontation between a native island tribe and white British traders—the first such meeting for either side—*Dawn Island* suggests how the Civilizing Mission might be accomplished by imperial representatives with altruistic moral and ethical standards, people . . . committed to promoting the socio-economic values of western culture."[34]

As Martineau elaborates a vision of commerce as an ethical method of imperial expansion, she reinforces the principle of free trade at the heart of the League's political stance. Yet she does not stop there. Though at first glance the tale seems to have little to do with the bazaar itself, a closer examination reveals Martineau's engagement with the gendered rhetoric circulating in League publications at the same time she was writing the book. In order to accept and implement international commerce, the people of Dawn Island must revalue the labor performed by its women.

We learn that on Dawn Island "women . . . [are] regarded as an inferior race" (15) and are required to serve their fathers, husbands, or sons:

> They were required to cook for their masters at the superior oven provided for the better abode [where the men lived], to carry in the baskets of food and wait on the eaters, and at night to sleep in the most comfortless corner of the larger dwelling; but further than this they were not indulged. They must eat only when others had done, must not touch anything particularly good nor complain of anything particularly bad, must always be within call, and wait standing, must not lie down at night till all the animals were asleep, and must, without fail, be busy at the oven before their masters awoke in the morning. (15–16)

Martineau paints such a stark picture of the gendered division of labor that

---

Imagination: Culture, Knowledge, and Power, ed. Jan Nederveen Pieterse and Bhikhu Parekh (London and Atlantic Highlands, NJ: Zed Books, 1995), 43–56; Brantlinger, *Fictions of State: Culture and Credit in Britain, 1694–1994* (Ithaca, NY, and London: Cornell University Press, 1996), 186–87; and Brantlinger, *Dark Vanishings: Discourse on the Extinction of Primitive Races, 1800–1930* (Ithaca, NY, and London: Cornell University Press, 2003), 30–32. Ayse Celikkol, in *Romances of Free Trade: British Literature, Laissez-Faire, and the Global Nineteenth Century* (Oxford and New York: Oxford University Press, 2011, 67–82), puts forward a related argument, asserting that Dawn Island represents a mystical land outside of national boundaries, where free trade can be associated with a feminized fertility and abundance.

[34] Logan, *Civilizing Mission*, 99.

the women are portrayed as virtual slaves: they are considered "an inferior race" who keep "their masters" clothed, fed, and housed.

Martineau was an ardent abolitionist, and she considered free trade the best means to eliminate slavery in the world, as she argued in "Demerara" (1834), a tale dealing directly with West Indian slavery.[35] Whether or not she was correct, her logic was in line with that of League leaders. As the *League* reported, "Convince the slaveowner that by free labour a greater quantity of sugar can be produced at the same or at less cost than by slave labour, and when he is made to feel that slavery is unprofitable he will not be long in discovering that it is inhuman."[36] In *Dawn Island,* Martineau exemplifies this principle; she depicts slavery as ultimately unprofitable. Within this rhetoric of abolitionist free trade, *Dawn Island* depicts a proto-Demerara, before slavery and economic exploitation had rendered free-labor and free-trade matters for complicated political maneuvering and intricate international trade negotiations. *Dawn Island* depicts first contact as it should have been according to Martineau. It is her version of an abolitionist text in that it addresses the problem of the enslavement of women on Dawn Island by offering Western colonial trade as its solution.

Emancipation comes about when the Captain and his men begin to trade for goods. The items the Captain and his men want to acquire are the types of products that Idya and the other women usually procure for their families—fish, hogs, and coconuts. Now that these goods have exchange value, the work done to produce them is respected and respectable. Whereas before the arrival of the ship Idya had done all of the work to sustain herself and her husband while he "did little but bask on the shore, or bathe in the inlet" (41), as soon as the sailors begin to trade, he "himself promised to go fishing" (74). Indeed, the men in general set aside their aversion to women's work and begin to participate in it, and the women vow to work even harder (74, 87). The people of the island make plans to provide raw resources, to implement agricultural cultivation, and to fabri-

---

[35] Harriet Martineau, "Demerara, A Tale," in *Illustrations of Political Economy,* vol. 2 (London: Charles Fox, 1834), 142–43.

[36] "How Slavery May Be Abolished—The Sugar Monopoly and the Anti-Slavery Society," *League,* 8 February 1845, 306–7, 306. To demonstrate his belief in the power of free trade to eliminate slavery, one donor to the League bazaar boasted that he was sending "fifteen hogsheads of New Orleans slave-grown sugar" to be sold at the bazaar in order to protest the government's refusal to lift the tariff on foreign sugar (William Brown to Sir, 11 May 1845, *Bazaar Gazette,* 7, 3). Consistent with this reasoning, Richard Cobden, one of the leading free-trade Members of Parliament, had taken a controversial stance in 1844, supporting Robert Peel's effort to lower the duty on slave-grown sugar. His support helped keep Peel in office (see McCord, *The Anti-Corn Law League, 1838–1846,* 192–93).

cate goods such as rope and mats (87). True to Martineau's claim that free labor is more productive than slave labor, the islanders show every indication that their productivity will increase with the introduction of commerce. Even more significantly, there is no question that both men and women will contribute to this work. Though there is no official Emancipation Proclamation, trade has radically changed the women's place in society. It has freed them from their slave status solely by reconceiving the value of their work.

In addition, trade brings a fundamental change in the value of women's reproductive labor. Since the first three children of each couple traditionally have been sacrificed to the god Oro, Martineau portrays infanticide as the main cause of the island's population decline: Miava ponders, "Those who are born should be more than those who die; but if every man has one or two living children, and many more dead, how are our valleys to be peopled again?" (47).[37] In his discussion of *Dawn Island,* Patrick Brantlinger argues that depictions of depopulation by colonial authors are "one of the most frequent rationalizations for the 'vanishing' or 'passing' of non-Western peoples. [. . . It] is also the most extreme form of 'blaming the victim.'"[38] This is exactly Martineau's approach; she depicts the islanders as at fault for their population decline. Brantlinger astutely argues that Martineau is portraying "a reversal of the Malthusian nightmare," in which "non-Western peoples" commit "auto-genocide."[39] Ironically, though, in one respect Martineau is following Malthus's lead. Malthus, referencing Hume, posits the practice of infanticide as a method of birth control that "generally contributes to increase the population of a country. By removing the fears of too numerous a family, it encourages marriage, and the powerful yearnings of nature prevent parents from resorting to so cruel an expedient except in extreme cases."[40] In Tahiti, however, he surmises that the practice was prevalent enough to have "a contrary tendency."[41] Martin-

---

[37] Martineau most likely drew her ideas for infanticide on Dawn Island from accounts of infanticide among the arioi societies on Tahiti. The arioi were groups of traveling ritual performers who practiced sexual freedom before marriage and who practiced abortion and infanticide in cases of premarital pregnancy. See Anne Salmond, *Aphrodite's Island: The European Discovery of Tahiti* (Berkeley; Los Angeles; London: University of California Press, 2009), 35, 112, 116, 315.

[38] Brantlinger, "'Dying Races,'" 43.

[39] Brantlinger, "'Dying Races,'" 43.

[40] T. R. Malthus, *An Essay on the Principle of Population; or A View of Its Past and Present Effects on Human Happiness; With an Inquiry into Our Prospects Respecting the Future Removal or Mitigation of the Evils Which It Contains,* 1803, 2nd ed., ed. Patricia James, vol. 1 (Cambridge: Cambridge University Press, 1989), 50.

[41] Malthus, *An Essay on the Principle of Population,* 50.

eau uses this same logic when she emphasizes infanticide as the main cause of Dawn Island's decreasing population. By depicting a shrinking population with an extreme form of birth control that must be eliminated, Martineau was able to represent the Malthusian stance on infanticide while advocating for a domestic ideal of maternal and filial love that combined a thoroughly feminine and respectable position with a new emphasis on the labor value of motherhood.[42]

Idya is haunted by the memory of her infant who was ritually sacrificed. The Captain validates her emotional response by insisting that the islanders' god must be displeased with these infant sacrifices if he is causing the population to decline (82–83). Instead of sacrificing their children, the Captain suggests, the islanders should raise them to be productive workers who can trade for industrialized goods (88). Within the logic of commerce, women's reproductive labor has increased value because it generates future workers. These new workers will then be able to barter for trade goods, which will become the new sacrifices to offer the islanders' gods: "'Lay before them,' said the captain seriously, 'an axe, and a knife, and a looking-glass, and a garment of cotton'" (88). By using industrial goods to replace ritualized human sacrifice, the Captain places trade at the heart of the society's moral and religious code.

As part of this new moral code, the Captain preaches a gospel of domesticity. He revokes the "taboos" that mark certain people, homes, and battlegrounds as untouchable, set aside for the gods. Instead, he taboos the taking of human life and invokes the establishment of a domestic space as the end result of free trade. As his last act before leaving the island, the Captain lifts a taboo on the house of Idya's mother-in-law, announcing that the home "'is for her and for Idya to live in, and for . . . Miava, . . . that all may see that the taboo is taken off'" (92). Establishing a newly hallowed domestic space becomes the moral result of introducing free trade to the island. The Captain offers a home, a new market value for women's (and now men's) work, a growing labor force, and industrial trade goods as the moral prescription both for satisfying the islanders' gods and for successful trade.

By the end of the tale, women who had previously lived in their own "hovels" now live in honored homes. Women who had provided subsistence for their fathers and husbands now contribute to a trade economy. Men who had considered war and sacred ritual their only responsibilities

---

[42] Martineau had been criticized for depicting Malthusian population control in her *Illustrations* tale, "Weal and Woe in Garveloch" (see *Quarterly Review,* 49 [April 1833]: 136–52). In *Dawn Island* she broaches the same topic more circumspectly.

now participate in making trade goods. Parents who had sacrificed many of their infants now plan to raise all that are born to them. These fundamental changes to life on Dawn Island required the revaluing of women's labor. Thus, Martineau insists that women's contributions are integral to the functioning of a moral and successful marketplace and that the impetus behind that marketplace is the creation of an idealized home.

III. CONCLUSION

Martineau therefore writes an idealized tale of free trade, emancipation, imperial commerce, and gender cooperation. In this milieu, free trade is a means, but not an end in itself. The end results of free trade in this tale are a reconception of women's productive and reproductive labor, and the establishment of a religious and moral domestic ideal as a justification for commerce. Thus, the issues associated with free trade in this narrative align themselves with the issues regarding gender and the marketplace at the League bazaar, where the value of women's labor was in flux, and the moral and domestic associations of a ladies' sale became a justification for seeing free trade as a philanthropic endeavor. In the tale, Martineau takes a decided stance on these issues. Women's work, of all varieties, is to be valued. Industrial production goes hand in hand with domestic production; the moral associations of domesticity (and the women's work so often associated with it) are not antithetical to a competitive marketplace. Instead, they are the moral impulse driving the marketplace; they are the rationale legitimating economic gain.

By placing domesticity and women's work at the heart of free-trade ideology, Martineau offers an alternative to viewing the ladies' sale and the industrial exhibition as antithetical elements of the bazaar. From the point of view given in *Dawn Island,* these elements are complementary. The ladies' sale offers the exhibition a moral justification, and the exhibition offers the ladies' sale a means of showing that men's and women's mutual work is essential to the healthy functioning of the market and the home. This may well have been the reason Martineau herself was pleased to discover that a tablecloth she had embroidered and sent to an American anti-slavery bazaar had been sold for $100, an exorbitant price. Though Martineau would surely have upheld the notion of a free market in principle, she did not bemoan the inflated market that had raised substantial money for a good cause. Instead, "'So many of my thoughts and feelings,' she said, 'are wrought into that table-cover, that I dreaded lest it should pass into unknown hands. But now—How much pleasure this has given me! Thank every one of the "chivalry" for me!'"[43] Her tablecloth was worth the exorbitant price because of the "thoughts and feelings" that were embroidered into it and because the price paid for it was a compliment to her from friends and fellow abolitionists. Martineau understood the labor theory of value that drove the typical ladies' sale—it did not result in an inflated market, it resulted in a market priced according to philanthropic, domestic, and moral value.

---

[43] Chapman, *Memorials,* 444.

CHAPTER 3

Sacrificial Value

BEYOND THE CASH NEXUS IN GEORGE ELIOT'S *ROMOLA*

ILANA M. BLUMBERG

*I*n the early years of the decade that offered George Eliot her highest selling price for fiction, misers and thieves became central figures in her work. Silas Marner, Brother Jacob, and the lesser-known figures of Bardo and Tito in her 1862 Italian romance, *Romola,* all bear troubled relations to wealth. Economics and ethics are inseparable in these portraits, since these characters are also described as needing the education in sympathy that Eliot famously saw her novels as providing. I want to suggest that in the 1860s, economics functioned for Eliot not merely as a convenient metaphor for ethics but as a personal and historically rooted challenge to her avowed ethics of free-flowing sympathy among mutually responsible human beings. As Eliot continued to collect royalties on *Silas Marner,* her best-selling fable of a miser and his gold; as she negotiated with George Smith, who had offered her £10,000 for serial publication of *Romola* in the *Cornhill,* an offer Eliot believed to be "handsomer than almost any terms ever offered to a writer of Fiction"; and as she came to recognize the commercial failure of that project and, in response, to offer Smith the gift of her short story "Brother Jacob," the tale of a faithless son who robs his mother of her small, private savings, Eliot's fiction enacted and reflected

I am grateful for the influences of Linda C. Dowling and Peter Stallybrass on this essay.

on questions shared by other major novelists and political economists of her day.¹ What sort of economic exchange might be productive of ethical human relations? What forms of wealth might be best suited to escape the risks of unethical possession or circulation? And, even more significantly, how might capable women become the ethical agents of such exchanges rather than their objects? Describing the intensive labors that attended her composition of *Romola,* Eliot said that she had written it "with [her] best blood."² It was this notion of sacrificial exchange that enabled Eliot to merge the private aims of literary entrepreneurship with the public aims of social sympathy and to imagine an ethical economics in the early 1860s.

Romola, Eliot's ambitious novel of the Italian Renaissance, was recognized by some of her more astute contemporary readers as a veiled meditation on the Victorian woman question.³ Yet neither readers past nor readers present have noted how thoroughly the novel considers the related conjunction of ethics and economics in Victorian terms. In *Romola,* Eliot associated marketplace exchange and the characterless liquidity of money with the dangerously self-seeking tendencies of utilitarianism and the worst abuses of the cash nexus; the province of this high-stakes marketplace is exclusively male. Meanwhile, the novel establishes its alternative to the marketplace in the space of the private library, another male domain. In this space, the aim to retain private property beyond circulation and to calculate value not as a function of exchange but by purely individual standards results in an equally self-concerned, antisocial ethic and economic practice. These two alternatives pose special threats to women, who run the risks of becoming either objects of exchange or prized private property that loses rather than gains value in retention. Against these troubling alternatives, Eliot offered sacrifice as a female form of exchange that could embrace the inevitably transformative power of the marketplace while refusing the moral fungibility it had previously threatened.

If sacrifice tends to evoke the self-lacerating and inhibiting forms of repression we have been used to associate with Victorian female experience, I use it here in a more particular sense. As the sociologist Georg Simmel defines it, sacrifice is the exchange of one precious value for a second equal

---

¹ George Eliot, *Letters of George Eliot,* ed. Gordon S. Haight, 9 vols. (New Haven, CT, and London: Yale University Press, 1954–78), 4:34–35.

² As quoted in Andrew Sanders, Introduction to *Romola,* by George Eliot (London and New York: Penguin, 1980), 7–31, 10.

³ The *Westminster Review*'s anonymous reviewer of 1863 stated, "We cannot but think . . . that this long and elaborate disquisition on the relations between the sexes as a moral question is set forth by George Eliot too much in the colours of the nineteenth century." See Anonymous, "Unsigned Review, *Westminster Review,*" October 1863, lxxx, 344–52 in *George Eliot: The Critical Heritage,* ed. David Carroll (London: Routledge and Kegan Paul, 1971), 213–20, 216.

or greater value: "the value that a subject sacrifices can never be greater, in the particular circumstances of the moment, than the value that he receives in return."[4] Paradoxically similar to self-interested exchange, then, sacrificial exchange also seeks its end in a surplus of value, rather than the sheer loss that at first seems to define it. Painful loss is a requisite of sacrifice, yet when we consider the results of sacrifice as much as the process, we can see that the loss functions to heighten the potential value of its replacement. In *Romola,* the surplus generated by sacrificial exchange is not just personal female agency but also a transformation "upward" in forms of value. Not all forms of value are equal, Eliot suggests, not even values that come to seem commensurate because they can be exchanged for one another. In *Romola,* when a capable woman becomes an agent of exchange, dead or desiccated forms of value are exchanged for life-giving and nourishing forms of value in a sort of "trading up" that mirrors the evolution of social relations Eliot hoped to encourage with her novels of sympathy. As we will see, the heroine Romola, betrayed by her husband, Tito, redeems the money realized from his treacherous sale of her late father Bardo's library, amassed and tended over a lifetime and planned as a bequest to the city of Florence. Romola uses this money to attend to yet another betrayal of Tito's, as she feeds the vulnerable bodies of Tito's extralegal wife and illegitimate children. In so doing, she realizes a kind of surplus value we might call sacrificial. Sacrificial value dissolves the lines between self and other that have previously divided ethical from economic practice. In short, sacrificial exchange transforms private value into more collective forms in a fashion particularly appealing to Victorian thinkers intent on ideals of wide, yet effective, human sympathy. As Eliot narrated her way to an ethically viable, female form of commercial and textual exchange, she cannily took advantage of the immense cultural authority and personal meaning located in the mid-Victorian ideal of sacrifice, even as she radically transformed its meaning. Sacrificial exchange, predicated on loss and renunciation, realized its profits as it shared them.

I. HOARDING AND EGOISM: ROMOLA IN THE LIBRARY

At the outset of Eliot's historical novel, the narrator asserts that while politics, scholarship, and trade have changed dramatically since the high

---

[4] Georg Simmel, *The Philosophy of Money,* trans. Tom Bottomore and David Frisby (London: Routledge and Kegan Paul, 1978), 87. For an extensive discussion of the objective and subjective dimensions of value, see Simmel, "Value and Money," 59–130.

Renaissance, men "still own *that* life to be the highest, which is a conscious voluntary sacrifice."[5] Yet beyond the poetry of the Proem, *Romola* is strikingly short on conscious voluntary sacrifice. In fact, it seems all concentrated into one character, Romola herself. When the novel opens, we first encounter Romola as the dutiful Miltonic daughter, sequestered in a dim library, where she aids Bardo de' Bardi, her blind, moneyless father, in his Casaubon-like exertions on the rare manuscripts he has spent his lifetime collecting, copying, and emending. Disappointed in his passionate scholarly ambitions by the loss of his son's assistance (Dino has converted to a life of monastic Christianity among the Franciscans), Bardo dedicates himself to protecting the library and collection of antiquities from claims and debt, and wishes to bequeath it in its integrity to the city of Florence as "an everlasting possession to my fellow-citizens" (53).

Yet Bardo's desire, noble as it may sound, also reflects his need "to leave a lasting track of his footprints on the fast-whirling earth" (46). Like his Bardi ancestors before him, Romola's father possesses the "old family pride and energy, the old love of pre-eminence" (53). Bardo may eschew the "vulgar pursuit of wealth in commerce," but his own ascetic life and his devotion to "collecting the precious remains of ancient art and wisdom" are their own vulgar pursuit; Bardo's self-importance occludes his understanding of the lessons offered by the ancient art and wisdom (53). Though stoical teachings of worldly renunciation pepper Bardo's speech, the narrator describes these as "lip-born maxims . . . powerless over the passion which had been moving him" (56). Bardo cannot forget what the world owes him: "'I have a right to be remembered,'" Bardo proclaims (55):

> "I claim my right: it is not fair that the work of my brain and my hands should not be a monument to me—it is not just that my labour should bear the name of another man. It is but little to ask," the old man went on, bitterly, "that my name should be over the door—that men should own themselves debtors to the Bardi library in Florence." (57)

Bardo fears the theft of credit and memory, and rejects the single most likely avenue for preserving his work—printing—a marvel of modernity that Bardo laments but the narrator celebrates: "the first sheets of that fine Homer which was among the early glories of the Florentine press" (7). Bardo's fear that some other scholar will claim the credit for his work has prevented him from yielding to "the wish of Aldo Manuzio when he sets up his press at Venice, and giv[ing] him the aid of my annotated manu-

---

[5] George Eliot, *Romola* (Oxford and New York: Clarendon-Oxford Press, 1993), 9.

scripts" (55). The pathos of Bardo's situation is that his work is likely to be remembered *only* if he lends the printers his manuscripts. Bardo's retention of his own manuscripts and his refusal to share any of his emendations guarantee that his insights will be buried in an unmarked grave.

Remarkably, Eliot tethers Bardo's rejection of print technology not so much to his historically limited perspective but to his culpable egoism, especially noxious because it operates in a sphere where it least belongs, a sphere dedicated to the production of knowledge. Bardo has zealously hoarded what he owns, all the while insensitive to its teachings and even to his own avowed commitment to provide a "far-stretching, lasting light which spreads over centuries of thought, and the life of nations, and makes clear to us the minds of the immortals who have reaped the great harvest and left us to glean in their furrows" (51). Yet, like light, earth, and recurring natural cycles, what Bardo has collected is not his alone; what he has emended, he has not himself written. The library has mistakenly come to reflect the man more than its contents. The objects have become "a scenario of the personal," as Susan Stewart puts it in her description of collecting: "The ultimate term in the series that marks the collection is the 'self,' the articulation of the collector's own identity" (162).[6]

Bardo describes the risk to his intellectual property in the most material of terms, appropriately reflecting the coincidence of material and intellectual possession in manuscript culture.[7] His inability to separate knowledge from its material form and its memorial function opposed Eliot's own typically Victorian ideal of the transgenerational, shared pursuit of knowledge in which individual contributions were imagined to be subsumed by a collectively owned, abstract product. John Ruskin, sharing Eliot's sense of the ongoing life of the dead in the quest for wisdom, described the project of inheritance and bequest as "exchange [. . .] between the living and the dead":

> We, as we live and work, are always to be thinking of those who are to come after us; that what we do may be serviceable, as far as we can make it so,

---

[6] Susan Stewart, *On Longing: Narratives of the Miniature, the Gigantic, the Souvenir, the Collection* (Durham, NC, and London: Duke University Press, 1993).

[7] In what was soon to be his classic account, *The Civilization of the Renaissance in Italy* (1860), Jacob Burckhardt had contextualized the term "fame," emphasizing that its Renaissance associations were intensely material. The markings of fame included an honored gravesite, perhaps a preserved birthplace, home, or library. See Jacob Burckhardt, *The Civilization of the Renaissance in Italy* (1860; New York: Modern Library–Random House, 1995), 108–15. Local competition over such monuments makes it even clearer that fame was rooted in singular objects and specific locations.

to them, as well as to us. Then, when we die, it is the work of those who come after us to accept this work of ours with thanks and remembrance, not thrusting it aside or tearing it down the moment they think they have no use for it. And each generation will only be happy or powerful to the pitch that it ought to be, in fulfilling these two duties to the Past and the Future. . . . Its own possessions will never be enough for it, unless it avails itself gratefully and tenderly of the treasures and the wisdom bequeathed to it by its ancestors.[8]

For Eliot and Ruskin, such collective knowledge could not be conceived apart from the dominant value of sympathy and the altruistic ethic that they imagined superseding egoism. Human sympathy, fellow-feeling on both its vertical and horizontal axes, was their corrective for corrupt individual ambition and their safeguard for a vivifying collective knowledge.

In the case of *Romola*, Bardo resembles most of the other important male figures in the novel who lack the "human sympathies which are the very life and substance of our wisdom" (164).

II. CIRCULATION AND EGOISM: ROMOLA IN THE MARKETPLACE

Eliot links both Bardo's refusal to share his manuscripts with printers and his insistence on their memorial value to his underappreciation of Romola, the one object in his library that is not "lifeless," but a living treasure (54). Like the inanimate objects and hoarded manuscripts of the library, Romola does not circulate beyond the confines her father sets for her. She is entirely unaware of the world beyond her father's library. The novel brilliantly dramatizes the unsympathetic, male alternatives of utter hoarding or undifferentiated circulation as they converge tragically upon Romola, who is transformed in the early pages of the novel from hoarded object to an object of trade between two men. Bardo's ethos of hoarding and retention yields to the unrelenting pressures of trade and circulation when Tito Melema appears in Bardo's library fresh from the rush of the Florentine marketplace. Tito needs money and is eager either to trade upon his scholarly services or to sell precious gems that were gifts from his adoptive father, Baldassarre. Tito's decision to sell the gems represents the son's callousness toward the aging father who generously adopted him years ear-

---

8 John Ruskin, *A Joy Forever* [1857], *Complete Works of John Ruskin*, vol. 19 (New York: Bryan, Taylor and Company, 1894), 181–82.

lier. The sale is callous not only because of the sentimental value of the rings, but because Tito sells them for his own profit rather than to finance a search to redeem Baldassarre, who was reputedly taken captive by Turks. Tito knows what is expected of him by "Public opinion"—to "make sacrifices, take voyages again and again" (98)—yet Tito asks himself, "'Do I not owe something to myself?'" (100). Tito, it seems, will sell anything—even his father—if it serves his personal advantage; he is "equal to any sacrifice that was not unpleasant" (281).

Not surprisingly, in this scene where the ethos of profit-oriented exchange rules the day, Romola too becomes reconstituted in the novel's gaze as a commodity. As Jeff Nunokawa claims, Victorian novelists wrote within a new economy that threatened to commodify and alienate even what was imagined to be sacred and inalienable. Responding to such cultural anxieties, novelists often represented women as "feminine treasure[s] that elude[d] the vicissitudes of capital."[9] Yet like all "inalienable" treasures, women, too, were finally alienable. The marriage market was one exceptionally important form of such daughterly alienability, with its financial proceeds and losses accruing largely to men, while affecting women's lives profoundly. Romola, with her golden hair, "a rare gem of [Bardo's] own" (74), is precisely that feminine treasure which at first seems to have no price, but soon enough is sold. It is no coincidence that Romola's dowry, along with the debts that might preclude the bequest of the family library, comes to interrupt her father's reverie over the spiritual estate he seeks to leave to Florence. For Bardo, Romola is associated with material demands, trivial and base, and yet ever pressing, and he chooses her circulation as the means for preserving his library, abdicating his responsibilities as her father to investigate the stranger who seeks her hand. After a short courtship between Romola and Tito, characterized by the mutual delusion so common to Eliot's courtships, Tito accepts Romola without a dowry (the price he pays for being a stranger with no leverage to make claims), and the two marry.

Tito is the novel's most complex figure, embodying a market culture's dominant value of circulation, with all its ethical risks, yet at the same time, with significant social possibilities. As the sale of his father's rings reflects, he is an unforgivable egoist. Yet solely by virtue of his entrance into the novel and his deeply unethical exchanges—his thefts and sales—does Romola find her way out of the confining space of her father's library toward an ethical understanding and practice beyond her own unques-

---

[9] Jeff Nunokawa, *The Afterlife of Property: Domestic Security and the Victorian Novel* (Princeton, NJ: Princeton University Press, 1994), 13.

tioned, fierce sense of loyalty to family and the past. Soon after Tito marries Romola, Bardo dies disappointed, having come to see that Tito will not replace his lost son by devoting himself to Bardo's scholarship. On the heels of Bardo's death, Romola, troubled by guilty fears that she pursued her own happiness before her father's, becomes consumed with fulfilling Bardo's dying wish to bequeath his library to the city. Even as Romola works to secure the library from Bardo's debts, Tito enters into his own negotiations to divide it and sell its components to French and Milanese bidders. Having learned that Baldassarre is in Florence, having denied the relationship and the man to secure his own comfort and reputation, and imagining, in consequence, that he might have to leave Florence, Tito seeks the funds to do so in comfort. Without any advance warning to Romola, Tito sells the library for three thousand florins, dismissing Romola's piety to the dead as "sentimental scruples which . . . had no relation to solid utility" and which needlessly "deprived himself and Romola of substantial advantages" (280). Eliot's forceful association of Tito with her own contemporary utilitarianism was unambiguously negative. Tito's convenient respect for utility entails his dismissal of any sympathetic or altruistic relations, especially those that might require self-sacrifice.[10]

In selling the library, Tito asserts himself against the wishes of his deceased father-in-law and takes advantage of his legally and physically defenseless wife, going so far as to lock her in when she seeks to leave the house to reverse the sale. As the novel's spokesman on behalf of circulation (as engineered by men), Tito provides a full and articulate, if terribly flawed, countertheory to the novel's praise for Romola's pious, retentive aims. Tito responds to Romola's need to "keep our silent promises on which others build because they believe in our love and truth" with an argument for wider sympathies (289–90):

> the notion of isolating a collection of books and antiquities, and attaching a single name to them for ever, was one that had no valid, substantial good for its object: and yet more, one that was liable to be defeated in a thousand ways. See what has become of the Medici collections! And, for my part, I consider it even blameworthy to entertain those petty views of appropriation: why should anyone be reasonably glad that Florence should possess the benefits of learned research and taste more than any other city? . . . what possible good can these books and antiquities do, stowed

---

[10] Eliot's treatment of utilitarianism is markedly negative, especially given its more sophisticated explications by the early 1860s. See J. B. Schneewind, *Sidgwick's Ethics and Victorian Moral Philosophy* (Oxford: Clarendon Press, 1977), 139.

together under your father's name in Florence, more than they would do if they were divided or carried elsewhere? Nay, is not the dispersion of such things in hands that know how to value them, one means of extending their usefulness? The rivalry of Italian cities is very petty and illiberal. The loss of Constantinople was the gain of the whole civilized world. (288–89)

In this passage, Eliot marshals her full arsenal of historical knowledge against a chronologically handicapped Tito. From her reading and her Italian journeys, she knew that the private collections of citizens, painstakingly built and retained against threats of debt, war, famine, and flood, were to form the core of invaluable, public Italian libraries. As Burckhardt noted in 1860, the "celebrated Medici library," which Tito takes here as his example of vain and useless collection, "had to be recovered piecemeal" after the plundering in 1494; it then became the foundation of Florence's public Uffizi galleries.[11] Yet ethical implications overshadow the historical ones. Tito's speech, with the hyperarticulate, sophistical arguments whose processes of self-convincing so interested Eliot, is easily seen through by Romola. Instinctively recoiling from Tito's self-justifications, Romola condemns his "hopelessly shallow readiness which professed to appropriate the widest sympathies and had no pulse for the nearest" (289).

III. SACRIFICIAL EXCHANGE: ROMOLA AND THE EDIBLE SCROLLS

Yet Tito's critique of "those petty views of appropriation"—the avowed preferential loyalty to city, nation-state, and family—sets in relief the narrowness of Romola's own sympathies, which barely extend beyond her father. Likewise, Tito's political engagement, unethical as it is (he is a double agent), allows us to see more vividly Romola's lack of interest in just those public concerns that will shape her future along with those of her fellow Florentines. The sale of the library marks a turning point in the novel. It occasions Romola's attempt to leave Tito, her passage beyond the walls of her home, and her subsequent life-changing meeting with Savonarola, who teaches her to accept the bonds of "simple human fellowship" rather

---

[11] Burckhardt, *The Civilization of the Renaissance in Italy*, 142. Influenced by Michelet and then Burckhardt, the dominant position of nineteenth-century historians was that the "rivalry" scorned by Tito had been responsible for spurring the great productions of the Renaissance. The division of materials was, contrary to Tito's claims, not at all useful to scholars who needed to do comparative work.

than those of her nearest affections alone (361). It is Savonarola who challenges Romola's assumption that "wide sympathies" must be Tito's shallow or false sympathies, erected as a defense against the real claims of those nearby.

As Romola attempts to flee her marriage and her city, Savonarola confronts her in language that is unusually suited to cast Romola into doubt but also to recall to the reader the ethical misapprehensions of both Bardo and Tito. Savonarola demands of Romola, "Who is so base as the debtor that thinks himself free?" (361) and tells her she cannot abandon her city in its time of need since she bears to others the "debt of a fellow-citizen" (363). While Tito and Bardo imagine the debts others owe them—pride, fame, pleasure, ease—and hoard, steal, and sell accordingly, Romola is asked to imagine an inverted ethical paradigm. Given the conjunction of ethics and economics in the novel, the inverted ethical paradigm Romola must imagine demands an economic correlative as well: What sort of exchange relation might match an ethical position that imagines oneself in debt to others who are not one's family but are also not sheer strangers? What sort of exchange relation would enact an authentic and appropriately measured sympathy? As we will see in the final pages of this essay, *Romola* dramatizes ethical exchange as the willingness to sacrifice one's own capital so that it anonymously supports transgenerational and extrafamilial beneficiaries; such exchange expresses the conviction that the future of humanity supersedes any one individual's claims. In establishing this model of self-sacrifice, Eliot reflects on writing, her chosen career, as a model site for sacrificial relations.

The central object of sacrifice in *Romola* is the library. After a complicated series of political and personal events, Tito meets his retribution, dying at his adoptive father's hand. Romola, inheriting his property, and "distrust[ing] the cleanness of that money," makes the funds over to the State, "except so much as was equal to the price of her father's library" (572). With this particular, consecrated sum, Romola sets out to find Tito's second family, whom she vows to support with the library money. The designation of the library's purchase money to feed and shelter Romola's rival offers an alternative to indiscriminate exchange and hoarding as expressions of greed, egoism, and private aggrandizement. Redressing her father's failures, Romola gives up her own wealth and forgoes any personal renown: "a more noble sensitiveness made her shrink from assuming an attitude of generosity in the eyes of others by publishing Tessa's relation to Tito" (571).

Further, Romola does not invest her money in enduring material possessions such as bronze and marble fragments or the parchment manuscripts that, when cared for correctly, could last over a thousand years in perfect condition. Romola does not invest at all. Instead, she buys food, the least staying of all commodities. Where Bardo desires to leave a mark, Romola buys what will assuredly leave no mark but instead will find itself incorporated into the bodies for which she cares, bodies which themselves will yield to future generations, a theme Eliot makes central to her historical novel. If the telos of print is memory and survival, the telos of food is incorporation and absorption. While Bardo depended on writing to leave what Stewart has called "a trace beyond the life of the body," to promise "the immortality of the material world in contrast to the mortality of the body" (31), Romola turns to food, which, as Peter Stallybrass writes, "rapidly *becomes* us and disappears."[12] That Eliot turns the exchange money of the library into the provision of nourishing food makes especially good sense since her novel has also developed the scriptural metaphor of knowledge truly acquired as something ingested and absorbed.[13] Romola's absorption of the humanist wisdom of sympathy enables her to share rather than hoard her wealth.

Romola's exchange of the library money for food also redresses Tito's failures. Where his easy exchanges have destroyed human links and denied the claims of the past, Romola's exchanges create new ties that uphold human obligations, particularly those the strong owe to the weak. Circulation here accepts the original debts of human sympathy that Romola's father and husband never acknowledged and does so in an excessive sacrificial mode that cannot be explained or circumscribed by Tito's utilitarian political economy. As Romola later explains to Tito's pleasure-loving young son, ethical life characterized by "this sort of happiness often brings so much pain with it, that we can only tell it from pain by its being what we would choose before anything else, because our souls see it is good" (587).

In adopting Tito's family, Romola also resolves the novel's problem of competing sympathies. Strangers, Tessa and the children are objects of Romola's "wide sympathy"; yet since they are linked to Romola through Tito, the second wife and children are simultaneously objects of "near sympathy." Adoption allows Eliot to trace this moderate path of sympathy, in which the fierce animal attachments for which Savonarola early on criti-

---

[12] Peter Stallybrass, "Worn Worlds: Clothes, Mourning, and the Life of Things," *Yale Review* 81.2 (1993): 35–50, 37.

[13] In contrast with Bardo's "lip-born maxims," Eliot imagines scrolls that require eating in order to nourish humanity. When Dino narrates an apocalyptic vision of the hunger and thirst left by inedible scrolls, Eliot implies a contrast with the prophecy of Ezekiel: "And He said to me, 'Son of man, feed your stomach and fill your insides with this scroll which I give you,' and I ate it and it became in my mouth as honey for sweetness'" (Ezek. 2:5–3:3).

cizes Romola ("'you are without a law, without religion: you are no better than a beast of the field when she is robbed of her young'" [364]) merge with the undifferentiated "simple human fellowship" which the novel's late village scenes suggest do not suffice either.

IV. SACRIFICIAL EXCHANGE: ROMOLA AND "PUBLICATIONS IN PRINT"

Even as the character Romola exchanges the library's material value for the means of human sustenance, the author Eliot transforms the library as the novel's central image of literacy; in the process, Eliot offers us a model for an ethical economics especially relevant to women writers in the mid-nineteenth century. With the sale of the library, the novel moves from the past, the realm of "history," to a modernity continuous with Eliot's own times. In a striking shift, Eliot exchanges the novel's predominating images of singular and desiccated manuscripts and scrolls with a new image: multiple copies of printed publications. The monumental library thus yields not only to mortal, human bodies but also, in its imagistic "exchange-value" in the novel, to a new form of inexpensive, public literacy. At the political climax of the novel, handbills arguing for and against the death of so-called conspirators are sold and circulate, still wet, in the hands of "eager readers" (491–92), and Savonarola's confessions, in two editions, also pass into the hands of "eager readers" (575). In these scenes, contemporary social, political, and economic life becomes inseparable from print.

Romola's new, sympathetic interest in the life of her city is doubly represented in the novel by her feeding Tito's family (along with many of the poor and hungry) and her purchase and avid reading of the printed news, alongside many others in Florence. Her independent reading makes a dramatic break not only in her history of submission to male authority but also in the larger cultural history the novel traces. Like the nineteenth-century novel itself, the handbill could be purchased cheaply, shared by many readers, and read by nonscholars.[14] George Eliot responded ambivalently to the objects of mass literacy, noting in *Romola* the unreliability and sensationalism of handbills. In her own day, she worried that major

---

[14] As Roger Chartier notes, in societies of the ancient regime, even those classed as "illiterate" may have been able to read signs, posters, news-sheets, or chapbooks. See *The Order of Books: Readers, Authors, and Libraries in Europe between the Fourteenth and Eighteenth Centuries*, trans. Lydia G. Cochrane (Stanford, CA: Stanford University Press, 1994), 19.

advances in printing technology would degrade the intellectual climate.[15] Yet even as she alluded to the "spawn of the press," she recognized the social possibilities of making print available to an unprecedentedly large audience.[16] In a letter of 25 June 1861, G. H. Lewes's son, Thornton, noted to his father and stepmother that the "cheapest books ever published" had just been issued in London and simultaneously cheered the sale of 8,000 copies of *Silas Marner*, writing, "the more the merrier."[17] Eliot's own hope in the increased, cheap availability and circulation of printed forms was deeply connected to her belief in the efficacy of realist art to evoke social sympathy. While neither printed confessions nor handbills are a form of realist art, they are the texts in *Romola* that most closely approach the mass-circulating novel of the nineteenth century. Technologically closest in their shared distinction from manuscripts, the handbills and confessions resemble novels as well in the reading practice Eliot imagines them engendering in the heroine.

The link between sympathy and modern, mass forms of textuality is dramatized by Romola's conscientious, discerning, and impassioned reading: an image of Eliot's own artistic aims realized. The narrator stresses Romola's attention not only to the bold headlines but to the "smaller type" of the handbills (491). Meanwhile, Romola attends to Savonarola's published confessions with great care, repeatedly reading a "memorable passage, which may perhaps have had its erasures and interpolations" (578). Here, Eliot seems consciously to rework Bardo's scribal relation to his manuscripts, his devoted search for any "error or indistinctness" and his specialized work to resolve it (50). Yet Romola's reading differs from Bardo's because she evaluates the document not in an intellectual exercise divorced from or repressive of personal experience. Instead, she applies her hard-earned understanding of human life and human voices, in all their tragic and sympathetic dimensions. Romola leaves behind the "lip-born maxims" of Bardo's manuscripts to evaluate Savonarola's transcript in light of what she knows of the extraordinary man himself: "Looking at the printed confessions, she saw many sentences . . . in striking opposition, not only to Savonarola, but also to the general tone of the confessions, [which] strengthened the impression that the rest of the text represented . . . what had really fallen from his lips" (578). At stake in Romola's exemplary

---

[15] On the print revolution of the nineteenth century, in particular the transition from the printing press to printing machines, see Allan C. Dooley, *Author and Printer in Victorian England* (Charlottesville and London: University Press of Virginia, 1992), 79–83.

[16] George Eliot, *Selected Essays, Poems and Other Writings*, ed. A. S. Byatt and Nicholas Warren (London and New York: Penguin Books, 1990), 265.

[17] *Letters*, 8:286.

reading of this printed document is nothing less than the ethical validation of the novel's other tragic figure of sympathy and sacrifice: the martyr Savonarola himself.

V. "PAINFUL JOY": ELIOT'S SACRIFICIAL PROFITS AND PROFITABLE SACRIFICES

Eliot's alignment of modern forms of textuality with sympathy, circulation, collective benefit, and female agency offers a satisfying novelistic resolution to the problems of the novel. Yet did it offer any meaningful practical lessons for developing an ethical economics in the mid-nineteenth century? As a professionalizing female writer, Eliot especially needed a way to reconcile sympathy with self-concern, collective profit with individual profit, and circulation with retention. In the balance were the risks to women when they functioned as objects rather than subjects of exchange. Texts became the special objects around which Eliot invented a female form of exchange that would allow for retention and circulation at the same time; that would allow for sacrificial activity, writing with one's "best blood," while vivifying the self; and that would trade upon an object close enough to the self to be a true offering, but distinct enough from the self to preserve an independent female agent of exchange.

As N. N. Feltes has demonstrated, one of the defining issues for professionalizing Victorian writers was whether they were to retain control over the "terms, conditions, and content" of their work or whether those rights were to remain largely in the hands of their publishers.[18] As a legal *feme sole,* in control of her own property as married women were not, George Eliot had as much to lose or gain from the relations of production under which her books were published as any male author. Like her contemporaries Charles Dickens and Wilkie Collins, for instance, she was involved in detailed negotiations over the price and format of her novels. Between *Romola* and *Middlemarch,* as Eliot's sense of her career began to coalesce, she was more and more willing to take the financial risks of her work upon herself in a royalty system rather than sell her books and their rights for a prearranged sum of money. No longer willing to engage in petty-commodity trade, Eliot came to relate to her novels less as "commodity-books," than as the "commodity-texts" of a capitalist culture, texts whose surplus value she sought to claim by altering the social relations of

---

[18] N. N. Feltes, *Modes of Production of Victorian Novels* (Chicago: University of Chicago Press, 1986), 45.

PART I. THE ETHICS OF EXCHANGE

their production.[19] The idea of royalties, of course, is dependent upon mass production and circulation. There are no royalties in a culture of singular manuscripts. Whatever profit an author makes comes from her capacity to give up her text to the public. And yet, this giving-up is not really a form of giving-up but of keeping-while-giving, the sort of sacrificial exchange along vertical and horizontal axes that Eliot took so much trouble to imagine against the alternative male models she described in *Romola*.[20]

What should we make of the fact that with all its sacrificial rhetoric *Romola* was a high watermark in Eliot's earning capacity? As a result of her decision to switch publishers in order to realize the extraordinary sum of £7,000 for *Romola,* Eliot was judged by her former and future publisher, John Blackwood, to be especially "mercenary."[21] Yet Rosemarie Bodenheimer has made the critical point that the money raised from the sale of Eliot's novels was not only the mainstay of Lewes and Eliot, but also went to supporting Eliot's stepchildren, the sons of G. H. and Agnes Lewes, and even, to some extent, the children Agnes bore with her lover, Thornton Hunt.[22]

A female writer should be no more obligated than a male to justify the money she makes for her work, yet it is remarkable that in publishing *Romola,* George Eliot acted out the part of her heroine, taking the equivalent of the "purchase-money" of her own precious text to support the second and even third family of the man she loved and lived with outside of legal marriage. Breaking down the lines between self and other, between kin and non-kin, and between personal and collective benefit, Eliot pursued profitable exchange without betraying her own ethical imperative. The salability of a precious text and then the fungibility of the money made from it became in her hands a very real mechanism for increasing and spreading value. Later, when George Eliot returned to reread *Romola,* the novel written with her "best blood," she described the "painful joy" of reencountering her own sentences, now faded from her memory.[23] Eliot's "painful joy" of simultaneous possession, loss, and repossession defines for us the paradox of sacrificial value Eliot invented in *Romola*.

---

[19] Feltes, *Modes of Production of Victorian Novels,* 49.

[20] The phrase "keeping-while-giving" belongs to Annette Weiner, who uses it in an anthropological context rather than emphasizing its metaphorical and literary possibilities. Annette Weiner, *Inalienable Possessions: The Paradox of Keeping-While-Giving* (Berkeley: University of California Press, 1992).

[21] As quoted in Feltes, *Modes of Production of Victorian Novels,* 46.

[22] Rosemarie Bodenheimer, *The Real Life of Mary Ann Evans: George Eliot, Her Letters and Fiction* (Ithaca, NY: Cornell University Press, 1994), 286, n18.

[23] Sanders, Introduction to *Romola,* 10.

PART II

Political Economy

CHAPTER 4

Florence Nightingale's Contributions to Economics

MARY POOVEY

Florence Nightingale was not an economist. A wealthy woman by birth, Nightingale tended to address the subjects we associate with economics primarily in terms of their social and moral implications: she was, for example, worried about poverty because she considered this a root cause of crime, not because she was interested in the rate of wages in the abstract. Indeed, when we think about the contributions Nightingale can be said to have made to the modern discipline of economics, we have to acknowledge that, even though she formulated her suggestions in the terms that governed political economy (the nonmathematical version of economics that prevailed during her most active years), she actually helped advance not the moral practice of nineteenth-century political economy but the "scientific" (mathematical) form that economics took after her death in 1901. To address the relationship between Florence Nightingale and economics, then, means that we have to describe the transformation of economics from a moral practice into a mathematical science. It also means that we have to understand how a contribution formulated in one set of terms came to look, in retrospect, quite different from its creator's intentions.

To see how Nightingale's moral—even theological—formulations can be said to have enhanced a discipline that came to pride itself on its superiority to all nonscientific agendas, we need to begin with her effort to improve the health of the British army. Today, as in her own time, Nightingale is credited primarily with improving nursing by making this a reputable profession for middle-class, as well as working-class, women. Despite her undeniable contributions to nursing, however, her campaign to reform military hospitals arguably had a more significant impact both during her lifetime (on determining the mortality rate of soldiers) and in ours (on applied statistics). Before examining her contributions to statistics—and, indirectly, to economics—we need to recover the details of her engagement with hospital reform.

I. THE CAMPAIGN TO IMPROVE MILITARY HOSPITALS

Florence Nightingale's relatively brief experience in the Crimea—she embarked for Turkey in October 1854 and returned to England in July 1856—anchored her lifelong commitment to improving conditions in military hospitals. As we will see in a moment, while in the Crimea, Nightingale became convinced that more soldiers were dying from "zymotic" (preventable) diseases such as dysentery and infection than from the wounds they received on the battlefield. Upon her return, with the help of the physician John Sutherland and William Farr, Compiler of Abstracts at the General Registry Office, Nightingale began to compile documentation that supported her view. Even though her sex prevented Nightingale from directly participating in the official commission that Queen Victoria appointed to investigate hospital conditions, the appendix she contributed to the Royal Commission Report (Appendix 72), along with two privately printed books Nightingale prepared for the government—*Mortality of the British Army* (1858) and *Notes on Matters Affecting the Health of the British Army* (1858)— helped convince legislators that something needed to be done. In 1859, in response to a pamphlet that accused her of exaggerating the mortality rate in military hospitals, Nightingale augmented her data with *A Contribution to the Sanitary History of the British Army*. Also in 1859, upon Nightingale's urging, Harriet Martineau recast Nightingale's more recondite work into a "slight sketch," *England and her Soldiers,* which was intended to arouse public outrage.[1] Largely as a result of Nightingale's efforts, four subcommissions were appointed, the Royal Commission issued its report *Army Medical*

---

[1] Harriet Martineau, *England and her Soldiers* (London: Smith, Elder, & Co., 1859), vi.

Statistics in June 1858, and the *First Annual Statistical Report on the Health of the Army* appeared in March 1861. Opposition to this report led Nightingale to publish the two addresses she had delivered to the National Association for the Promotion of the Social Sciences as *Notes on Hospitals* (1861); and, as conditions similar to those in the Crimea reappeared in India in the wake of the 1857 uprising, Nightingale successfully urged the queen to appoint a Royal Commission to investigate army mortality there. The "greater part" of this Commission's 1863 report was "Nightingale's handiwork," and the ten years she devoted to improving Indian sanitation and hospital management helped lower army mortality rates there as well.[2]

Of all these documents, Nightingale's *Notes on Matters Affecting the Health of the British Army* best represents her method and goals. Composed in just six weeks, this 800-page book was printed at Nightingale's expense and distributed privately to influential politicians and writers. The work struck various of its first readers as "a treasury of authentic fact" and "a gift to the Army"—even though, as we will see, Nightingale's mode of presentation made absorbing the information it contained challenging.[3] For the argument I am developing here, it is also important to note that this volume reprinted the (revised) versions of three graphics that had initially appeared in her 1858 contributions to the government commission. These graphics, which are now referred to as polar-area diagrams, also appeared in Martineau's *England and her Soldiers*. They provide a visually arresting representation of the month-by-month mortality at hospitals in Scutari, Kulali, and Manchester, which allows the viewer to compare both the rate of mortality before and after the introduction of sanitary reform and the relationship between the rate of mortality in the East and that at a domestic hospital (see figures 4.1 and 4.2).[4]

Notes on Matters Affecting the Health of the British Army is characterized by a remarkable degree of ardor, capaciousness, and redundancy. Intended as a survey of conditions in the military hospitals of the East, an indictment of the administrative system of the army, and a passionate plea for sanitary reform, *Notes* juxtaposes lists, tables, diagrams, excerpts from official documents, and editorial commentary in an effort to make the

---

[2] Edwin W. Kopf, "Florence Nightingale as Statistician," *American Statistical Society*, December 1916, 400.

[3] Quoted in Kopf, "Florence Nightingale as Statistician," 391.

[4] An animated, interactive version of Nightingale's graphics can be found at "Nightingale's Coxcombs," http://understandinguncertainty.org/node/213 (accessed 2 July 2010). While Nightingale's diagrams were (obviously) neither animated nor interactive, this digital representation is extremely helpful for understanding the value of these graphics.

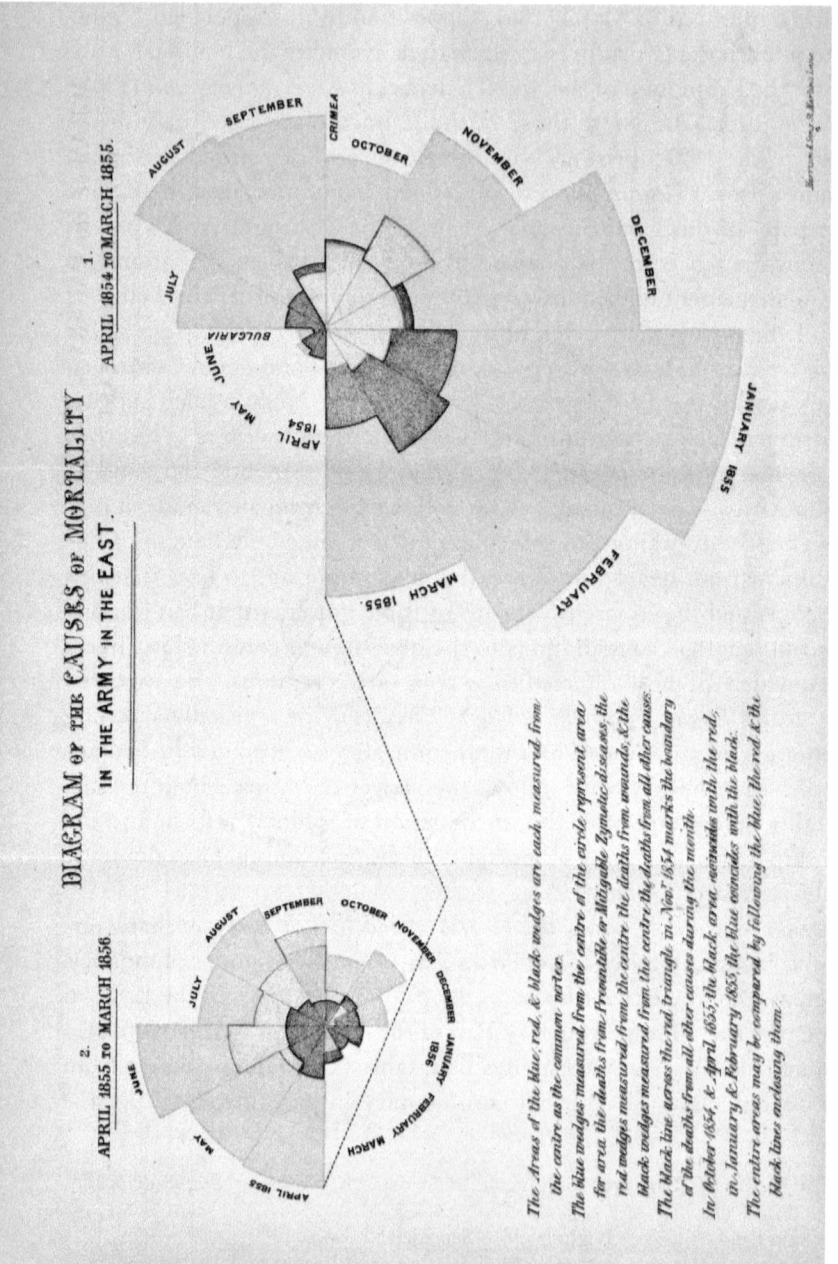

Figure 4.1
Nightingale's Diagram of the Causes of Mortality in the Army in the East.
Left: April 1855–March 1856. *Right*: April 1854–March 1855. From Florence Nightingale, *Notes on Matters Affecting the Health of the British Army* (1858), Part II, following p. 314. Yale University, Harvey Cushing/John Hay Whitney Medical Library

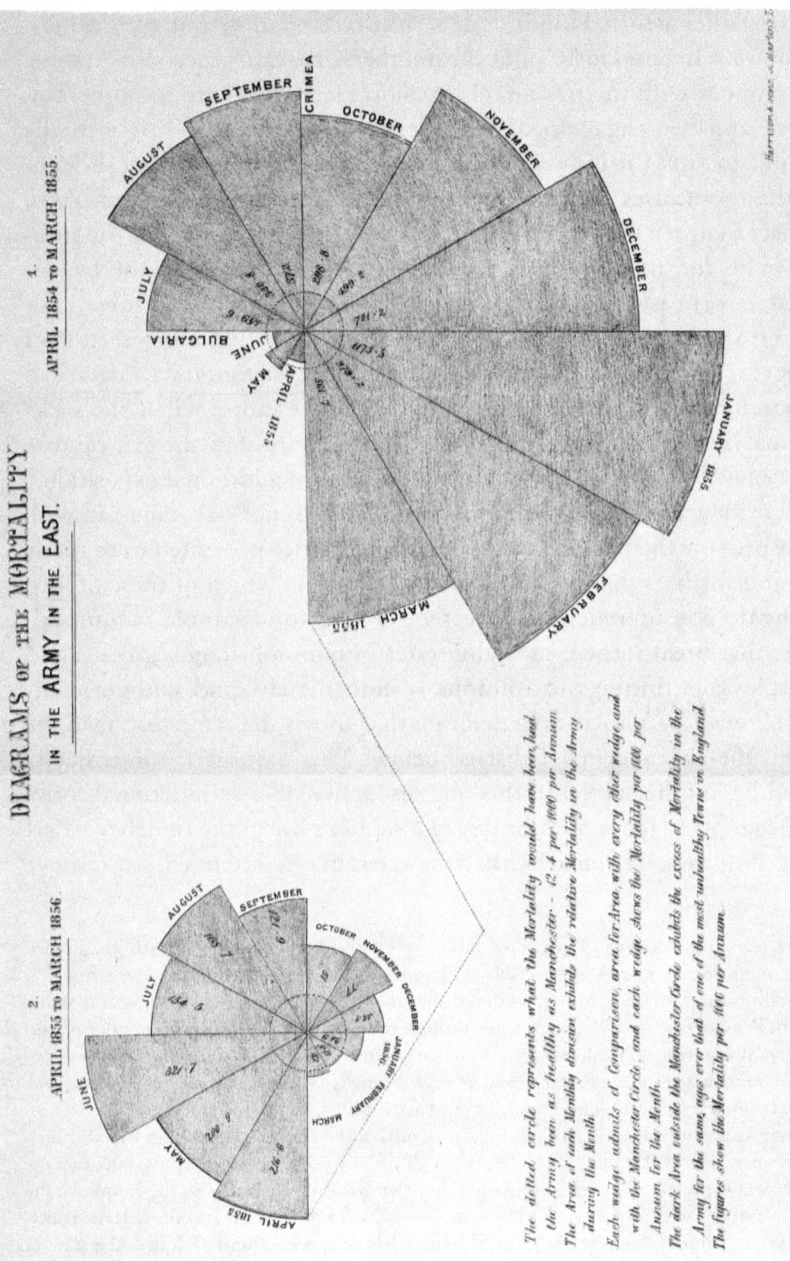

Figure 4.2

Nightingale's Diagrams of the Mortality in the Army in the East.

Left: April 1855–March 1856. *Right*: April 1854–March 1855. From Florence Nightingale, *Notes on Matters Affecting the Health of the British Army* (1858), Part II, section ix, following p. 320. Yale University, Harvey Cushing/John Hay Whitney Medical Library

PART II. POLITICAL ECONOMY

evidence irrefutable. At times, Nightingale seems aware that her tendency to heap together assorted kinds of data risks redundancy,[5] but, for the most part, she unselfconsciously piles on numbers, narrative accounts, tables, and harangues with the passion of a zealot. Her targets are so numerous, however, and her engagement with detail so intense that it is virtually impossible to rank the injustices she chronicles or to identify what she considers the root causes of the army's mortality.[6] At the beginning of *Notes,* she insists that her target is the "system" of army hospitals (not the individuals who run them), but, in her account, the system seems so byzantine that reform is impossible to imagine. To indicate the additive logic that informs her presentation, we might simply note that every section of the report is followed by one or more appendices, memoranda, "detached memorand[a]," sketches, or notes. Typically, once more, when she seeks to summarize her findings in section vi, every claim that she can capture her case in a "few words" begets page after page of additional exposition.[7]

The evidence Nightingale summons in *Notes* is not only amassed with scant respect for the reader's attention span; it is also presented in so many genres and formats that it is difficult to determine which of these, if any, Nightingale considered most effective. Thus, for example, a numerical table that breaks down mortality rates into month-long segments and that displays its findings in columns is immediately (and without comment) followed by a polar-area diagram that shows the same results in the exploded pie-chart format I discuss below. This graphic is immediately followed by another account, this one discursive, in a semifictional form, which attempts to focus on "one day of a soldier's life in the trenches" (Part II, 316). Nightingale remarks that the narrative is intended "to remove

---

[5] After providing dozens of pages of tables, eyewitness accounts, and testimonials, for example, Nightingale erupts into a self-conscious commentary on her own method: "it appears vain to heap evidence upon evidence that this [the deplorable conditions at Scutari] was so; if the evidence already given is not enough to make people believe it, 'neither would they believe if one rose from the dead!'" *Notes on Matters Affecting the Health, Efficiency, and Hospital Administration of the British Army, Founded Chiefly on the Experience of the Late War* (London: Printed by Harrison and Sons, 1858), Part I, 140.

[6] Among the scores of targets Nightingale identifies, we find the following: the administrative organization of the war office, the nature of provisions given the soldiers, bureaucrats' lack of respect for science, general ignorance about sanitation, conditions in the hospitals, the chain of command within the army, the forms with which information is collected, the transport ships that bring in wounded soldiers, the cubic feet of space around each bed, the state of the privies, discipline in the wards, the number and kinds of items washed each week in the hospital, the quality of the cooking at Scutari, the number of shirts issued to each soldier, and the regimental system of hospital management.

[7] See pp. 164–76.

any surprise which the above statistics may have created" (Part II, 316). The supplemental nature of this narrative—it both complements the tabular and graphic displays of information and calls attention to their insufficiency—is confirmed when Nightingale segues from the individualistic narrative she promised ("*one* day of *a* soldier's life") to a collective narrative that seeks to capture both the generic experience of the typical soldier and the range of experiences of all British soldiers ("they breakfasted on their rum and biscuit," "he had on either a shirt, which he had worn for six weeks . . . or was without linen altogether," Part II, 318). This little narrative, which occupies four pages of the 800-plus-page document, ends in another set of statistics, which, Nightingale assures her reader, is "in no way unaccountable" after the story she has just presented (Part II, 320).

The tensions among the individual, the type, and the collective, which Nightingale's narrative enacts without comment, constitute the heart of the representational conundrum she tries to work through in *Notes*. In the face of evidence that threatens to overwhelm her (and the reader), that is so heterogeneous in kind and content, and that contradicts most of the available reports about conditions in the East (both official and anecdotal), how was she to convey both the suffering of the individual and the overall condition of the army? And how could she formulate her litany of injustices and ills so as to make them felt without convincing the reader that reform was impossible? In the next section I argue that Nightingale approached a solution to these challenges through her presentation of statistical data—that is, through her embryonic recognition that what statistical representation could do was to simultaneously capture the conditions individuals suffered and compare these conditions with others that readers might know firsthand. Whether presented in graphical or numerical format, in other words, statistics promised to link the individual to the collective and to display data in a form that would identify the root causes of deaths in the East. Once they could identify the causes of mortality, Nightingale fervently believed, legislators would find the will and the resources to remedy them.

Before I turn to Nightingale's engagement with statistics, it will be helpful to look briefly at Harriet Martineau's attempt to render Nightingale's findings in a form more palatable to ordinary readers, the "vulgar public" that Nightingale occasionally scorned.[8] From Martineau's re-presentation

---

[8] Hugh Small cites Nightingale's reference to the "vulgar public" in "Florence Nightingale's Statistical Diagrams," http://www.florence-nightingale-avenging-angel.co.uk/GraphicsPaper/Graphics.htm (accessed 2 July 2010). This is a presentation that Small delivered at the Nightingale Museum, St. Thomas's Hospital, London, on 18 March 1998. From

of Nightingale's data and conclusions in (largely) narrative form, we can see that the contest between statistical data (whether iterative, tabular, or graphic in format) and discursive prose, which makes Nightingale's document so challenging, *could* be resolved at midcentury simply by excising the statistics.

Writing three years after the end of the Crimean War and at Nightingale's urging, Martineau wanted to produce "not a work of invention" but another version of the evidence contained in various unofficial and official reports (including Nightingale's).[9] As with her *Illustrations of Political Economy,* which had helped disseminate the principles of political economy, *England and her Soldiers* was designed to abstract, simplify, and animate data that appeared elsewhere in less accessible form. "Few people read Blue Books; and very few have time to go through the mass of evidence collected by the various authorities who have reported on the state of the army," Martineau acknowledges in her prefatory remarks. "I have selected what seemed fittest to illustrate a slight sketch of the experience of our troops in the late war. This much may be quickly read; and my trust is, that it may suffice to rouse the public to claim the complete fulfillment of the programme of reform, laid down by the Royal Commissioners, and assented to by all rational persons who have considered the particulars" (vi–vii).

For the most part, Martineau's "slight sketch" (which approaches 300 pages in length) consists of a discursive rendering of Nightingale's litany of administrative shortcomings, sanitary horrors, and suggestions for reform, but Martineau shapes Nightingale's barrage into an organized, relatively uncluttered, and generically homogenous presentation of evidence and advice. Throughout *England and her Soldiers,* Martineau focuses primarily on administrative reform: "The thing further wanted is that every advance should be secured by the well-grounded establishment of a complete system, in which every individual should know his own place and his own duty" (280). For her, the tension between the individual and the collective, which surfaces repeatedly, but without comment, in Nightingale's text, can best be addressed by recognizing that, within a well-ordered system, every individual has a place. Within such a system, both narrative and administrative, the individual becomes a type—an orderly, for example, or a patient—not an idiosyncratic, fully characterized person and not simply a data point.

Small's quotation, which is taken out of context and not referenced, it is not clear whether this phrase refers to ordinary readers or to those legislators and government officials who were not "scientific men"—that is, those who could not appreciate and understand statistics.

[9] *England and her Soldiers,* v.

We see Martineau's preference for the type both in the work's only approach to fictional realism and in the way she deals with Nightingale. The first focuses on a fictional character, "Bob," who enters the military and falls ill in a military hospital. As in the individual tales that make up her *Illustrations of Political Economy,* this story is self-consciously presented as a fiction ("I have in my mind's eye," 28) and is immediately followed by a moral designed to redirect the reader's imaginative engagement away from the story to the lesson Martineau wants to stress (30). Far from being an individuated character, Bob simply stands for all the soldiers who have fallen ill in military hospitals—all of the soldiers who are reduced to numbers in Nightingale's tables and graphs. When Martineau engages the one figure, moreover, whose larger-than-life reputation might make her a fully individuated character, if not a fictional one, she deliberately downplays both Nightingale's agency and the idiosyncrasies that distinguished her from every other person at Scutari.

Nightingale does not even appear in Martineau's text until page 197, well after Martineau has identified the problems, rehearsed many of the horrors of the Crimean War, and presented her imaginative scenario of a soldier's life. When she does admit Nightingale into her text, Martineau does not initially name her but simply personifies Nightingale's indifference to existing protocols in a formulation that also presents Nightingale's intervention as a programmatic dead end: "When the state of things mended, it was not by means of any substantial reform which we can point to now as a security against the same calamity recurring. The soldiers were saved by a preemptory breaking through all rules, and the most lavish expenditure of money ever witnessed in our military history" (251). Martineau's closest approach to distinguishing Nightingale from the other nurses quickly subsides into the collective representation that renders even Nightingale simply a type, if an unusually wealthy one, of the benevolent nurse. "It would be more painful than profitable to detail the condition in which the Scutari patients lay before it was possible to institute those reforms which made all clean and comfortable at last. . . . An effort was early made to give assistance to the Barrack Hospital; and Miss Nightingale's washing establishment supplied 2000 clean (really clean) shirts per month" (206–7). While Martineau does momentarily single Nightingale out for praise—"What a change it was when Miss Nightingale and the nurses appeared, with hands full of good things at the right time!" (214)—she more generally subsumes all of the nurses into a collective entity, characterized principally by their unforgettable hands: "The long lane had its turning at last. The wounded from Inkerman who survived the first crowding, the hospital gangrene, and other causes of mortality, could not forget, if they were to live a thousand years, the first approaches of comfort, the first sensations of convalescence.... Some were kept alive, when given over from the severity of their wounds,—kept alive by watchful hands administering spoonfuls of nourishment through the night, and strengthening them for surgical treatment in the morning" (254).

In addition to simplifying and providing both narrative coherence and generic homogeneity to Nightingale's presentation of data, Martineau also twice makes a point that Nightingale only mentions in passing—even though we might imagine that this point would have appealed to budget-minded legislators (and overtaxed readers). Martineau's point is that greater efficiency in the administration of military hospitals would save the nation money. "We now lavish life, means, and hard money, for very poor results, as regards the maintenance of an adequate military force," Martineau declares in her preface (vii). "We now see how we may maintain an adequate military force at a much smaller cost in every way; and to do this, all that is necessary is such a vigorous expression of the national will as may overcome the obscure resistance in official quarters which always impedes reform in any department of the State" (vii). As she nears the conclusion of her work, Martineau returns to the theme of expense—money as well as lives—now underscored by the revelations that mortality in military hospitals in India has begun to approach the levels at Scutari.

> History has nothing to show that can compare in clearness with the illustration that the Crimean war affords of the results of wisdom and folly in the administration of our military resources. We have seen a complete and undisguised exemplification of the loss and the renovation of our national armies. The lesson cost us 18,000 men, for whose loss our ignorance was answerable. Such an experiment cannot be tried repeatedly by a nation in warfare, as a scientific one by a philosopher in his laboratory; but one would think that we intended it, by our hesitation in practically adopting the instruction. After three years, while we have, and must continue to have, a large army in India, and while the hum and murmur of warfare is growing louder with every shifting wind, what have we done towards renovating and preserving our military strength? We saved the remnant of our soldiers by a total disruption of forms and regulations, and by a wild waste of money. We set to work to learn the right method of preserving our army by means of wise regulations, and that generous economy which proves the best thrift in the end. The right method is ascertained and disclosed, and a few desultory reforms have been instituted; but our system is

still unfavourable in a high degree to the health and longevity of the soldier, and there is no approach to completeness in our care of the *physique* of the British army. The thing has to be done. There is no time to lose in doing it. Why is it not done? (268–69)

Nightingale's own wealth, which allowed for the "wild waste of money" to which Martineau alludes, may have led the self-proclaimed savior of the ill soldiers to slight the monetary saving that increased hospital efficiency could be expected to yield. Nightingale was too enraged by the loss of lives, the ignorance (or indifference) of administrators to the basic facts of sanitary science, and the redundancy and incompetence of military chains of command to focus on the financial benefits that her proposed reforms might yield. For Martineau, by contrast, who had been forced to scrape for every penny (before *Illustrations* made her fortune), monetary saving ranked high in the reasons for pursuing administrative reform. The type of the soldier, the nurse, and the imaginatively embodied "British army" could be saved, she insisted, even if individuals perished—with the reduction in cost that should appeal to everyone.

II. APPLIED STATISTICS: ANOTHER APPROACH TO REFORM

When Martineau insists that nations cannot conduct experiments in warfare (or in hospital care), she indirectly alludes to one of the challenges that long prevented social scientists from incorporating statistical methods. As Stephen M. Stigler has argued, nineteenth-century social scientists lacked the ability to control experiments that had allowed contemporary psychologists to adopt the statistical methods used so effectively by contemporary astronomers.[10] Then, too, the variables with which social scientists worked were so numerous and different in kind that they could not be reduced to a single, disciplining law—like the law of gravity, which disciplined the physical sciences. While Florence Nightingale did not solve this theoretical problem or successfully integrate statistics into those social sciences that most closely approximated her interests (demography and public health), she did both champion the method that Francis Galton refined in the 1880s and produce an example of one form in which comparative situations could

---

[10] Stephen M. Stigler, *The History of Statistics: The Measurement of Uncertainty before 1900* (Cambridge, MA: Harvard University Press, 1986), 7.

be graphically represented. In doing so, she also helped push the study of social problems, such as the possible correlation between sanitation and mortality, away from the ethical and theological terms in which she formulated them and toward the kinds of formulations that would repudiate ethical considerations entirely.

As we have seen, one of Nightingale's many attempts to convince legislators that poor sanitation was responsible for more hospital deaths than battlefield injuries consisted of a series of graphics now called polar-area diagrams. The only reference I have seen to Nightingale's opinion of these diagrams suggests that she considered them something of a sop to readers too impatient or ignorant to understand the accompanying lists and tables. Hugh Small cites Nightingale's reference to *Mortality of the British Army,* where the diagrams first appeared, as a "coxcomb" intended to engage the "vulgar public," who lacked the sophistication of "scientific men."[11] Whatever Nightingale thought of them, the diagrams have fascinated historians, who see them as an early contribution to the field of data visualization.[12] I want briefly to describe these diagrams and to show how they conveyed data about hospital mortality before turning to Nightingale's theoretical understanding of statistics, which she largely borrowed from the Belgian Adolphe Quetelet.

Nightingale's three diagrams, as they appeared in revised form in 1859,[13] were intended to illustrate two conclusions: more fatalities occurred

---

[11] "Florence Nightingale's Statistical Diagrams," http://www.florence-nightingale-avenging-angel.co.uk/GraphicsPaper/Graphics.htm (accessed 2 July 2010). Small speculates that this phrase, which Nightingale uses to refer to the entire 1858 book, not just the diagrams, is the source of the term many subsequent analysts have applied to the diagrams—"coxcombs." A coxcomb is the florid, fleshy crest that adorns the head of a rooster.

[12] In addition to Small, see Ian Short, "Mathematics of the Coxcombs," http://understandinguncertainty.org/node/214 (accessed 2 July 2010); Paul J. Lewi, *Speaking of Graphics,* chap. 5, http://understandinguncertainty.org/node/213 (accessed 2 July 2010); Zachary Forest Johnson, "indiemaps.com/blog," http://indiemaps.com/blog/2008/10/nightingales-roses-in-actionscript-3 (accessed 2 July 2010); Julie Rehmeyer, "Florence Nightingale: The Passionate Statistician," *ScienceNews,* http://www.sciencenews.org/view/generic/id/38937/title/Florence_Nightingale_The_passionate_statistician (accessed 1 June 2010); "Florence Nightingale's Coxcomb Diagrams *SAS re-creation,*" http://www.math.yorku.ca/SCS/Gallery/historical.html (accessed 27 December 2009); and I. Bernard Cohen, *The Triumph of Numbers: How Counting Shaped Modern Life* (New York: Norton, 2005), chap. 9.

[13] The revisions were necessary because, as Small explains, the original diagrams imply that the shaded area that appears in each wedge, not the length of the radial lines, is proportional to the death rate. Nightingale inserted errata sheets in this volume, but in the revisions, which were printed in *A Contribution to the Sanitary History of the British Army* (1859), she cleared up the ambiguity by opting for what Small calls "wedges." In these diagrams, areas, not the lengths of the radial lines, represent variation in the death rate. See Small, "Florence Nightingale's Statistical Diagrams."

in the Eastern hospitals from illness than from wounds; improvements in sanitary conditions could dramatically reduce the death rate in any hospital. To represent both conclusions, Nightingale conveyed the mortality figures in pie-shaped units, each of which represents a month's worth of mortalities, and which fan out to various extents from a stationary vortex in two partial-circles printed side by side. The areas that represent preventable deaths, from "mitigable zymotic diseases," are colored blue; they grow successively larger from April 1854 through January 1855 and then diminish in size from February through May of 1855 (see figure 4.1). (These wedges increase in area in June 1855 and then decrease again in July.) Red wedges show the deaths that were caused by wounds, and black wedges indicate deaths from all other causes. In addition, a relatively small dotted circle, which does not vary in size and which appears at the center of each partial circle, represents "what the Mortality would have been, had the Army been as healthy as Manchester." As Nightingale's legend explains, "Each wedge admits of Comparison, area for Area, with every other wedge, and with the Manchester Circle, and each wedge shows the Mortality per 1000 per Annum for the Month."[14] By comparing the blue area that lies outside the Manchester circle in each wedge with the area inside the dotted line, one can immediately see the degree to which preventable mortality in the Eastern hospitals exceeded what is here presented as a norm. (Manchester was not the norm for domestic mortality; as Nightingale notes, it was "one of the most unhealthy Towns in England.") By comparing the areas of each wedge around the two circles (the second circle begins in April 1855, and thus continues the story told in the first circle, which ends in March 1855), one can see how mortality increased month by month from July 1854 through April 1855, then began to decrease in March, after the Sanitary Commission arrived. After April, mortality levels fell off sharply, until they approached the Manchester level in February 1855.

Nightingale was not the first person to graphically represent data. William Playfair had invented the pie chart in 1801, and polar-area diagrams were introduced by A. M. Guerry, a contemporary of Quetelet.[15] Even if

---

[14] The best print representation I have found appears as a foldout insertion in Martineau, *England and her Soldiers,* after p. 282. These graphics reproduce those in Nightingale, *Contribution* and *Notes* (where the first diagram appears in part I, section I, appendix ii, after p. xxiii; the second diagram appears in part II, after p. 314; and the third appears in part II, section ix, after p. 320. Note: the page numbering in *Notes* is very complex, involving, as it does, Roman numerals as well as Arabic numbers, and often [but not always] beginning anew in each section).

[15] For a discussion of Playfair and the pie chart, see Small, "Florence Nightingale's Statistical Diagrams"; Kopf discusses Guerry's use of polar-area diagrams in "Florence Nightingale as Statistician," 292.

they were not completely original, her diagrams constituted an advance for what would become the scientific practice of economics because, unlike a bar graph (which might have rendered her evidence more clearly), Nightingale's diagrams were essentially *mathematical* demonstrations. As Ian Short and Paul J. Lewi have demonstrated, Nightingale's diagrams display a relatively sophisticated mathematical understanding.[16] Like pie charts, the polar-area diagrams display frequency by area, but, because Nightingale's diagrams keep the angles of the vectors constant and vary the radius, they actually perform a square root transformation of the data.[17]

In *Notes on Matters Affecting the Health of the British Army,* Nightingale offered two criticisms of the way army officers calculated mortality rates in Scutari. First, they used "the system of averages," which tended to efface the fact that different conditions led to differential rates of mortality. "What we want to know is, where the conditions vary, what the result is of each successive condition, *not* what is the *average* of the whole" (Part I, section x, xxv). Second, army officials underestimated the mortality rate by inflating the number of soldiers who passed through the wards (or died there). "This method counts the cases remaining every month, or twelve times a year, and adds to them the cases admitted. So that, in addition to the cases really treated, it obtains also fictitious cases, simply by counting the same man a certain number of times, that is, by counting the patients remaining twelve times annually, and adding them to the new patients admitted" (Part I, section i, appendix ii, xxiii–xxiv). This method of counting, Nightingale pointed out, yielded a mortality rate of around two percent, instead of the much higher rates her figures showed. (In Scutari, for several months, 88 out of every 100 soldiers admitted to the hospital died.) Since she introduces her first polar-area diagram immediately after this second critique, it seems likely that she viewed her mathematical diagram as a corrective to what was both a conceptual and arithmetic error on the part of British officials.

Nightingale's juxtaposition of the polar-area diagrams to both complaints about other modes of counting and her own statistical tables suggests that she viewed these diagrams as an abstract mode of quantitative reasoning, not simply as decoration or as suggestive pictures of proportionalities. As we will see, it was this view of the mathematical treatment of

---

[16] Short works through the mathematics of the diagrams in "Mathematics of the Coxcombs"; Lewi's analysis appears in "Florence Nightingale and Polar Area Diagrams," esp. 14–16.

[17] Lewi, "Florence Nightingale and Polar Area Diagrams," 22. Since the area of a circle is πr^2, the area is proportional to the square of the radius, not the length of the radial line.

statistical data that practitioners of economics were to take up at the end of the century, even though they did not rely heavily on polar-area (or any other kind of) diagrams. Despite their intrinsic interest (and visual appeal), in other words, Nightingale's diagrams were less important, in the long run, than was her view of mathematics more generally.

Nightingale's understanding of statistics as a form of mathematics was heavily indebted to Adolphe Quetelet, whose work she had first encountered in the late 1830s. Quetelet's most influential book, *Physique social,* was published in 1835; the book was translated into English in 1842, and this, along with Quetelet's other work on statistics, was reviewed at length by John Hershel in the influential *Edinburgh Review* in 1850.[18] Nightingale initially read Quetelet's work in French; she admired his work throughout her life; and, when he died in 1874, she mourned his passing in an intense engagement with his theories and method. This text, finally titled "In Memoriam," had occupied Nightingale on and off since 1851, before she left for the Crimea; it was never published during her lifetime but, along with her annotations of *Physique social,* provides the best evidence of the influence Quetelet's work had on her understanding of statistics.

For Nightingale, as for Quetelet, statistics provided the bridge between simple observations and generalizable knowledge.[19] Quetelet used two methods to move from empirical observations to general claims: the "average man," and the notion that naturally occurring data, properly collected, follow a "normal" curve. Both of these methods sought to find regularities (or "laws") in large collections of data, and, even though, by the standards of modern statistics, each was deeply flawed, both proved influential for Nightingale and her contemporaries.

Quetelet described the "average man" in the essays published as *Physique social,* and he continued to refine this concept for the rest of his career. Methodologically, Quetelet arrived at the "average man" arithmetically, simply by adding all available data about any given characteristic (height, weight, number of crimes committed, and so on) and dividing by the number of individual data points in the set. The function of this concept was to

---

[18] This review was reprinted in 1857 in Hershel's collection *Essays from the "Edinburgh" and "Quarterly" Reviews.* Florence Nightingale annotated her copy of this book. See Lynn McDonald, Introduction to *Florence Nightingale on Society and Politics, Philosophy, Science, Education, and Literature,* ed. Lynn McDonald (Waterloo, ON: Wilfrid Laurier University Press, 2003), 14. Hershel's review initially appeared in the *Edinburgh Review* 185 (July 1850).

[19] One annotation to *Physique social* reads, "Number of observations necessary. All sciences of observation depend upon statistical methods; without these [they] are blind empiricism. Make your facts comparable before deciding causes." McDonald, *Florence Nightingale on Society,* 30.

smooth out the random variations individuals presented. The belief that informed it, according to Stigler, was "that if there is no change in any underlying causal relationship—if there is a 'persistence of causes'—then there will be a tendency for the average of large aggregates of even unhomogeneous data to be stable."[20] This concept immediately attracted the attention of social investigators and was used by both French and English reformers to generate profiles of everything from the rate of drunkenness in a given district to the characteristics of a racial group. Although controversial, the concept of the "average man" is visible in Nightingale's desire to convert large numbers of data points (the number of soldiers in possession of shirts, for example) into a "type" (the soldier bereft of a shirt). As we have already seen, Nightingale's treatment of the relationship between the individual and the type was not fully worked out in *Notes,* but some of that incoherence, as we are about to see, has to be attributed to the relative immaturity of Quetelet's conceptualization of statistical typicality.

The second method Quetelet used to relate individual observations to generalizations involves identifying a pattern that shows a mean, or "normal," distribution (which, following Laplace and Gauss, he graphed as a bell curve) and that indicates individual deviations from that norm. In his work, Quetelet subjected only the mean to intense scrutiny. Because individual departures from the norm were relegated to the category of deviations (or "outliers," in today's terminology), Quetelet generated a picture of lawlike regularity, which, given his applications, appeared not only in natural but also in social phenomena. The concept of social laws was one of the aspects of Quetelet's theory most appealing to Nightingale. "There is no doubt as appears from researches a type in God's mind for every nation and one for every individual," Nightingale wrote.[21] The idea that all such law-governed phenomena interact with each other, which Nightingale also extrapolated from Quetelet, formed the basis for her suggestions for reform and for the resilient hope she retained in spite of the government's foot-dragging. "Quetelet has shown this very plainly, has actually reduced to curves and numbers the deviations which revolve, as it were, round this type. And his curves concern, strangely enough, quite as much moral and intellectual as physical things." "The laws of the material world, the laws of the moral world, the political world, the action of government, the economic world, or the conditions of trade, commerce, manufacture, agriculture, act and react on each other," she wrote. "In this regularity and certainty, which makes our hair stand on end, lies in fact our best, our only

---

[20] Stigler, *History of Statistics,* 171.

[21] McDonald, *Florence Nightingale on Society,* 65.

hope for the future. For were the results not certain, how could we foresee them? How could we modify, change them?"²²

Modern statisticians have found serious weaknesses in Quetelet's theories (and, by extension, in Nightingale's use of them). Most significantly, Quetelet had no method for conceptualizing the effects—much less the interaction—of multiple variants.²³ He also lacked any method for determining whether the classifications he used to identify data points were sufficiently fine and/or precisely the ones needed in any given situation.²⁴ Beyond these two shortcomings, which also afflicted Nightingale's statistical work, she has also been faulted for failing to factor in the possibility that some of the observations from which she took her data could have been due to chance alone. "On purely statistical ground," Paul Lewi explains, "the main objection [to Nightingale's polar-area diagrams] would be directed to the lack of randomization."²⁵ For the purposes of my argument, however, it matters less that Nightingale followed Quetelet down theoretical and methodological paths that modern statisticians would not take than that she supplemented his generally secular social physics with her own powerful religious convictions. This meant that, where Quetelet saw natural laws, Nightingale saw evidence of God's hand.

We can see how Nightingale's religious faith colored her use of Quetelet's theories in the annotations with which she made his book her own. Next to Quetelet's statement "From the past one may predict the future," for example, Nightingale wrote, "All is under God."²⁶ We also see this in her memorial to Quetelet, which is filled with references to God's laws (or

---

[22] "In Memoriam," in McDonald, *Florence Nightingale on Society*, 53, 54.

[23] "He showed no inclination toward a simultaneous unwinding of multiply categorized data. He was, like the astronomers before Laplace, unable to take the conceptual step of combining measurements taken under a variety of conditions into one analysis. He could write of marginal relationships, and within categories he could seek relations across other variables (such as male height across age); but he could not go further. His elimination of individual variation was at bottom reduced to an assumption of *ceteris paribus*—that all other things are equal" (Stigler, *History of Statistics*, 173). Lewi makes a similar observation about the limitations of Nightingale's statistics: "In Nightingale's days ... one did not possess the sophisticated modeling techniques, such as the analysis of variance and covariance that are available to the modern statistician" ("Florence Nightingale and Polar Area Diagrams," 15).

[24] "Quetelet's method failed to solve the problem that was the main stumbling block to the advancement of statistics in the social sciences. It did not provide the key to evaluating and finding useful ways of classifying data for analysis, except in very specialized situations. It was ... too successful in revealing patterns—in almost all cases where it was tried it revealed the same pattern" (Stigler, *History of Statistics*, 219).

[25] Lewi, "Florence Nightingale's Polar Area Diagrams," 16. "In defense of Nightingale," he continues, "one can say that, in her time, the calculus of probabilities was only in its beginning" (16).

[26] McDonald, *Florence Nightingale on Society*, 23.

"God's thoughts"), whereas Quetelet was content with invoking natural laws.[27] Indeed, as Lynn McDonald has remarked, Quetelet's work provided Nightingale with the theoretical and methodological means necessary to convert her religious faith into social activism.[28] It was this religious coloring that indelibly marked Nightingale's commitment to statistics—her conviction that "the study of statistics is . . . a religious service"—as part of the essentially ethical practice of nineteenth-century political economy, not the disinterested science that economics was soon to become.[29]

III. THE SECULARIZATION OF NINETEENTH-CENTURY POLITICAL ECONOMY

Many of Florence Nightingale's contemporaries would not have considered political economy to be an ethical, much less a theological, practice. Famously caricatured by Thomas Carlyle as "the dismal science," political economy was engaged with topics such as labor, land, and capital, but not in a manner that necessarily implied a moral or religious attitude. Quetelet's application of statistics to moral questions continued to spark controversy, for example, and the one large-scale application of statistics to a matter directly involving religion—the religious census of 1851—was widely resisted and ridiculed in Britain. Yet, not only did Nightingale view statistics as "a religious service"; when we contrast it with its modern descendent, nineteenth-century political economy looks distinctly like a moral, not a mathematical, science. For, as Daniel Breslau has argued, the questions that preoccupied almost all nineteenth-century political economists before the 1870s implicitly involved class relations. For political economists such as John Stuart Mill, "the components of wealth—wages, rent, and profit—represented the returns to labor, land, and capital, respectively, and any discussion of how these were derived was inevitably a discussion of the terms of exchange among the various classes."[30] In Victorian Britain, no topic had more profoundly ethical implications than the ques-

---

[27] McDonald, *Florence Nightingale on Society*, 42, 65.

[28] McDonald, Introduction to *Florence Nightingale on Society*, 13. "Quetelet's methodology . . . is the link between her faith and her social activism."

[29] "The Passionate Statistician" (video recording), Milton Keynes: Open University Educational Enterprises (1995); cited in John Maindonald and Alice M. Richardson, "This Passionate Study: A Dialogue with Florence Nightingale," *Journal of Statistics Education* 12.1 (2004), http://www.amstat.org/publications/JSE/v12n1/maindonald.html.

[30] Daniel Breslau, "Economics Invents the Economy: Mathematics, Statistics, and Models in the Work of Irving Fisher and Wesley Mitchell," *Theory and Society* 32.3 (June 2003): 394.

tion of what classes owed to each other. Indeed, Nightingale's insistence that conditions in military hospitals be improved implicitly addressed this very topic, for the vast majority of soldiers were working-class men, and the majority of those entrusted with hospital oversight were not. The ease with which questions about class relations could be translated into apparently disinterested economic formulations is also obvious in the frequency with which descriptions of the healthy economic "body" or "system" constituted thinly veiled references to questions about the deservingness of the lower classes and what measures should be taken (by the well-to-do) to ensure their economic productivity.[31]

Beginning in the 1870s, this ethical component was very gradually stripped from the practice of British political economy. In general terms, what I am calling the secularization of political economy was a result of practitioners' attempts to incorporate mathematics, including statistics and mathematical formulations of probability, into political economy. The two English theorists generally credited with applying mathematics to economic problems are William Stanley Jevons, who considered mathematics to be the heart of any genuine science, and Francis Galton, who developed a statistical approach to heredity; the former is now associated with the marginalist revolution in economic theory, and the latter is largely responsible for naming and promoting regression analysis.[32] The reorientation of British political economy away from ethical questions and toward mathematical methods took more than a single decade (and required that the discipline be incorporated into the university system), but, by the third decade of the twentieth century, political economy had become the almost fully mathematicized discipline of economics. As practiced by Alfred Marshall and his students, this science had all but completely discarded the class-specific, ethical inquiries of its predecessor.

Florence Nightingale repeatedly argued that statistics, especially what she called "applied statistics," should become part of the university curricu-

---

[31] See Mary Poovey, *Making a Social Body* (Chicago: University of Chicago Press, 1995), especially chaps. 2 and 3.

[32] Jevons's first influential book was *The Theory of Political Economy* (1871), which Irving Fisher said began the use of mathematical modeling in economics. Galton's major works on heredity were published in the nineteenth century. In addition to naming regression analysis, Galton also created the statistical concept of correlation. Jevons was a professor of logic and the Cobden Professor of Political Economy at Owens College, Manchester; Galton was a lecturer in logic at King's College, London. Regression analysis is a method of describing in statistical terms the relationship between a dependent variable and one or more independent variables. Such statistical models show, for example, how the dependent variable changes when one independent variable changes while the others remain fixed.

lum in Britain, but, even though she aggressively lobbied Francis Galton, one of Britain's leading statisticians, she was not successful in this campaign. Only after her death was the first department of applied statistics created, at University College, London, in 1911 by Karl Pearson. Because the chair of this department was named for Galton (the Galton Chair of Eugenics), we can see a faint trace of Nightingale's influence in establishing the academic credibility of the discipline. Pearson's successors in the Galton Chair, Ronald Fisher and Egon Pearson (Karl's son), with the help of Jerzy Neyman, did the mathematical work necessary to formulate modern hypothesis testing. In the chain of connections whose first link was forged outside the university, then, in the barrack hospitals of the East, and which acquired new strength in the cauldron of academic succession and disciplinary change, we can see that Florence Nightingale left her mark on what has become the modern discipline of economics.[33]

IV. CONCLUSION

What might Nightingale have thought of modern economics, with its disciplinary indifference to ethical questions, its preference for theoretical over applied modalities, and its nearly universal antipathy to theology? Given the deep faith that informed all of her comments about her work, it is hard to imagine that she would have approved of the academic discipline of economics. Yet it is also difficult to imagine that she would have objected to what the field of statistics has become in the hands of academic economists and other social scientists. As "a logic and methodology for the measurement of uncertainty and for an examination of the consequences of that uncertainty in the planning and interpretation of experimentation and observation,"[34] modern statistics seems well suited for the enterprise closest to Nightingale's heart: finding the laws that could lead to social reform. "Mankind can modify, can reform mankind, can almost create mankind," she insisted, "by discovering and applying the laws which register (we will say govern) the movements of the moral world."[35]

---

[33] In 1933 the Department of Applied Statistics at University College, London, split into two separate academic units: eugenics and biometrics. In this same period, economists at some U.S. universities were applying the kind of mathematical modeling associated with various diagrams and graphs to financial topics, such as interest rates, uncertainty, and the capitalization of income. Irvin Fisher at Yale was a leader in this area of economic research.

[34] Stigler, *History of Statistics*, 1.

[35] "In Memoriam," in McDonald, *Florence Nightingale on Society*, 56.

CHAPTER 5

The Cost of Everything in *Middlemarch*

GORDON BIGELOW

The first tremor that shakes Dorothea Brooke's youthful absolutism, in the opening pages of *Middlemarch,* is an insight into the theory of value. She has been taught by her family's "hereditary strain of puritan energy" to abjure the vanity of ornament, but when prompted by her sister Celia to look through the jewels left to them by their mother, she is struck by the power of these objects, a power that has nothing to do with either the self-love of the wearer or the admiring glances of any observer.[1] "How very beautiful these gems are!" she exclaims, as she is caught by "a new current of feeling" (13). She reflects, "It is strange how deeply colours seem to penetrate one, like scent" (13). Out of these observations, she hatches a new desire to keep some of the jewels for her own use, in order "to feed her eye at these little fountains of pure colour" (14).

Before this close consideration, Dorothea seems to have held to Adam Smith's view of gemstones, a view he retails in an important early passage of the *Wealth of Nations* on the difference between "value in use" and "value in exchange." "A diamond," he writes, "has scarce any value in use; but a

---

[1] George Eliot, *Middlemarch: A Study of Provincial Life,* ed. Rosemary Ashton (1871–2; London: Penguin, 1994), 8. All further references are to this edition and are cited in the text.

very great quantity of other goods may frequently be had in exchange for it."² Dorothea is looking at amethysts and emeralds here, as well as "brilliants" (12), but the point is the same: before this moment, she regards the stones as useful for nothing in themselves, valuable only in the social network of exchange. But her reflections here seem to affirm that gemstones do have "value in use." Their capacity to concentrate and refract light, to radiate pure color, gives them a sensuous power to "penetrate" consciousness and to "feed the eye." In this she follows J. S. Mill, who chided Smith mildly on the same point in 1848. Mill argues here that, when Smith claims diamonds have no "value in use," he is

> employing the word use, not in the sense in which political economy is concerned with it, but in that other sense in which use is opposed to pleasure. Political economy has nothing to do with the comparative estimation of different uses in the judgment of a philosopher or a moralist. The use of a thing, in political economy, means its capacity to satisfy a desire, or serve a purpose. Diamonds have this capacity in a high degree, and unless they had it, would not bear any price.³

A thing which merely gives pleasure, according to Mill, must itself be considered useful. And its value as a useful thing cannot be separated categorically from the value of something that performs necessary work but gives little pleasure, like the gift of new socks. Smith, Mill implies, falls into this error because of a moral mistrust of pleasing things; Mill, a loyal student of Bentham's, counts human pleasure as moral good.

In *Romola* (1863) Eliot gave considerable attention to the powers of gemstones and the sometimes outlandish meanings assigned to them in human history.⁴ There, as in *Middlemarch,* part of what was implied is a refutation of charges of feminine vanity attached to the ornaments of dress. In showing that jewels have unique and powerful characteristics in themselves, characteristics that appeal keenly to the senses, the text rejects the suggestion that their value is simply a concoction of the female imagination,

---

² Adam Smith, *An Inquiry into the Causes of the Wealth of Nations* (1776), ed. Edwin Cannan (1904), online ed., http://econlib.org/library/Smith/smWN.html, I.4.13. Smith later remarks, "The demand for the precious stones arises altogether from their beauty. They are of no use, but as ornaments; and the merit of their beauty is greatly enhanced by their scarcity, or by the difficulty and expence [sic] of getting them from the mine" (I.11.84).

³ J. S. Mill, *Principles of Political Economy with some of their Applications to Social Philosophy* (1848), ed. William J. Ashley (1909), online ed., http://econlib.org/library/Mill/mlP.html, III.1.3.

⁴ See Ilana Blumberg's essay in this volume.

authorized by husbands and fathers via the process Veblen would label vicarious consumption. But the jewels in question at the start of *Middlemarch* evoke a specific argument about the theory of value, and they signal a persistent interest in questions at the center of mid-Victorian economic thought.[5] What emerges is an understanding of the complex and mixed nature of economic value, a phenomenon that arises from the social embeddedness of useful objects. It is a view aligned with Mill, but one that, more than Mill, emphasizes the power of social meanings, a power that often overwhelms and obscures particular characteristics.

Perhaps we should not be surprised to find this detailed meditation on value in *Middlemarch*. It is after all a book whose narrative climax is signaled when Dorothea, in promising to accept the penniless Will Ladislaw, declares that she will "learn what everything costs" (812). Between the opening discussion of jewels and this final declaration, there is much attention to the cost of everything in *Middlemarch,* and much attention to the ways characters make decisions about debt, spending, investment, and work. Eliot did read Mill's 1848 *Principles of Political Economy,* but from the evidence of her letters and notebooks she seems to have read little else on the subject.[6] Her well-documented interest in philosophy and the natural sciences has led critics to focus on these areas, and, as I argue below, recent attempts to consider her fiction in relation to economics have resulted in some missteps. But the 1870s, the decade in which *Middlemarch* was published, saw an effort to transform political economy through the application of methods from the natural sciences. In Eliot's intellectual sphere, this new effort was associated most closely with logician and mathematician William Stanley Jevons. Eliot, I will argue, remained skeptical of Jevons's vision of an economic science, holding more closely to the classical political economy of Smith and Mill than to the "neoclassical" school that emerged in the later decades of the nineteenth century, while at the same time modifying their view through her attention to the social meanings of valuable things.

---

[5] In this, I am suggesting that the novel takes up a problem different from the one that John Plotz posits in *Portable Property: Victorian Culture on the Move* (Princeton, NJ: Princeton University Press, 2008). Despite their status as an inheritance from the mother, the jewels signify here neither as "heirlooms" nor "simply as alienable bits of potential cash"—the polarity of meanings Plotz highlights (9). The "depth" Dorothea perceives in them derives not from their family association, nor from their profound exchange value. It is the purely sensuous character of the objects that strikes her, and that evokes this particular problem in Smith's theory of value.

[6] Eliot to Elizabeth Stuart Phelps, 13 August 1875, *The George Eliot Letters,* ed. Gordon Haight (New Haven, CT: Yale University Press, 1978), XI.163.

PART II. POLITICAL ECONOMY

I. MYSTERIOUS MIXTURE

In February 1878, Eliot and G. H. Lewes encountered Mark Pattison at Edith Simcox's house, and their conversation turned to a recent attack that Jevons had published against Mill. Eliot, in response, pointed out "a dangerous tendency among 2nd and 3rd rate thinkers to go on inventing something that shall catch disciples."[7] In a letter dated a few weeks earlier, Lewes had thanked George Croom Robertson for his harsh review of Jevons's attack; Lewes called the review "calmly crushing."[8] These offhand remarks might make us at least initially skeptical when critics link Eliot's later work with Jevons's ideas.[9]

While it is true, as Catherine Gallagher points out, that Eliot and Jevons shared a range of interests,[10] their resulting portraits of economic life are quite distinct. Eliot's implicit stance in the fight that Jevons is picking with Mill comes at the very start of *Middlemarch,* with its description of human history as a "mysterious mixture" subject to "the varying experiments of time" (3). The phrase is now familiar enough to humanists as to appear unexceptionable, but in fact it suggests a position hostile to that which Jevons was working out. It had been Mill's long contention that a pure empiricism could never be applied to political economy.[11] In the physical sciences all the factors giving rise to a phenomenon could be isolated and measured individually; this was impossible in political economy, since one

---

[7] Edith Simcox, *Autobiography,* quoted in *George Eliot Letters,* IX.217. Jevons's essay is "John Stuart Mill's Philosophy Tested," *Contemporary Review* 31 (December 1877): 167–82.

[8] George Henry Lewes to George Croom Robertson, *George Eliot Letters,* IX.211. Ashton seems to misread this in her biography of Lewes, assuming that Jevons had reviewed Lewes's *Physical Basis of Mind* (Rosemary Ashton, *G. H. Lewes: An Unconventional Victorian* [London: Pimlico, 2000], 272).

[9] In *Victorian Relativity* Christopher Herbert gives much attention to Jevons's mawkish claim that Mill's authority within the field of political economy was stifling the free exchange of ideas. Jevons is one of the heroes of what Herbert sees as an emerging relativist standpoint in Victorian thought, and in a brief but suggestive paragraph he seeks to bring Eliot into this new camp. Christopher Herbert, *Victorian Relativity: Radical Thought and Scientific Discovery* (Chicago: University of Chicago Press, 2001). The claim is deftly disassembled by the Irish political economist John Eliot Cairnes ("New Theories of Political Economy," *Fortnightly Review* 61 [1 January 1872]: 71–76). I am grateful to Tadhg Foley for this reference.

[10] In her discussion of *Daniel Deronda* in *The Body Economic,* Catherine Gallagher argues that Eliot's interest in the role of physiological sensation in the formation of human motives, and also her interest in the sales figures for her novels, brought her very close to Jevons's position on how economic actors make choices in the market. See Catherine Gallagher, *The Body Economic: Life, Death, and Sensation in Political Economy and the Victorian Novel* (Princeton, NJ: Princeton University Press, 2008).

[11] J. S. Mill, *Essays on Some Unsettled Questions of Political Economy* (1844), in *Collected Works,* vol. 4, ed. J. M. Robson (Toronto: University of Toronto Press, 1967), 322.

cannot know whether the thing being measured is itself the result of multiple causes. Wage rates, profit margins, panics: the origins of these phenomena are human decisions, and no single causal factor in these events could be isolated from other "disturbing causes."[12] For this reason Mill held that "the laws of the mind" and "the laws of matter" are essentially distinct, and because of this, political economy could never hope to deduce fixed laws akin to gravitation or temperature. "There are hardly any of the processes of industry," Mill writes, "which do not partly depend upon the properties of the lever; but it would be a strange classification which included those properties among the truths of Political Economy."[13]

As Harro Maas demonstrates in a recent study, it was the burden of Jevons's career to show that the laws of mind and the laws of matter were the same. He solidified his views on the question of "disturbing causes" while working in Australia as a gold assayer, where he needed to measure minute amounts of gold using a balance scale. He became an expert on the use of the instrument and eventually wrote a small treatise on it.[14] "When we operate with sufficient care," he later observed, "we cannot perform so simple an experiment as weighing an object in a good balance without getting discrepant numbers."[15] His 1871 *Theory of Political Economy* offers a direct rejoinder to Mill: "We can calculate the effect of a crowbar provided it be perfectly inflexible and have a perfectly hard fulcrum,—which is never the case."[16] The properties of matter are themselves subject to multiple factors, and material phenomena never result from a single cause. Thus the levers of the engineer are no different from the metaphorical levers of the mind: neither could be totally isolated from "disturbing causes." The point was crucial for Jevons, for it led him to conclude that Mill was wrong in separating the mental from the physical sciences. Quantities in physics and chemistry were always prone to variation resulting from "disturbing causes"—contaminants, air currents, barometric pressure—and were thus no different from economic phenomena such as a decline in prices.

In a novel focused on the "mysterious mixture" that results in human civilization, Eliot from the start emphasizes the complex and manifold factors that result in human choices. Dorothea's choice of plain dress, we're

---

[12] Harro Maas, *William Stanley Jevons and the Making of Modern Economics* (Cambridge: Cambridge University Press, 2005), 8.

[13] Mill, *Unsettled Questions*, 322; quoted in Maas, *William Stanley Jevons*, 178.

[14] Maas, *William Stanley Jevons*, 254.

[15] William Stanley Jevons, *Principles of Science* (1874), quoted in Maas, *William Stanley Jevons*, 174.

[16] William Stanley Jevons, *Theory of Political Economy* (1871), 3rd ed. (1888), online ed., http://www.econlib.org/library/YPDBooks/Jevons/jvnPE.html, I.8.

told, "was due to mixed conditions" (7), a phrase that signals both the difficulty in ascribing Dorothea's taste to simple causes, and also the possibility that these "conditions" are themselves subject to the kind of change Dorothea experiences later, when she discovers a beauty in ornaments that she had never before valued.

II. THE REQUISITE THINGS

The result of Jevons's physicalism was a radically subjective theory of economic life. Where classical economics from Smith to Mill had emphasized the social and historical dimensions of wealth and poverty, Jevons emphasized individuals. For him, a large market itself provided a sample size big enough that "disturbing causes" would cancel each other out. While the factors prompting the decisions of each consumer, employer, or worker might be impossible to calculate, the market provided an overall image of the results of their choices, in a profile distant enough to filter out anomalies. "We can no more know nor measure gravity in its own nature," Jevons writes, "than we can measure a feeling; but, just as we measure gravity by its effects in the motion of a pendulum, so we may estimate the equality or inequality of feelings by the decisions of the human mind. The will is our pendulum, and its oscillations are minutely registered in the price lists of the markets."[17] Through this bit of reasoning, Jevons reorients the theory of value around the subjective perceptions of individuals in the market, but at the same time he establishes this theoretical subject as radically isolated: as inaccessible to the speculations of the political economist as she is to the influence of other actors in the market. "The mind," Jevons famously concluded, "is inscrutable to every other mind."[18] In the market, the "disturbing causes" created by disturbed consumers will tend to factor each other out. Shoppers who are irrationally obsessed with a particular commodity—like diamonds—will be counterbalanced by those irrationally repelled by it, and the bulk of purchasers will show, in the prices they are willing to pay, how much a diamond is truly worth to humans. (On rationality, more below.) Thus in the record of market fluctuations, we have a true record of human need and human desire.

From one perspective, Jevons's insistence on the "inscrutability" of the mind might be seen as sympathetic to Eliot's aims in *Middlemarch*. With its

---

[17] Jevons, *Political Economy*, I.17.
[18] Jevons, *Political Economy*, I.20.

protomodernist focus on the inner world, the novel has provided one of the nineteenth century's most famous metaphors—the pier glass—for subjective detachment (264). With each life viewed from within its own "center of self" (210), the world is subjected to an inevitable distortion whereby random events around us seem to be arranged for our particular use. Characters in *Middlemarch* repeatedly find the minds of others "inscrutable" to them, particularly in the disastrous marriages the novel studies, marriages in which spouses are always "missing [. . .] each other's mental tracks" (587). Of course the burden of the novel, as readers have recognized in different ways since its first publication, is for its characters to overcome this mental isolation, to recognize the "mental track" of the other, and to reject the subjective distortion that colors the world. But even so, it is important to notice that these isolated "mental tracks" are typical of the book's description of human relationships. Its depiction of economic life, and in particular of human relations to things, is quite different.

When Tertius Lydgate sets out to buy the necessities of married life, his aim is simply to live "in the usual way," the "ordinary way" (348), with "the requisite things" (355) prescribed by "hereditary habit" (349). He proceeds "without any notion of being extravagant" (348), disdaining showy display as much as "he despises a man who calculated the effects of his costume" (589). In his dress he does what is "a matter of course" (589), and his knowledge of what is usual and ordinary and habitual to families of the minor aristocracy is perfectly evident to Rosamond Vincy, who sees that Lydgate always "seemed to have the right clothes on by a certain natural affinity, without ever having to think about them" (267). What is emphasized again and again is the social context of Lydgate's otherwise private judgments. He acts not on his own perception of utility but on his lifelong awareness of the perceptions of others. And as is clear from the reactions of Rosamond, he is no outlier in this. His views of clothing, furniture, and literature are seen not just as admirable, but indeed as *typical*; they are praiseworthy because they indicate how much his feelings are similar to those of others of his class. But these feelings, as is clear from the examples above, originate not within himself but out of his relation to others.

In these passages, Lydgate's thoughts fall into the same category of impressions and judgments that Dorothea initially holds about jewels. It is not the character of these things that is important—indeed their inherent characteristics seem to him trivial; rather, what bestows value on these things is the judgment of others. It is not that he is unaware of the distinctive characteristics of these objects—as Dorothea initially was. He "hates ugly crockery" (353) and is clearly unwilling to experience this ugliness in his household. But the emphasis within this portrait of Lydgate's economic imagination is clearly on the social contexts that shape what ultimately look like deeply private desires. As a consumer, Tertius resembles Mr. Casaubon at Rome: when confronted with the works of Raphael, he has difficulty in saying what things he "care[s] about," and is only aware of what is "highly esteemed" by others (197).

The market force exerted by others' esteem is a central problem in *Middlemarch*. In Jevons's model, economic choices are always based on the private perception of utility; Eliot's model of life shows that perceptions of utility are never private. Jevons argued in 1871, "it will be readily admitted that pleasure is the opposite of pain."[19] The passive construction here indicates the axiomatic status of this assumption. The mind works as a metaphorical balance scale, with market actors weighing the opposing forces of pleasure and pain anticipated in any action.[20] Conceiving of the mind in this way, he concludes that all economic decisions are made according to the "mechanics of utility and self-interest."[21]

However, in *Middlemarch* pleasure is not in any clear way the opposite of pain. Eliot insists on the point in an extended sketch of the market for horses. On his trip to the Houndsley horse fair, Fred Vincy suffers the pains of bad weather, bad food, and bad company, company that is not just "monotonous" (236) but deliberately corrupt. As Eliot's narrator suggests, it was only "the sustaining power of nomenclature which determined that the pursuit of these things was 'gay'" (236). It is only through this force of conventional meanings that the sharp-trading Mr. Bambridge, who succeeds in duping Fred, is regarded by others in the town of Middlemarch as "a man of pleasure" (237). Pleasure, in other words, is here shown to be thoroughly unpleasant. But in this example, the pain produced in these actions is dulled through their citation of pleasure, their associative reference to the habits of the leisure class. The novel's emphasis on the customary associations of language opens the way to a position sharply critical of Jevons's theory of economic motives. The things of this world cannot be lodged in permanent categories of pleasure and pain, even by the variable lights of individual minds. They will always be subject to the "power of nomenclature," to the force of metaphor, and any theory that misunderstands this force will present a faulty view of human behavior.

---

[19] Jevons, *Political Economy*, II.7.
[20] Maas, *William Stanley Jevons*, 276–77.
[21] Jevons, *Political Economy*, "Preface to the Second Edition," 7.

III. THE MARKET'S PULSE

So far I have argued that *Middlemarch* rejects the simple subjectivism of Jevons's theory of the market, presenting instead a view of human economic behavior that stresses the complex social meanings that attach to economic choices. This contextualist view of economics is reinforced as well in a telling moment from *Daniel Deronda,* a fragment of dramatic verse that Eliot uses as the epigraph to chapter 10. Here two speakers debate the metaphor of marriage as market. A "1st Gent." asks, "What woman should be?" and he provides his own answer as follows:

> Sir, consult the taste
> Of marriageable men. This planet's store
> In iron, cotton, wool, or chemicals—
> All matter rendered to our plastic skill,
> Is wrought in shapes responsive to demand:
> The market's pulse makes index high or low,
> By rule sublime.[22]

In this vision of the market, the external world is "responsive" to subjective tastes and desires, as commodities are "wrought in shapes" dictated by the hearts of a mass of individual consumers. The speaker asks, "What woman should be?" From his point of view, there is no *should;* there is only what women *are:* a creation of "plastic skill" applied to suit the orders of bachelor consumers everywhere. It is a peculiarly late-nineteenth-century redaction of misogynist myth, with its touchstones of fickleness and cosmetic artificiality. Or, as this first speaker puts it, epigrammatically, "Men's taste is women's test."

Encapsulated here is the abandonment of the social and ethical foundations of classical political economy for the implicit amorality of the models advocated both by Mill and by Jevons. Mill considers it irrelevant whether we should or should not derive pleasure from diamonds; what matters is that they command a price. The theory of value from Mill forward is not concerned with the "comparative estimates" of the "moralist or philosopher," but rather with the comparative judgments cast up daily by consumers in the market. Its business is not with how people should be, but only with how they are.

---

[22] George Eliot, *Daniel Deronda,* ed. Terence Cave (1876; London: Penguin, 1995), 99. Epigraphs in *Middlemarch* featuring these same disputants open chapters 9, 13, and 28.

But the "2nd Gent." undoes the first, overturning his easy formula:

> Nay, but turn it round.
> Give us the test of taste. A fine *menu*—
> Is it to-day what Roman epicures
> Insisted that a gentleman must eat
> To earn the dignity of dining well?[23]

The rhetorical question suggests that economic behavior is born out of a mixed assembly of motives, for consumption is always understood as social indicator, a conspicuously public proof of character as well as a private experience of satisfaction or pleasure. Here the force of compulsion works in the opposite direction. It is not the market that takes its shape from our desires, but rather our desires that are shaped by the market. A gentleman *must* consume as a gentleman, must consume what already carries the mark of dignity and taste. Sir James Chettam buys Dorothea a Maltese puppy despite their shared aversion to the dogs because "ladies usually are fond of [them]" (30). This is the proposition explored in *Middlemarch*: every purchase is a citation of a previous purchase, and its social meaning is always to some degree fixed, before the consumer begins to calculate his or her pleasures.

According to the 1st Gent., the rise and fall of prices represents "the market's pulse," slowing and speeding up in direct response to the input it receives from the behavior of market actors, just as the heart responds to stimulus from all the body's systems. The word "pulse" then works here in just the sense that Neil Hertz has suggested, indicating "a small, replicable unit of vitality."[24] Each "pulse" or heartbeat would represent one tiny increment of this response, as the external world of the market is "wrought" moment to moment by human desire.[25]

In Hertz's reading, the word "pulse," with all of its related terms, always signals something "equivocal" in Eliot's work, allowing it to "artic-

---

[23] Eliot, *Daniel Deronda*, 99.

[24] Neil Hertz, *George Eliot's Pulse* (Stanford, CA: Stanford University Press, 2003), 13.

[25] Finding a "replicable unit" with which to measure the human will was a problem for Jevons: "I hesitate to say that men will ever have the means of measuring directly the feelings of the human heart. A unit of pleasure or of pain is difficult even to conceive" (*Political Economy*, I.17). But Jevons's mathematical method makes the need for such a unit clear, and his friend Francis Ysidro Edgeworth did his best to supply one in *Mathematical Psychics: An Essay on the Application of Mathematics to the Moral Sciences* (London: C. K. Paul, 1881). Edgeworth was the nephew of Anglo-Irish novelist Maria Edgeworth and founding editor of *The Economic Journal*.

ulate conflicting vocabularies of motivation," where, for example, vital "impulse" can become a deadly "compulsion."[26] It is this kind of conflicting view of human motivation that is carried by the epigraph here. From one point of view, markets seem subject to our impulses, registering in their infinite "plasticity" the shapes of human desire. This is Jevons's point of view: markets bend to our will, and thus in the mathematical patterns of the market, we can find a legible record of the human soul. But from a different perspective, it is human desire itself that appears infinitely malleable, as it conforms to the changing patterns of work and consumption. Jevons argues that market prices follow our desires. The alternative view, given voice in Eliot's work, shows that desire follows price.

IV. MAKING YOURSELF UNCOMFORTABLE

Celia notes with an apt succinctness at the start of the book that Dorothea "likes giving up" (18). The novel's early descriptions of Dorothea could suggest that Celia is right: since Dorothea derives a pious pleasure from self-denial, she may simply be charting her own unique path to happiness when she gives up riding and devotes herself to unremitting labor at Casaubon's side. But Celia repeats the judgment at the close of the novel, when she accommodates herself to Dorothea's love match by saying "you must always be making yourself uncomfortable" (820). While we may agree with Celia's insight on the renunciation of horses, her vision of Dorothea's match with Will as a mere expression of Dorothea's odd taste for displeasure is shown to be inaccurate and simplistic. Jevons, who read *Middlemarch* late in 1872, seems to have taken Celia's view himself: "I am much disappointed in the termination of *Middlemarch*," he wrote to a friend. "The introduction of Ladislaw is a blemish on the whole, and the novel would have been better with about half the characters."[27]

There is a self-reinforcing logic in Jevons's theory of self-interest that seems able to fend off any criticism. It asserts that, no matter what your private reasons may be, no matter what takes place in your inscrutable brain, you are always, ultimately, serving your own desires. It is this premise that allows Jevons to conclude that in the shape of the market we can always see "the quantitative effects of the feelings" of all members of a society. If diamonds fetch high prices, it is because they deliver real utility to the

---

[26] Hertz, *Pulse*, 13, 18.
[27] Jevons to E. J. Broadfield, 25 December 1872, *Letters and Journals of William Stanley Jevons,* ed. Harriet T. Jevons (London: Macmillan, 1886), 272.

marrying class. The more sinister implication of this view was summed up in 2001 by George Akerlof: "Neoclassical theory suggests that poverty is the reflection of low initial endowments of human and nonhuman capital."[28]

When you hold that market actors craft their choices in a private reality, and that their resulting circumstances are the authentic representation of that private world, then poverty and wealth end up looking like the accurate measure of human souls. But in the town of Middlemarch, no matter how much the world is subject to the private distortions of its individual residents, those residents craft their opinions and their desires in complex interplay with others. They do not regard the objects of the world—gemstones or horses—in direct encounters, but rather in scenes that are mentally populated by families and lovers and rivals. They evaluate resources not in isolation but from within a highly magnetized social field. In her recent book on emerging theories of space in the Victorian era, Alice Jenkins suggests a useful analogue for this aspect of Eliot's late work in the early field theory of Michael Faraday. Through the 1840s and 1850s, Faraday developed a vision of atoms not as acted upon by forces in space but as "centres of force" in themselves.[29] For Jenkins, *Middlemarch* offers a comparable "field in which people . . . are not bounded, self-contained units operating in a neutral space but extend as far as their influence does."[30] Jevons, and most economists who followed him in the twentieth century, viewed markets as neutral spaces in which self-contained and self-acting individuals were free to act. *Middlemarch* depicts things otherwise.

In showing how characters imagine each other and interact within the field of the market, Eliot's distinctive view of economic life anticipates some of the arguments made recently by economists interested in displacing the neoclassical model that has dominated the discipline for so long. Many of them emphasize "intersubjective" factors that condition tastes and choices.[31] Others, even more prominent in recent policy debates, stress the perennial irrationality of economic behavior. Examining the behavior of

---

[28] George A. Akerlof, "Behavioral Macroeconomics and Macroeconomic Behavior," Nobel Prize Lecture, 8 December 2001, http://nobelprize.org/nobel_prizes/economics/laureates/2001/akerlof-lecture.pdf.

[29] Alice Jenkins, *Space and the "March of Mind": Literature and the Physical Sciences in Britain, 1815–1850* (Oxford: Oxford University Press, 2007), 199.

[30] Jenkins, *Space and the "March of Mind,"* 199.

[31] For a useful overview, see Edward Fullbrook, "Descartes' Legacy: Intersubjective Reality, Intrasubjective Theory," in *Elgar Companion to Economics and Philosophy*, ed. John Bryan Davis, Alain Marciano, and John Runde (London: Elgar, 2004), 403–22; as well as Fullbrook's anthology *Intersubjectivity in Economics: Agents and Structures* (London: Routledge, 2001).

consumers, workers, and investors, they find little evidence that economic choice flows from the rational calculus of pleasure and pain, and they conclude that market models based on the actions of these rational calculators are bound to be inaccurate.[32] The last decades of Eliot's life coincided with the first formation of the neoclassical theory of markets and consumers. Her philosophical and literary sensibilities led her to resist the methodological individualism of this new economics, and to develop a very different way of imagining the inner life of capitalism.

---

[32] The most prominent figure here is Duke economist Dan Arielly, who helped to popularize a new "behavioral economics" in his *Predictably Irrational: The Hidden Forces that Shape Our Decisions* (New York: Harper Perennial, 2008).

CHAPTER 6

Demand and Desire in *Dracula*

DEANNA K. KREISEL

I. THOSE AWFUL WOMEN: THE PARADOX OF FEMALE DEMAND

In a now-classic analysis of economic themes in *Dracula,* Franco Moretti argues that the Count "lacks the aristocrat's conspicuous consumption: he does not eat, he does not drink, he does not make love, he does not like showy clothes. . . . Dracula, in other words, is a saver."[1] While Moretti's insight has intuitive force (it certainly seems to explain part of Dracula's puzzling behavior, at least *chez lui*), it fails to capture other contradictory elements of the economic logic of the novel. For while Dracula may not indulge in conspicuous consumption of the aristocratic human variety, and while his blood-drinking may seem measured (he "sucks just as much as is necessary and never wastes a drop"), certainly there is something curious about labeling a practice that ends in the agapic death of its objects "ascetic."[2] Later critics have in fact emphasized other consumptional aspects of the Count's activities; for example, Gail Turley Houston argues

---

[1] *Signs Taken for Wonders: On the Sociology of Literary Forms* (1983; New York: Verso, 2005), 90–91.

[2] Moretti, *Signs Taken for Wonders,* 91.

that Dracula and the English vampire hunters compete "to the death for a complete monopoly on circulation and consumption."[3]

The stakes of the disagreement for an economic reading of the novel—and of late-Victorian culture generally—are not trivial. While classical political economy focused on the production end of commercial activity and enshrined the labor theory of value, the interest in consumption intensified with the rise of the marginal-utility school in the latter decades of the century, when the demand theory of value waxed triumphant. The question of what, how, and why Dracula consumes is intricately connected to new cultural formations regarding appropriate levels of economic demand. Yet these concerns are not new to the latter decades of the century: anxieties about stagnation and general glut—the possibility of an economic slowdown caused by insufficient consumer demand—shape much professional and amateur economic discourse in the Victorian period. John Ruskin was a particularly important contributor to a midcentury economic heterodoxy that argued that insufficient consumption, particularly in the form of hoarding or overinvestment in capital goods, posed a threat to the continued growth of the British economy. While the rise of the marginal-utility school in the 1880s and 1890s brought these issues to the forefront, concerns about consumer demand formed an emergent discourse in the middle decades of the century; we can thus trace, in the anxieties of earlier writers such as Ruskin, the same complex of issues that reach their apotheosis in *Dracula*.

These concerns were also gendered. As many historians and cultural critics have argued, in the Victorian period the long-standing impressionistic connection between women and consumption (economic, domestic, and sumptuary) intensified; images of shopping, saving, and hoarding women also became the locus of widespread anxiety about consumption in general and the functioning of economic demand in particular. Victorian ideology imagined women as caretakers of domestic wealth, administering household resources in order to maximize the moral and spiritual health of their families: "Every wife is a steward of her husband's wealth, and should consider herself in that light. Every little act of carefulness . . . becomes a sacred duty."[4] Yet the image of the managing woman was not always so saintly and benign. Ruskin, for example, imagines a more sinister version of the household administratrix; in "The Ethics of the Dust" he admonishes schoolgirls to "either be house-Wives, or house-Moths. . . . In the deep sense, you must

---

[3] Gail Turley Houston, *From Dickens to Dracula: Gothic, Economics, and Victorian Fiction* (Cambridge: Cambridge University Press, 2005), 117.

[4] "Our Households and Homes," *Englishwoman's Domestic Magazine* 15 (1873): 75–76, 76.

either weave men's fortunes, and embroider them; or feed upon, and bring them to decay."[5] We already see here the association of errant womanhood with the consumption and death that are so insistently present in the image of the vampire.

Yet for Ruskin the problem is not consumption *qua* consumption. On the contrary, Ruskin, as iconoclastic critic of the labor theory of value, worried more about economic stagnation and insufficient demand than about luxurious expenditure:[6] as the rest of this essay demonstrates, these concerns were precursors to the economic anxieties attendant upon the rise of the marginal-utility school that we see in *Dracula*. As Ruskin opines in *Munera Pulveris,* the hoarder is the real figure of revulsion, a figure that is also strikingly gendered and sexualized: "the holder of wealth . . . may be regarded simply as a mechanical means of collection; or as a money-chest with a slit in it, not only receptant but suctional, set in the public thoroughfare."[7] In his denial of the universal benefit of saving, Ruskin rhetorically equates images of transgressive female sexuality with the horrors of unwise economic management. By withdrawing capital from the circulatory stream, the hoarder expends value by shrinking aggregate consumer demand and thus threatening the smooth operations of the young capitalist economy.[8] And the selfish miscreant guilty of this transgression, as with the figure of unwise spending, is figured, paradoxically, as a sexually rapacious woman.

This complex of issues returns in force in *Dracula,* where signs and tokens of deviant demand become literalized in the form of the vam-

---

[5] John Ruskin, *The Works of John Ruskin,* ed. E. T. Cook and Alexander Wedderburn, 39 vols. (London: George Allen, 1903–12), 18: 337.

[6] See John Ruskin, "Home and Its Economies," *Contemporary Review* 21 (1873): 927–37.

[7] *Works,* 17:169.

[8] For a helpful discussion of the paradox of hoarding, see Walter Benn Michaels's *The Gold Standard and the Logic of Naturalism: American Literature at the Turn of the Century* (Berkeley: University of California Press, 1987), chap. 5. For a discussion of scarcity and the marginal-utility school, see Regenia Gagnier, *The Insatiability of Human Wants: Economics and Aesthetics in Market Society* (Chicago: University of Chicago Press, 2000), 4; and Catherine Gallagher, *The Body Economic: Life, Death, and Sensation in Political Economy and the Victorian Novel* (Princeton, NJ: Princeton University Press, 2006), 127. As numerous other critics have argued, the concern with instilling new tastes and desires and with catering to the newly crowned consumer became paramount in the final decades of the Victorian era. See Thomas Richards, *The Commodity Culture of Victorian England: Advertising and Spectacle, 1851–1914* (Stanford, CA: Stanford University Press, 1990); Lawrence Birken, *Consuming Desire: Sexual Science and the Emergence of a Culture of Abundance, 1871–1914* (Ithaca, NY: Cornell University Press, 1988); and Erika Diane Rappaport, *Shopping for Pleasure: Women in the Making of London's West End* (Princeton, NJ: Princeton University Press, 2000).

pire. The novel is obsessed, above all else, with consumption and failures thereof. *Pace* Moretti, the Count *does* consume: generally, the blood (and life) of his victims, and in particular the blood of Lucy Westenra and Mina Harker—along with the blood from the three suitors that flows briefly through Lucy's veins before being withdrawn nightly by the vampire. This particular act of consumption is markedly "aristocratic," invoking through the novel's discourse of marriage and husbandly rights the mythical privilege of *droit de seigneur*. Yet the vampirization *process* (not just its results) also turns both its female victims, strangely, into consumers: Lucy imbibes the blood of the men in love with her, while Mina is later forced to drink Dracula's own blood directly in a depraved parody of consumer desire. By acting as conduits for the Count's "consumer goods," both Lucy and Mina dramatize and trouble the model of woman as caretaker of resources—albeit in very different ways. The heterodox—and largely repressed—anxiety about insufficient demand and economic stagnation we see in Ruskin is resurrected at the end of the century in the form of the vampire. For while vampiric women in particular might seem to resolve anxieties about insipid consumption, in fact their methods are unsustainable—and so the fear persists, for Stoker and his readers, that the depredations of *fin-de-siècle* consumer culture are ultimately unsustainable as well.

II. LUCY'S EXTRAVAGANCE

The paradoxical image of the vampiric female consumer reaches its apotheosis in Lucy Westenra, the first of Dracula's English targets. While Lucy's vampirization marks her, quite literally, as object of consumption, she is also an extravagant consumer in her own right, both as the "Bloofer Lady" vampire and as wasting victim requiring nightly blood transfusions from her devoted male suitors. This confusion of consuming and being-consumed is one we see throughout the Victorian discourse of womanhood, where wives are expected to act simultaneously as thrifty managers of household resources and as decorative objects of male choice. This paradox, along with persistent anxiety about inappropriate (including insufficient) consumption, is a rhetorical side effect of the discourse of economic demand,[9] of which the vampire metaphor is a particularly condensed version.

---

[9] I elaborate further on this idea in Deanna K. Kreisel, *Economic Woman: Demand, Gender, and Narrative Closure in Eliot and Hardy* (Toronto: University of Toronto Press, 2012).

It is thus not surprising to see these images appear throughout the writings of demand theorists, both after the rise of the marginal-utility school and in midcentury heterodox theorists such as Ruskin. In the lengthy dialogue-essay "The Ethics of the Dust" I quoted above, Ruskin whimsically educates a group of "Little Housewives" about the proper duties of womanhood, using geological formations as extended metaphor. As I noted, Ruskin's warning to young women that they prepare to be proper "House-wives" and avoid "feeding" on their husbands' fortunes presents the mismanaging woman as a species of monster. Elsewhere in the essay, Ruskin invokes vampires both indirectly and directly; the former occurs during a discussion of the formation of agates in the veins of rock:

> The veins themselves, when the rock leaves them open by its contraction, act with various power of suction upon its substance . . . while water, at every degree of heat and pressure . . . congeals, and drips, and throbs, and thrills, from crag to crag; and breathes from pulse to pulse of foaming or fiery arteries, whose beating is felt through chains of the great islands of the Indian seas, as your own pulses lift your bracelets. (333)

The word "veins" is not a dead metaphor for Ruskin: the arteries of evolving crystal thrill and throb and pulse with life just like those within the wrists of his young interlocutors. The processes of crystal production are intimately intertwined with violent processes of consuming raw materials, and all under the sign of the vampire: the "open" veins in the rock exerting their "power of suction" align this image rhetorically with the "receptant yet suctional" hoarder/prostitute of *Munera Pulveris*. He does not belabor the point, but the mention of the girls' bracelets invokes an association between crystals as natural formations and crystals as gems, objects of luxurious feminine consumption: all this tumult and steam and pressure and decomposition are the unseen obverse of decorative femininity.

While obfuscating his own vampiric interest in the veins of young girls, Ruskin makes crystal clear the connection between vampirism and capitalism; in a long passage in which he likens varieties of geological formations to caricatures of people, he notes: "sometimes you will see fat crystals eating up thin ones, like great capitalists and little labourers; and politico-economic crystals teaching the stupid ones how to eat each other, and cheat each other; . . . and vampire crystals eating out the hearts of others; . . . and parasite crystals living on the means of others" (335). This is a somewhat different capitalism–vampirism linkage than the classic one we see in Marx, where "capital is dead labour which, vampire-like, lives only by sucking living labour, and lives the more, the more labour it sucks."[10] Ruskin personalizes the connection and moralizes it even more pointedly than Marx: the vampire is the capitalist himself, and thus the blame for the evils of the system can be laid squarely at his feet rather than attributed to a historical process.

For Ruskin proper consumption is not merely a matter of quantity (thus simple rapacity is not the solution); the questions of production, consumption, and supply are also deeply ethical. Ruskin required consumers to be attentive to the social effects of their tastes and desires: "wise consumption is a far more difficult art than wise production."[11] It is important to consume lavishly and not to "spend" selfishly through hoarding, but it is also important to consume objects that contribute to the health and well-being not only of their manufacturers but of their purchasers and the economy in general. This responsibility was one Ruskin particularly marked out for women, as his lectures to schoolgirls attest. And this means he also marked out for them particular ire, in the form of images of monstrosity and vampirism, when their consuming practices were immoderate in any way.

Ruskin's paradoxical image of the vampiric female consumer is perfectly embodied in Lucy Westenra. Lucy's own acts of blood consumption are, as innumerable readers of the novel have noticed, markedly sexual.[12] Yet it is also her "super-sensitivity" (86) that initially sets her apart as Dracula's ideal victim: her powerful unconscious drive to be vampirized leads to her nightly sleepwalking, just as her irresponsible flirtation leads to her confession of three marriage proposals in one day.[13] In other words, it is not only after she has been converted (or is in the process of being converted) to a literal bloodsucker that she betrays a predilection for rapacious desire: Dracula's predation only literalizes and makes visible a tendency that has been present all along. Thus the logic of her consumption: Lucy feeds on the blood of her victims not only as a full-fledged vampire, but also during the course of the transfusions in which her stalwart, and largely discarded, suitors (plus Van Helsing) give up the "blood of four strong men" (138) for her maintenance. This is also a process that is

---

[10] Karl Marx, *Capital: A Critique of Political Economy*, trans. Samuel Moore and Edward Aveling (New York: Modern Library, 1906), 257.

[11] *Works*, 17:98. See also *Fors Clavigera* (*Works*, 27:31ff.).

[12] For example, see Phyllis A. Roth, "Suddenly Sexual Women in Bram Stoker's *Dracula*," *Literature and Psychology* 27 (1977): 113–21.

[13] Bram Stoker, *Dracula*, ed. Nina Auerbach and David J. Skal (1897; New York: Norton Critical Ed., 1997), 86.

explicitly sexualized by the donors, who insist that to give and accept blood is to be "really married" (157) and that Lucy has been made a "polyandrist" (158) by accepting their bodily fluids. Lucy's femininity is thus always characterized as extraordinarily expensive and her "tastes" as extravagant, to say the least.

Yet perhaps the more interesting aspect of Lucy's vampirization is the strange way in which she acts as "index" to the Count's own desires. The word "index" is used twice in reference to Renfield, whose lunatic excitability waxes and wanes with the proximity of his "master," the Count. Once the vampire hunters discover the connection between the two, they realize they can use the psychological state of the patient "in an indexy kind of way" (219) to track the Count's activities.[14] What the focus on Renfield obscures, however, is the much more reliable and direct way in which Lucy acts as "index" to the Count's grotesque consumption: this is an unacceptable connection that must be obscured by the text. The relationship between indexing and blood becomes apparent, however, upon close reading: Lucy's cheeks, their pallor or ruddiness, indicate distinctly when she has been fed upon and when she has been allowed to recover. Before the arrival of Dracula in Whitby, Mina's journal attests that Lucy "has got a beautiful colour since she has been here" (65); that her "cheeks are a lovely rose pink" (72); and that she has "lost that anæmic look which she had" (72). Later, when Dracula begins to feed on her, she becomes "paler than is her wont" (91); we are told that "the roses in her cheeks are fading" (92), and later that she is "ghastly pale" (103). The novel is, at least superficially (and as we shall see in a moment, not always logically), meticulous on this point: dates are carefully collated so as to create a "secret" index of the Count's comings-and-goings, which is corroborated by the more histrionic index of Renfield's zoophagous activities and rantings about his master.

There are two crucial ways in which Lucy's index intersects with the pervasive economic concerns of the novel. First of all, her changing cheeks stage an up-to-date, *fin-de-siècle* version of the Romantic ideology of the

---

[14] The only other time the word "index" is used in the novel is when Jonathan describes the blue flames that appear on the eve of St. George's Day to mark the location of buried treasure in Dracula's own country. As the Count explains to Jonathan, "That treasure has been hidden . . . in the region through which you came last night, there can be but little doubt. For it was the ground fought over for centuries by the Wallachian, the Saxon, and the Turk. Why, there is hardly a foot of soil in all this region that has not been enriched by the blood of men, patriots or invaders" (27). In a very direct way, the "index" here points to the existence of blood, or blood-as-treasure: treasure as a literalization of the spoils of rapine and imperial exploitation very similar to the metaphor employed by Marx.

blush, one that is attuned to the specific concerns of the new economic theories taking hold at the end of the century: consumption and the "scientization" of economic discourse. As Mary Ann O'Farrell has argued, blushes in the nineteenth-century novel straddle the somatic and the semiotic, enacting a "demand for interpretation" that is also an "invitation to narrative."[15] In the case of Lucy, what the blush demands is a species of scientific interpretation: in this sense it is more of an invitation to medical case history than to imaginative narration. This precise measurement of Lucy's process of vampirization—this index—is of a piece with the overall scientization that grips the characters in the novel. As many readers have noted, *Dracula* enacts an almost obsessive need to professionalize and technologize the practices and accoutrements of monster-hunting: from phonography, shorthand, typewriting, and hypnosis to telegrams, railway timetables, and double-entry bookkeeping, the novel aggressively (and paradoxically) presents late-Victorian vampire fighting as thoroughly methodical and relentlessly empirical.[16] While critics have thus traced the influence of multiple professional or newly professionalized disciplines—such as accounting, psychiatry, and medicine—in *Dracula,* none has discussed marginal-utility theory, the newly scientific version of political economy contemporaneous with Stoker's novel.

The theory of marginal utility was simultaneously "discovered" in 1870 by three theorists working independently, W. Stanley Jevons in England, Léon Walras in France, and Carl Menger in Austria.[17] The principle states that the satisfaction or benefit (utility) to a consumer of an additional unit of any good is inversely related to the number of units of that good she already has. The value of a commodity is no longer seen to be determined by its cost of production, or the cost of the labor required to produce it, but in terms of its desirability to the consumer. The rise of the marginal-utility school thus marked a shift both in content (the demand theory of value) and in methodology (the mathematical model). "Economics," as the study was starting to be called, was becoming a professional discipline requiring highly specialized knowledge and advanced mathematical skills.

---

[15] Mary Ann O'Farrell, *Telling Complexions: The Nineteenth-Century English Novel and the Blush* (Durham, NC: Duke University Press, 1997), 4.

[16] For analyses of the technologies and modernity of *Dracula,* see Jennifer Fleissner, "Dictation Anxiety: The Stenographer's Stake in *Dracula,*" *Nineteenth-Century Contexts* 22 (2000): 417–55; and Jennifer Wicke, "Vampiric Typewriting: *Dracula* and Its Media," *English Literary History* 59 (1992): 467–93.

[17] For a good discussion of the strange phenomenon of this theory appearing in three separate places simultaneously, see Marc Blaug, *Economic Theory in Retrospect,* 5th ed., Cambridge: Cambridge University Press, 1996, 277–92.

We can see most clearly the mathematization of consumer desire in the figure of Renfield: his meticulously kept records—the long columns of figures and tallies of insects, spiders, and birds he plans to consume—function as a grotesque parody of the calculation of consumer desire "at the margin." Yet once again, Renfield here functions as the more visible textual function, obscuring the fact that Lucy is engaged in a more furtive version of the same activity. Lucy's index, or rather Lucy-as-index, stages a quasi-scientific quantification of the occult practice of vampirism; her blush and pallor are both scientific "evidence" of Dracula's activities and a sexualized version of the rigorously *measurable* desire to consume insisted upon by marginal-utility theory.

The second way in which Lucy's indexing reveals the economic concerns of the novel is an extension and amplification of the first, and has to do with the way in which the index directly reflects the operations of demand itself. The Count husbands his resources in Lucy; he allows her body to restore its supply of nourishment before he feeds on her again. But the timeline of Lucy's "indexing" of the Count seems a bit peculiar. The very night after the arrival of Dracula, Mina remarks that Lucy has "more colour in her cheeks than usual" (86). The morning after we are certain that the Count has begun feeding on Lucy—the morning after Mina rescues her from the "something dark" (88) bending over her "snowy white" (88) figure in the churchyard in Whitby—Mina notes in her diary: "The adventure of the night does not seem to have harmed her; on the contrary, it has benefited her, for she looks better this morning than she has done for weeks" (89).

Has Dracula drunk only enough to stimulate the color in Lucy's cheeks, but not enough to enervate her? As soon as she does start to become pale from his ministrations, he leaves Whitby and travels to London, allowing his favorite victim to recover—for the "roses" in her cheeks to return and even for her to get "fat" (101)—before he begins to feed on her again in London. Only when the "stalwart men" begin restocking her artificially does Dracula get greedy and apparently feed on her nightly, to such a degree that she cannot survive even with the artificial prop of the transfusions. What is important about the logic of the transfusions is the way it displaces "demand" from Dracula (the "end user") to Lucy—she is the one who appears insatiable. As long as Dracula and Lucy are engaged in good, measured, up-to-date economic activity—using resources only when the added utility of each additional unit warrants its consumption—the system seems sustainable. Yet vampirism, as we shall see, is exactly that activity that exposes an anxiety about the *unsustainability* of the capitalist system.

For if demand is what is required for the operations of the economy, then those operations are simultaneously threatened in two directions by the figure of the vampire: first, as Moretti argues, demand can be inadequate; and second, demand can be so robust as to evacuate productive capabilities. In both cases, the anxiety is particularly focused on transgressive female figures.

III. MINA'S TRANSGRESSION

Mina is an even more interesting case study in anxieties over improper consumption than her more flamboyant friend. While Lucy is figured as pure-yet-transgressive, demure-yet-rapacious, Mina is depicted as unalloyedly loyal, discreet, hard-working, and sensible; her process of vampirization is thus more complicated and circuitous than that of the susceptible Lucy. However, even though Mina is a late-Victorian update of the "angel in the house" (helping her husband in his work through her knowledge of shorthand), she is not immune to the kind of anxious gender critique we saw levied at the earlier incarnation of domestic femininity. As Mina herself is at great pains to emphasize, after she and Lucy tuck into a "capital" afternoon tea, she is *not* a "New Woman": "I believe we should have shocked the 'New Woman' with our appetites" (86).[18]

Mina's anxious disavowal marks both women as potentially monstrous consumers. For Ruskin and other commentators on the Victorian discourse of proper womanhood, the idealized woman does not, vampirelike, clamor for her fair share of comestibles. She is instead a *source* of consumption for others—a fertile, maternal, *lactating* body, with a free-flowing supply of fluid sustenance: "Calm and quiet, refreshing as a fountain in the desert, as the charm of a rock in a weary land, is the true mother. . . . But with all these essentially womanly qualities she is an excellent manager, and displays business-like abilities."[19] This passage could serve as a description of Mina Harker, with her "so good combination" of a "man's brain" and "a woman's heart" (207). Yet during the course of her vampirization, Mina changes utterly. Not only does she cease to be the rock upon which

---

[18] The locus classicus is Carol A. Senf's article "*Dracula*: Stoker's Response to the New Woman," *Victorian Studies* 26 (1982): 33–49. For a more recent treatment of the topic, see also Charles E. Prescott and Grace A. Giorgio, "Vampiric Affinities: Mina Harker and the Paradox of Femininity in Bram Stoker's *Dracula*," *Victorian Literature and Culture* 33 (2005): 487–515.

[19] "Our Households," 75–76.

the menfolk lean when they need to weep and be comforted in solitude; she also becomes a consumer herself, a grotesque reversal of the lactating mother who is forced to feed on the liquid sustenance of Dracula's own breast:

> On the bed beside the window lay Jonathan Harker, his face flushed and breathing heavily as though in a stupor. Kneeling on the near edge of the bed facing outwards was the white-clad figure of his wife. By her side stood a tall, thin man, clad in black. . . . With his left hand he held both Mrs. Harker's hands, keeping them away with her arms at full tension. His right hand gripped her by the back of the neck, forcing her face down on his bosom. Her white nightdress was smeared with blood, and a thin stream trickled down the man's bare chest which was shown by his torn-open dress. The attitude of the two had a terrible resemblance to a child forcing a kitten's nose into a saucer of milk to compel it to drink. (246–47)

Several critics have discussed the connection between lactation and bloodsucking in *Dracula*;[20] I would argue further that this connection is inflected by an understanding of the particular economic meanings of breast milk (and blood) in the Victorian period. These two bodily fluids (which are symbolically conflated in the lactating-Dracula scene), when considered as items of consumption, are particularly cogent emblems of the operations of demand: they are the only "products" that are "manufactured" solely *in response* to demand.[21] Milk is replenished by the body in direct response to its withdrawal; the obverse of this causal relationship is that milk ceases to be produced when demand itself ceases. While the renewal of blood does not normally work in this same way, it does in *Dracula*: it is presented in the logic of the novel as another special object of consumption that is infinitely replenishable under conditions of optimum demand—not too robust and not too feeble.

Vampirism seems to be a perfect solution to the conundrum of production and allocation of resources: to consume only products that are replenished "naturally" as a direct response to the act of consumption is to return to a Physiocratic fantasy of self-sustaining, circular economic activity and thus to resolve the central anxieties of the capitalist economic organization.[22] As Catherine Gallagher notes, both Ruskin and Dickens, as adher-

---

[20] For a fascinating psychoanalytic study of vampirism and breastfeeding, see, for example, Joan Copjec, "Vampires, Breast-Feeding, and Anxiety," *October* 58 (1991): 25–43, 34.

[21] See Kreisel, *Economic Woman*, chap. 5.

[22] For the eighteenth-century French school of economics known as Physiocracy, the only

ents of sanitary reform, fantasized a self-sustaining system in which bodily products and remains (including corpses, human waste, and blood products) would nourish further production in a closed and infinite cycle of renewal.[23] We can see, then, how a perverse kind of logic would render vampirism another such closed and self-sustaining system. In the case of Mina, the logic of her feeding on Dracula—he tells her that it functions magically to place her under his power (252)—constitutes her as a conduit between Dracula and the hunters, who later hypnotize her in order to learn of his movements, just as Lucy acted as conduit for the delivery of the suitors' blood to Dracula. Both circulatory "systems," under optimum conditions of demand, seem to be perfectly self-contained and self-perpetuating.

The most remarkable aspect of this scene is the way it reverses the usual terms of vampirism: the consumer becomes the consumed, and vice versa. We see this reversal as well in the case of Lucy. After her death Lucy is transformed into a vampire who terrorizes the area around Hampstead Heath near where she is buried: she specializes in feeding on the bodies of young children whom she lures to her with an ersatz maternal manner, and who have nicknamed her the "Bloofer Lady." The horrifying image of a young woman clutching an infant to her breast not to feed it but to feed *on* it is described in terms markedly similar to those used to detail her growing sexual rapaciousness during her slow process of vampirization:

> The sweetness was turned to adamantine, heartless cruelty, and the purity to voluptuous wantonness. . . . With a careless motion, she flung to the ground, callous as a devil, the child that up to now she had clutched strenuously to her breast. . . . When she advanced to [Arthur] with outstretched arms and a wanton smile he fell back and hid his face in his hands. She still advanced, however, and with a languorous, voluptuous grace, said, "Come to me, Arthur. Leave these others and come to me. My arms are hungry for you. Come, and we can rest together. Come, my husband, come!" (187–88)

The "voluptuousness" (Stoker's favorite word for female vampires) of her sexual advance to Arthur is juxtaposed with the voluptuous wantonness of her consumption of the child's blood. Lucy's vampiric integration of perverse sexuality and perverse acts of consumption (she is "hungry" for her lover) is an extension of the dynamic we see at work in the three "weird

---

source of economic surplus was agriculture—produce extracted from the land that is greater than the amount needed for subsistence. For summaries of the work of the Physiocrats, see M[ax] Beer, *An Inquiry into Physiocracy* (New York: Russell & Russell, 1966).

[23] See Gallagher, *The Body Economic,* 100–107.

sisters" who terrorize Jonathan Harker in Dracula's castle: they, too, subsist on a diet of infantine flesh, and their acts of blood consumption are also described in sexualized terms. After the Count rescues his guest from the "languorous ecstasy" of the "soft, shivering touch of the lips" (43) of one of the sisters, he placates them:

> "Well, now I promise you that when I am done with him you shall kiss him at your will. Now go! Go!" . . . "Are we to have nothing tonight?" said one of them, with a low laugh, as she pointed to the bag which he had thrown upon the floor, and which moved as though there were some living thing within it. For answer he nodded his head. One of the women jumped forward and opened it. If my ears did not deceive me there was a gasp and a low wail, as of a half smothered child. (43–44)

In the case of both Vampire Lucy and Dracula's three minions, there is a smooth and seamless substitution of food for sexual "prey," and vice versa. Yet even more importantly, that food is itself not just a substitution but also a reversal: just as with the breastfeeding tableau between Mina and Dracula, the relationship between nurturer and nurtured is exposed as structurally reversible. When we consider the special status of breast milk and blood in the novel—as "products" whose bodily manufacture literalizes the metaphorical operations of economic demand—we can begin to see how these perverse scenes of feeding both destabilize and resolve the contradictions of consumption first isolated by Franco Moretti. In other words, if we take seriously the metaphoric connection between blood and capital that Marx himself first insisted upon, then the feeder/fed reversal makes perfect sense. The fantasy of a capitalist body grown munificent, a bloodsucker who freely gives rather than taking, is a reaction not only to anxieties about sustainable production but also to anxieties about economic stagnation due to flaccid consumer desire.[24]

Mina and Lucy are perfect complements for each other: while Lucy's insatiability (which was of course really Dracula's) seemed to outstrip the productive capabilities of the system, Mina's desires are not robust enough to sustain it. Vampirism thus functions as the dark obverse of the expanding capitalist economy: just as the economic system of Count Dracula is ultimately unsustainable (once everyone is a vampire, who will remain to be consumed?), so the fear persists, for Stoker and his readers, that *fin-de-*

---

[24] This same vision of consumptional reversal is one that we find throughout economic writers concerned about the operations of demand. See, for example, Thomas DeQuincey, *The Logic of Political Economy* (1845; Boston: James Osgood, 1872), 170.

siècle consumer culture is ultimately unsustainable as well. It is in the figures of Lucy and Mina that this tension is examined and uneasily resolved: while both the Count and Lucy—as superconsumers whose appetites are irresponsibly rapacious—must be eliminated, Mina is successfully disciplined into a mode of consumption that seems sustainable. The ultimate irony of *Dracula* is that the model of vampirism, in which consumption actually brings new products into being, is the perfect resolution to the anxiety attendant upon a demand theory of value. It is a resolution that is inadmissible to middle-class Victorian values, as surely as middle-class, Victorian female vampires are inadmissible. As this essay shows, such vampire/women are horrifying in their consumption, not for the reasons that have traditionally been mooted, but because they suggest the untenable implications of capitalism (and the demand theory of value) itself.

PART III

Financing the Family

CHAPTER 7

"A *pauper* every wife is"[1]

LADY WESTMEATH, MONEY, MARRIAGE, AND DIVORCE IN EARLY NINETEENTH-CENTURY ENGLAND

JANETTE RUTTERFORD

*E*mily Nugent, the Marchioness of Westmeath, was one of the most famous and infamous women of her day. Pamphlets were written by her and about her as she attempted to separate from her abusive husband, fought his attempts to retain conjugal rights, and took him to court for maintenance payments and custody of her children. Her struggle to achieve financial independence before the Matrimonial Causes Act of 1857 and the Married Women's Property Acts of 1870 and 1882 highlights both the economic vulnerability of women, whose property and legal identity merged with those of their husbands at marriage,[2] and the striking

---

[1] Emily Nugent Westmeath, *A Narrative of the Case of the Marchioness of Westmeath* (London: James Ridgway, 1857), 136.

[2] Under common law, a married woman's property—whether acquired before or during marriage—was deemed to belong to the husband. Married women could neither own property nor make contracts in their own name. See Amy Louise Erickson, "Common Law Versus Common Practice: The Use of Marriage Settlements in Early Modern England," *Economic History Review,* 2nd series, 43 (1990): 24. If a married woman incurred debts, creditors could not obtain redress from her; they had to do so via the husband. Children were the legal property of their father. Under equity law, a married woman could benefit from a marriage settlement, which allowed the wife's family—or the husband—to settle a certain amount of property on her. The settlement specified what was to happen to the funds upon the wife's death and typically made provision for what was to happen in the event of the hus-

resilience they sometimes showed in their efforts to extricate themselves from those marriages[3] and to achieve economic security and even comfort.

Lady Westmeath's story challenges the conventional understanding that marriage offered women financial stability. Writing in 1857, a year before her death, Emily was clear that, from a financial standpoint alone, she would have been better off not marrying at all. Yet, as this essay shows, she was hardly a simple victim. In the various ways that she pieced together a living, we see an important case study of how women deployed a range of financial strategies—from exploiting personal and political connections to pursuing investments—despite their legal and economic subjection. Although Lady Westmeath's rank makes hers an exceptional case in certain respects, she recognized her situation as one brought about by a system of gender inequality, comparing herself to "every wife" and to "married women in this country" in general. Her archive includes a rich collection of pamphlets, legal cases, personal correspondence, and financial transactions. This unusually extensive paper trail offers unique insight into the social and economic impact of separation and divorce for a married woman before the 1857 Matrimonial Causes Act and the Married Women's Property Acts of 1870 and 1882.

I. THE WESTMEATH MARRIAGE

Emily-Ann-Bennett-Elizabeth Cecil was the second daughter of the first Marquis of Salisbury.[4] Before her marriage in 1812, she was used to court

---

band dying first. Since, under primogeniture, the eldest son inherited the "estate," money was usually set aside through the premarital contract out of which to pay the widow's jointure. Janette Rutterford and Josephine Maltby, "The Widow, the Clergyman and the Reckless—Women Investors before 1914," *Feminist Economics* 12 (2006): 111–38; Amy Louise Erickson, "Possession—And the Other One-Tenth of the Law: Assessing Women's Ownership and Economic Roles in Early Modern England," *Women's History Review* 16.3 (July 2007): 370. Marriage settlements, structured as trusts, were defensible under the law of equity only in the Court of Chancery. Common law did not recognize such premarital contracts, which were viewed as annulled on the subsequent marriage.

[3] Until the Matrimonial Causes Act of 1857, divorce could only be granted by private act of Parliament, which required proof of adultery. The ecclesiastical courts granted divorce *a mensa et thoro* (from bed and board) for such offences as adultery, desertion, or extreme cruelty. This was a form of separation and not dissolution of the marriage and consequently did not permit remarriage. Before a private divorce bill could be considered, a divorce *a mensa et thoro* had to be obtained through the ecclesiastical courts. See Sybil Wolfram, "Divorce in England, 1700–1857," *Oxford Journal of Legal Studies* 3.2 (Summer 1985): 155–86. Note that the wife was unable to defend herself in such a suit or to have legal representation.

[4] Charles Mosley, ed., *Burke's Peerage, Baronetage, & Knightage*, 107th ed., 3 vols. (Wilming-

life during the London season and to the splendors of her family home, Hatfield House, in Hertfordshire. She married George Nugent, Lord Delvin, heir to the Irish earldom of Westmeath and the son of a *divorcée*—not quite a *mésalliance* but a definite step down the social ladder. His father, the seventh Earl of Westmeath, had divorced his mother, Marianne Jeffereyes, for adultery in 1796.[5] George met Emily through her brother, Lord Cranborne, who had served with him in the army.

Although this was initially a love match, problems set in early, many of them rooted in the couple's financial life. During the first few years of the marriage, the couple lived in the isolated Clonyn Castle, near Devlin, a far cry from the bustle of London. Emily complained of being left alone, with not even enough pin money to be able to buy tea and sugar, or the other little luxuries that made life in the country bearable to her.[6] She asserted that George called her a "damned bitch" when she asked for pin money. When Emily was eight months pregnant with their first child, born in May 1814, George was so roused during an argument that he both hit Emily and threatened to disinherit their child in favor of his half-brother. Emily used his guilt at the violence to make him verbally retract the financial threat, a real one if the unborn child were a girl.[7] Marital disputes, frequently violent, persisted. George had acknowledged the existence of an illegitimate child to Lord Cranborne before his marriage. Another was conceived while he was paying his addresses to Emily, and she found out

---

ton, DE: Burke's Peerage [Genealogical Books] Ltd, 2003), vol. 3. She was the third daughter, but the first, Caroline, died young.

[5] A. P. W. Malcolmson, *The Pursuit of the Heiress: Aristocratic Marriage in Ireland, 1740–1840* (Belfast: Ulster Historical Foundation, 2006), 142; George Frederick Nugent Westmeath, 7th Earl of Westmeath, *The Trial at Large on an Action for Damages brought by the Right Hon. G.F. Earl of Westmeath against the Hon. A.C. Bradshaw for Adultery with . . . Mary Anne, Countess of Westmeath, etc.* (Dublin, 1796); and Lawrence Stone, *Broken Lives: Separation and Divorce in England, 1660–1857* (Oxford: Oxford University Press, 1993).

[6] The term "pin money" refers to an allowance given by the husband to the wife for her personal expenditure. For full details of the Westmeath marriage, see the judgment by Sir John Nicholl, 1827, reproduced in full by Lady Westmeath in her pamphlet *A Narrative of the Case of the Marchioness of Westmeath*, 1857. The Nicholl judgment can also be found in Proceedings of the Court of Arches, Hilary Term, 3d Session, 1827, Westmeath v. Westmeath, Haggard, 1830, Supplement, pp. 61 to 132 and as a separately printed pamphlet. The two pamphlets produced by Lord Westmeath—the first in 1828, in response to fifty-three pages of new material submitted (and later expunged from the record) that Lady Westmeath had submitted to the House of Lords, and the second, in 1857 in reply to her *Narrative*—also provide further details and opposing views as to what occurred. Additional details are also provided in Malcolmson, *Pursuit of the Heiress*, and Stone, *Broken Lives*.

[7] John Haggard, *Reports of Cases Argued and Determined in the Ecclesiastical Courts at Doctors' Commons and in the High Court of Delegates, Vol II Supplement* (London: Saunders and Benning, 1830), 66.

about this child's existence after she was married.[8] The affair threatened Emily's financial affairs as much as her feelings. Under an agreement drawn up and witnessed by a neighbor and sometimes conciliator Henry Widman Wood, George was never to see his mistress or their two children again, would give no more than a fixed sum in support to be transmitted by Emily's maid, and would receive no communications from them, in return for which Emily would remain silent on the subject. Emily was particularly incensed that George's mistress had received more money than she had in pin money, although, as George's wife, Emily had more—albeit limited—rights than George's mistress, whose financial and legal claims on the father of her children were nonexistent; what help she received was entirely discretionary.[9]

In the autumn of 1816, after more violent arguments, Emily and George moved to London, where relations deteriorated to such an extent that Lord Westmeath was persuaded to sign a prospective deed of separation in December 1817, which would take effect if his behavior worsened, and she would then be paid maintenance of an amount to be determined by friends. At the same time, George settled most of his Irish Nugent estates on their daughter, Rosa, in the event that he and Emily failed to produce a male heir. Things went well for a while, and Emily became pregnant with her second child, a son. Again, the good times were short-lived. Formal articles of separation were signed on 30 May 1818, by which Emily was to be paid her pin money of £500 a year plus a separation allowance of £1,300 a year and allowed to live separately.[10] Emily moved into a house of her own in Bolton Street, but her mother, Lady Salisbury, anxious to keep up appearances, persuaded her to allow her husband to have a room there and even to dine there and accompany her to social events. Allowing her husband bed (albeit in a separate room) and board was in direct contradiction to the common term for separation *a mensa et thoro,* that is, separation from bed and board. This meant that the public's perception, vital to Emily's mother, was that there was no separation—but, as I later show, it would also have financial repercussions for Emily when she tried to collect her alimony.

Emily's son, Lord Delvin, was born in November 1818. In early 1819 she moved into Stratford Place, where she also allowed George a bed-

---

[8] Haggard, *Reports of Cases,* 80–81; George Thomas John Nugent Westmeath, *A Sketch of Lord Westmeath's Case,* fn21. Emily unsuccessfully tried to arrange the emigration of the children and their mother to America in 1817.

[9] See Stone, *Broken Lives,* 302.

[10] Haggard, *Reports of Cases,* 44. The deed was initially destroyed by Lord Westmeath at the stationer's, where it was being copied. It was executed in August 1818.

CHAPTER 7. RUTTERFORD, "'A *PAUPER* EVERY WIFE IS'"

room and dining rights. However, in April, after further arguments, Emily refused to dine with George, and in June 1819 George opened Emily's personal papers without permission and threatened her physically. He refused her request to leave the house. Emily, fearing for her safety, moved out on 20 June. George took their son to Clonyn, where he died at the age of one, hours before Emily arrived with her brother to see him. Her daughter Rosa lived with her until 1821, when George kept her with him after a visit. Emily's mother, acting as a witness on the husband's side, confirmed that George then prevented Emily from seeing Rosa until at least 1824. Rosa continued to live with her father until her marriage in 1840. The fact that Emily never again spoke to her mother, even at her father's deathbed in 1823, and that by the mid-1820s Emily was no longer on speaking terms with her husband, father, mother, brother, sister, and cousin shows the high social cost of separation and divorce to the women involved.[11]

The case of Lady Westmeath's marriage confirms for us the economic difficulties that women faced within marriage as well as when they attempted to separate. Just as importantly, however, her case also reveals the ways in which the dissolution of a marriage could tax a husband, as well as the creative strategies wives such as Emily could use to overcome some of their gendered disadvantages.

II. THE LEGAL TANGLE

Litigation between Lord and Lady Westmeath lasted until 1837 in a number of different courts—relating to ecclesiastical, equity, and common law—and revealed the financial ramifications of a failed marriage for both. The cases involved deeds of separation, child custody and maintenance, and nonpayment of court costs. Ultimately, they led to a prison sentence for Lord Westmeath and witnesses, steep payments for all parties involved, and the longest running marital dispute of nineteenth-century England. Using the ecclesiastical courts, which covered the rules of marriage and separation, Lord Westmeath sued for restitution of conjugal rights in 1821.[12] Emily responded in 1822, detailing thirty-three separate incidents of cruelty supported by ten exhibits. After witnesses had been

---

[11] Haggard, *Reports of Cases*, 66. George Thomas John Nugent Westmeath, *A Sketch*, 38–39; Stone, *Broken Lives*, 299; Mosley, *Burke's Peerage*, 3504.

[12] Common law was primarily concerned with transmission of property, debt, and credit, and the ability to award damages; equity law was able to deal with marriage settlements, trusts, and enforcement of alimony. Lawrence Stone, *Road to Divorce: England, 1530–1987* (Oxford: Oxford University Press, 1992), 24–26.

examined and after Lord Westmeath's replies to the accusations, Emily submitted in 1823 further evidence, including five charges of adultery.[13] The adultery case was built around an assertion by the Irish gardener, subsequently employed by the Duke of Wellington, that Lord Westmeath was the father of "two suppositious children by a loathsome and filthy prostitute who was sworn by herself and her filthy associates to have been introduced into my house and my bed the very night of my only son's death." In court, the "prostitute" was unable to answer some of the questions posed because "By the Lord, I was so drunk I do not know." In 1825 three of Emily's witnesses for charges of adultery were convicted of conspiracy and fined and imprisoned in Ireland.[14] This did not help her case for separation, which she lost in 1826 on both counts of adultery and cruelty.[15] The first deed of separation was dismissed as invalid, as it related to a future and not present separation, and the second was deemed void due to subsequent cohabitation.[16]

On appeal, in 1827 the Court of Arches preferred to concentrate on Emily's accusations of cruelty, which had more reliable witnesses. Sir John Nicholl, in an unusual and much publicized verdict—deemed freak by Malcolmson[17]—found *for* Lady Westmeath not on grounds of adultery but on grounds of cruelty.[18] He expressed the view that where blows might have been acceptable to those

> in the lower conditions [where] amidst very coarse habits such incidents occur almost as freely as rude or reproachful words . . . if a nobleman of high rank and ancient family uses personal violence to his wife, his equal in rank, the choice of his affection, the friend of his bosom, the mother of his off-spring—such conduct carries with it something so degrading to the

---

[13] Haggard, *Reports of Cases*, 4.

[14] Anne Cornell, *A Full and Complete Report of the Trial, the King, at the Prosecution of the Marquis of Westmeath, against Anne Cornell, John Monaghan, Bernard Maguire, Patrick Farley and William McKenzie at Green-Street Dubline at the Commission of Over and Terminer, January 3rd and Two Succeeding Days* (Dublin: John Cummings, 1825).

[15] Haggard, *Reports of Cases*, 60.

[16] Richard Vaughan Barnewell and John Leycester Adolphus, *Reports of Cases Argued and Determined in the Courts of the King's Bench, Vol. III* (London: Saunders and Benning, 1833), 748–50; Stone, *Broken Lives*, 318. One of Emily's advisers on both deeds was Mr. Sheldon, the Cecil family lawyer. He was so mortified by the difficulties she had in obtaining maintenance from her estranged husband that he left her £1,000 in his will.

[17] Malcolmson, *Pursuit of the Heiress*, 144.

[18] The verdict and commentary on cruelty reproduced below was reported in the *Niles Register* of 31 March 1829, published in Baltimore, Washington, and Philadelphia.

husband, and so insulting and mortifying to the wife, as to render the injury itself far more severe and unsupportable.[19]

Both parties paid their own legal costs in the lower courts, but Lord Westmeath was ordered to pay both sides' costs for the final hearing. Both Lord and Lady Westmeath complained of poverty. Emily estimated her legal costs at £12,000 in 1831. George estimated his at £14,000 in 1831, rising to £30,000 in his 1857 pamphlet.[20] These costs were orders of magnitude greater than the £700 total estimated for uncontested divorces by the 1850 Royal Commission, although even the costs for uncontested divorces were far beyond the means of the "lower conditions."[21]

III. COPING WITH COVERTURE IN MARRIAGE

Under coverture, a wife's income and assets belonged to her husband, unless a premarital contract specified otherwise by putting money in trust to provide pin money during the marriage, a widow's jointure after the husband's death, and dowries for any younger children. Married women could also inherit assets if held in trust. However, as the Westmeath archive reveals, such precautions did not always work as planned.

In Emily's case, the premarital contract stipulated a dowry from Emily's father of £15,000, which was settled on the younger children of the marriage. Of this, only £5,000 was paid in cash, with the remainder being paid in the form of an annuity of £500, until the lump sum of £10,000 was paid at some undetermined future date. In fact, the lump sum was paid in 1823 by Lord Cranborne, soon after the death of his father and after his marriage to an heiress. In return, Emily was to have £500 a year pin money payable by George for her exclusive use.[22] In addition, a widow's jointure of £3,000 a year was agreed upon, to be paid from the income from her husband's estates. George told his future father-in-law that the Irish estates would yield over £10,000 a year, well able to finance the promised £3,000 a year widow's jointure. However, he was being economical with the truth. As late as 1828, the estate's income was still less than £4,800 a year, with

---

[19] Haggard, *Reports of Cases*, 73.
[20] Stone, *Broken Lives*, 331, 340. Emily asked her brother to pay Parliamentary agents the £4,000 to £5,000 legal costs she owed them.
[21] Wolfram, "Divorce in England, 1700–1857," 167.
[22] Stone, *Broken Lives*, 286.

outgoings of £1,650 in interest payments and a further £840 in annuities to family dependents.[23]

There was no formal settlement for Emily's jointure because, by some settlement made by the then Lord Westmeath on his second marriage after the divorce of his first wife, his son, George, had "no power to settle anything."[24] He would have to wait until his father's death. When his father did die, in 1814, no attempt was made by his son to provide for the widow's jointure, and his Nugent inheritance was not settled until 1822.[25] Indeed, as late as 1857 George was contesting the jointure amount. He asserted that it had been agreed to in Irish pounds, so that the £3,000 promised was actually £2,769 4s 7½ d in sterling terms.[26]

As a woman, Emily had no choice but to rely on her family and legal advisers to act on her behalf to assure her the proper premarital settlements. They failed to commit George to providing a widow's jointure immediately on his father's death, to check whether George would have sufficient funds to settle the promised jointure, and to clarify whether the jointure would be denominated in Irish or English pounds. As this example suggests, Emily could not rely on others to look out for her future financial security.

In 1813, after her marriage, Emily inherited all the plate, jewelry, and furniture of her aunt, Lady Anne Cecil, as well as the reversion on her father's death of trust funds of £12,500.[27] In 1817 Emily, on George's behalf, asked the trustees for a loan from her aunt's reversion, to pay off Paris expenses and to help with costs incurred in setting up house in London.[28] In this case, the trustees ensured that George signed an agreement to pay interest on the loan and repay the principal upon Emily's father's death. The £5,600 loan from the trustees was in the form of government stock and was expressed in nominal terms. After the Napoleonic Wars, with England highly indebted, the price of government stock was low. George sold the stock at well below nominal value—£66 to £67 per £100—to yield proceeds of £3,665 10s. He paid interest on the loan until the death of the Marquis of Salisbury, when an attorney "took proceedings against me in Ireland for the same sum without asking me to pay it." George complained that he

---

[23] Malcolmson, *Pursuit of the Heiress*, 28.

[24] Emily Nugent Westmeath, *A Narrative*, 78.

[25] Stone, *Broken Lives*, 287.

[26] George Thomas John Nugent Westmeath, *A Reply*, 8.

[27] George Thomas John Nugent Westmeath, *A Reply*, 23. Lord Westmeath also complained that the furniture was not worth the carriage to Ireland but that out of "respect to the donor [he] consented it should come" (23). Stone, *Broken Lives*, 287.

[28] Haggard, *Reports of Cases*, 99.

had to sell his half-pay annuity, raise money at 11%, and sell a life assurance policy to replace the government stock which cost, on 18 February 1824, £5,024 7s 6d. This was more than he had received in loan, as the price of government stock had by then risen to around £92 for £100 nominal. He also admitted to having had silver plate—engraved with the Duke of Wellington's crest and given by the Duke as a wedding present to Emily—melted down, raising £18 for the coffee pot and teapot alone.[29]

Emily also experienced difficulties in receiving her pin money as promised in the premarital contract. She complained that she did not receive the full pin money when in Ireland in the early years of their marriage. The 1816 and 1817 payments were also not made, with George arguing that the income from his Westmeath estates was insufficient.[30] Even a premarital contract and trust structures did not prevent a husband from failing to provide fully for his wife, with George, in this case, able to access funds designed to protect Emily from the disadvantages of coverture.

IV. COPING WITH COVERTURE AFTER SEPARATION

The indenture of separation signed in 1818 committed George to pay Emily £1,300 a year in maintenance, as well as £500 a year pin money from the original marriage settlement. From 1819 on, there were no maintenance payments. Furthermore, while George was suing to have the separation overturned, he was in no mood to support his wife. Emily did not receive her pin money of £500 a year for three years after 1823.[31] After legal separation in 1827, Emily became entitled to alimony. However, nonpayment of much of this money until the 1830s forced Emily to be proactive in seeking alternative sources of income. These consisted of income from earnings, a pension, and astute investment of the funds over which she had control.

Physically separated from 1819 on, Emily needed resources. And she procured them. As this section demonstrates, despite her legal disadvantages Emily was able to draw on a variety of resources to piece together a

---

[29] George Thomas John Nugent Westmeath, *A Reply*, 18, 22–23. Note that the teapot and coffee pot were given to Emily and could have been considered to be hers as "paraphernalia." Before the Married Women's Property Acts of 1870 and 1882, married women were usually allowed pin money and "paraphernalia" such as household goods and linen. See Anne Laurence, Josephine Maltby, and Janette Rutterford, Introduction to *Women and Their Money 1700–1950: Essays on Women and Finance*, ed. Anne Laurence, Josephine Maltby, and Janette Rutterford (Abingdon, Oxfordshire: Routledge, 2009), 7.

[30] Stone, *Broken Lives*, 303.

[31] Stone, *Broken Lives*, 317.

wealthy lifestyle. In 1821 Emily used a court order to get bailiffs to distrain George's land and personal property in Ireland, after Henry Wood, as her Trustee, had sued for nonpayment of maintenance. Tenants, encouraged by George to resist and even shoot the bailiffs, were prosecuted and sentenced to prison.[32] Emily then changed her tactics and ran up debts, since she was still technically married—albeit separated—and a husband was legally liable for his wife's debts. She spent lavishly, as George himself put it later, "denying herself nothing which she can obtain without payment, and exciting her creditors by a promise of paying the costs in failure to sue me for the value of these indulgences which I have been obliged to deny myself and my daughter."[33]

As a member of the elite, though, Emily had sources of income other than her husband. These derived from her connections with Lady Conyngham, George IV's mistress (and later, wife), and the Duke of Wellington, her brother-in-law from 1816 on.[34] Beginning in 1818 she received £250 as lady-in-waiting and, from 1826 on, she had her £500 pin money, £350 interest on the inheritance from her aunt, and £275 as extra lady of the bedchamber, plus free lodgings—a total income of £1,125.[35]

In 1826 the ecclesiastical court found that, because there had been cohabitation after the 1818 deed of separation had been signed, this invalidated the agreed-upon £1,300 alimony payment. In 1827, however, after judgment was found in Emily's favor and the ecclesiastical divorce *a mensa et thoro* was declared, George was ordered to pay £700 a year alimony as well as Emily's legal costs of £1,600 for Consistory and Arches Courts.[36] George refused to pay the legal costs and, after he was charged by Emily with contempt of court in 1829, it was decided that he could not be forced to pay because, by then, he was an Irish Representative Peer at Parliament and therefore could not be found in contempt.[37]

In 1829, with no alimony payments having been made, George IV was persuaded by his wife to ask the Duke of Wellington, then prime minis-

---

[32] Stone, *Broken Lives*, 294.

[33] George Thomas John Nugent Westmeath, *A Sketch*, 40. For married women's strategic use of credit, see Margot Finn, "Women, Consumption and Coverture in England, c. 1760–1860," *Historical Journal* 39.3 (September 1996): 703–22; and Joanne Bailey, "Favoured or Oppressed? Married Women, Property, and 'Coverture' in England, 1660–1800," *Continuity and Change* 17.3 (2002): 351–72.

[34] Emily's elder sister, Georgiana, married the Duke of Wellington's youngest brother, Henry Wellesley, in 1816.

[35] Stone, *Broken Lives*, 334.

[36] Stone, *Broken Lives*, 330.

[37] Haggard, *Reports of Cases*, 653.

CHAPTER 7. RUTTERFORD, "'A *PAUPER* EVERY WIFE IS'"

ter, to give Emily a pension from the Irish List. This caused a public outcry, so she was quietly given £385 a year on the English List, a payment that survived a government inquiry in 1833.[38] In 1834 George sued successfully to have Emily's £700 a year maintenance take account of her pension from the Civil List of £385, and so it was reduced to £315 a year. George was ordered to pay arrears of maintenance from 1827 to 1833 at the new rate, totaling £2,000.[39] This amount was finally paid to Emily on 10 April 1835.[40] With alimony being paid from 1835 on, Stone estimates that, by 1836, Emily's income totaled around £1,850 a year, plus a free apartment. George complained that Emily was so well-off after payment of the £2,000 arrears of maintenance in 1835 that she shortly thereafter added a ballroom to her house in Piccadilly.[41] Although Emily refers, in her 1857 pamphlet, to returning from abroad after an absence of six years and finding her creditors still unpaid, she was certainly not short of funds until her death in 1858.[42]

By the mid-1830s Emily had a variety of sources of income: court appointments, civil pension, income from her aunt's inheritance, and alimony. But the alimony came in a lump sum of £2,000, and she needed to make sure that this generated income too. So, part of Emily's income came from yet another source, canny investment of her surplus income and the arrears of alimony paid in 1835. There is evidence of investment in both British shares and foreign bonds. The evidence of British shares comes from her ex-husband, who refers to her jobbing in the shares of the Pibrow Patent Company, an English company. Her lawyers wrote to him to ask if they could use his name in legal proceedings that she wished to institute but which, as a married woman, she could not do in her own name.[43]

However, there is also evidence of Emily investing in overseas government bonds, in particular Spanish bonds, and this comes from the Barings Archive in the form of letters of hers in a bundle of correspondence from 1833 to 1846 between Lady Westmeath's friend, Miss Eliza Caton, and Joshua Bates of Barings Bank.[44] This bundle includes correspondence

---

[38] Charles C. F. Greville, *The Greville Memoirs: A Journal of the Reigns of King George IV, King William IV and Queen Victoria* (London; New York; Bombay: Longmans, Greene & Co, 1899), chap. 4: 161, 164, http://www.archive.org/details/grevillememoirsj01grevuoft; Stone, *Broken Lives*, 335.
[39] Stone, *Broken Lives*, 330–32.
[40] George Thomas John Nugent Westmeath, *A Reply*, 43.
[41] George Thomas John Nugent Westmeath, *A Reply*, 43.
[42] Emily Nugent Westmeath, *A Narrative*, 75.
[43] George Thomas John Nugent Westmeath, *A Reply*, 45.
[44] *The Barings Archive, General House Correspondence, HC1.11.*

between Lady Westmeath and Bates, dated 1835 to 1845. Bates was an American citizen and senior partner of Barings from 1828 until his death in 1864. He was responsible for maintaining Barings's role as the prime "American" house in London. Eliza Caton, born in 1787, was the extremely well-connected eldest of four daughters of a Baltimore, Maryland merchant. Marianne, one year younger, became the Countess of Mornington and sister-in-law to the Duke of Wellington on her second marriage in 1825 at the age of 37. Louise Catherine, born in 1791, became Duchess of Leeds on *her* second marriage in 1828 at the age of 37. The youngest sister married the British Consul in Baltimore in 1815. The two middle sisters, who became peeresses, were often at Court, and Marianne was Lady of the Bedchamber to Queen Adelaide from 1830 at exactly the same time as Emily, Lady Westmeath, who was also a sister-in-law to the Duke of Wellington.[45] Emily knew Marianne's unmarried elder sister, Eliza Caton, well.

Eliza Caton ran an active investment portfolio using her substantial personal wealth, sometimes following the advice of Joshua Bates, and sometimes imposing her own views. Eliza managed investments for her married sisters by holding investments in her own name.[46] She also assisted Lady Westmeath in a series of bold and profitable investments. Her portfolio included Spanish stock, Buenos Ayres bonds, and American railroads. Eliza had two types of sources for investment information. One was personal or political contacts. In 1833 she wrote to Joshua Bates: "one of the persons most likely to know says there will be no general war, but there may be a fight against the Spaniards. Sir Norbert Taylor is the person." In 1835 she cited Mrs. N. de Rothschild, who "told me the longer I kept the Spanish stock the better" (letter dated 18 March 1835). She also cites her mother: "Mamma . . . says they tell her whom she thinks well-informed that the Bank of New Jersey or York . . . will fall fifteen per cent by Christmas . . . but she has sold out all her own stock."[47] Her use of newspaper information resembled Keynes's view of investment as a beauty contest, in which items are appraised not for their fundamental value but in the context of how attractive others find them to be.[48] For example,

---

[45] *The Court Journal: Court Circular & Fashionable Gazette* 5 (23 March 1833): 186.

[46] *The Barings Archive, General House Correspondence, HC1.11*. For example, in a letter dated only 30 December, Eliza asks for a loan of £250 to buy shares, as her sister "does not like to sell her Spanish stock she has in my name, she feels confident it will rise."

[47] *The Barings Archive, General House Correspondence, HC1.11*, letter dated 9 August 1836.

[48] John Maynard Keynes, *A General Theory of Employment, Interest and Money* (1936; Chichester: Palgrave Macmillan, reprinted 2007), chap. 12.

CHAPTER 7. RUTTERFORD, "'A *PAUPER* EVERY WIFE IS'"

in the first place, do not let the house sell the four thousand Chilian bonds ... and, in the second, I entreat you to buy me ten thousand more because *The Standard* says "it goes without question there will be an early and equitable adjustment of the claims of the bond holders in this State" now it is possible this may not be true but the public will think so for a time at least, at any rate I can only lose a few hundreds and if it be true I shall make many thousands and a short time will decide it.[49]

One of the stocks favored by Eliza Caton was Spanish Cortez bonds. These were highly speculative stocks, as Spain was in the middle of a seven-year war between the supporters of Don Carlos and Queen Cristina. In September 1835, when the financier Mendizabal was called from exile in England to run the finance ministry, hopes—and bond prices—were high. In 1836, when Mendizabal's proposed new bond financing failed, Spanish bond prices plummeted to 80 percent below par. By 1837 Spanish bond prices had recovered some of their losses, and there was an end to "the most extraordinary series of price fluctuations that has ever occurred."[50] Eliza wrote to Mr. Bates during the honeymoon period after Mendizabal's return from exile: "I cannot help making one more attempt to soften your flinty heart and get you to buy me ten thousand Spanish Stock" (30 December 1835). Eliza also recommended these bonds to Emily.

Although Emily was legally separated from her husband by the 1830s, the law was not clear on ownership of investments, and any gains from investment could be used by George to reduce the maintenance payments, as he had already done with her Civil List pension. Lord Westmeath himself had pointed out her position: "a wife without a husband."[51] So Lady Westmeath was also wary of making her income public. Eliza Caton was the model of discretion:

Dear Mr Bates, Will you be so good as to see me and a lady who wishes you to make an investment for her at your banking house tomorrow between

---

[49] *The Barings Archive, General House Correspondence, HC1.11*, letter dated 1835 from the Clarendon Hotel. Eliza went on to say: "Where I say I, I mean me, and my partner, who thinks with me." It is not clear whether she is investing with one of her sisters or is already discussing investment with her future husband, Baron Stafford, whom she married the following year.

[50] For more information on Spanish bonds and the Spanish civil war, see Raymond Carr, *Spain, 1808–1939* (Oxford: Clarendon Press, 1975); and Brison D. Gooch, "Belgium and the Prospective Sale of Cuba in 1837," *Hispanic American Historical Review* 39.3 (August 1959): 413–27. The quotation is from J. Horsley Palmer, *Causes and Consequences of the Pressure on the Money Market* (London: 1837) cited in Carr, *Spain, 1808–1939*, fn171.

[51] George Thomas John Nugent Westmeath, *A Sketch*.

the hours of two and three. This is the lady of whom I spoke to you last spring ... to keep it all a profound secret.⁵²

All correspondence between Lady Westmeath and Mr. Bates was transmitted via Eliza Caton.⁵³ On 19 July 1835, Emily wrote to Mr. Bates to invest her arrears of alimony. "I expect the amount of £2,000 to be paid to me in the course of a week or ten days at furthest." She asked for Portuguese sixes or fives to be bought immediately on credit: "I am very anxious to buy in before those funds get higher as the interest is a great object." She calculated that if she bought the bonds at 92 per cent of the nominal value, she would get nearly 5½ percent, or £110 a year.⁵⁴

Emily wrote from Naples and Rome in 1836 on the subject of investment. She declared herself to be "delighted" with her investment in the United States Bank and glad that "I added the two thousand to the original investment." It would appear that Mr. Bates had counseled against the Portuguese bonds in such large size. He certainly prevented her from converting her Spanish debentures into Spanish stock, which she confessed was "in a very sorry state." Again, she was discreet, writing to Mr. Bates that "Of course [my Bankers] know nothing of the funds which will produce the £800. It is a profound secret."⁵⁵

Emily continued to write to Mr. Bates until at least 1845, when she was happy with her portfolio, "delighted" that she had not sold her Portuguese stock when she took fright, and "in good spirits about my Spanish stock ... it is not 40 and I intend to pursue it."⁵⁶ It is worth remembering that the nominal value of bonds was £100, so that a price of £40 meant a sixty percent drop in value from issue. But £40 was twice the value of £20 at the peak of the crisis in 1836, equivalent to a one hundred percent gain. Women at this time were relatively rare as investors, representing from five to twenty percent of shareholders in companies.⁵⁷ Most women held low-risk government bonds; along these lines, Green and Owens have estimated that, in 1840, forty percent of holders of British government debt

---

⁵² *The Barings Archive, General House Correspondence, HC1.11,* undated letter.

⁵³ It is worth noting that, although divorced in the ecclesiastical courts, Emily continued to sign her name as Lady Westmeath in all correspondence with Joshua Bates and, indeed, in her 1857 pamphlet.

⁵⁴ *The Barings Archive, General House Correspondence, HC1.11,* letter dated 19 July 1835.

⁵⁵ *The Barings Archive, General House Correspondence, HC1.11,* letter dated 2 March 1836.

⁵⁶ *The Barings Archive, General House Correspondence, HC1.11,* letter dated 1845.

⁵⁷ Mark Freeman, Robin Pearson, and James Taylor, "Between Madam Bubble and Kitty Lorimer; Women Investors in British and Irish Stock Companies" in Laurence, Maltby, and Rutterford, *Women and Their Money,* 95–114.

were female.[58] However, neither Eliza nor Emily was afraid to speculate in what were volatile investments, Eliza for fun as she already had a low-risk investment portfolio invested on her behalf by her father, Emily in an attempt to boost her capital and her income and to earn returns that were potentially much higher than could be obtained on British government bonds. This investment strategy also gave Emily the opportunity to increase her wealth well beyond that offered by more conventional female trust portfolio strategies.

V. CONCLUSION

Lady Westmeath's entire adult life was affected by the lack of protection afforded to married, separated, and divorced women until the legislation of 1857, 1870, and 1882. She suffered from the fact that it was almost impossible for a married woman to separate from her husband, that full divorce was only available to women who could prove both adultery and either incest or bigamy, that it was impossible to obtain custody of children, and that it was difficult as a married woman to sue a man for failure to pay monies owed. Even when women separated, their legal position with respect to money was precarious. Rather than offering her financial security, marriage stripped this wealthy woman of a substantial fortune. Unmarried, she asserted, she would have been given her £15,000 dowry, and would have received an annuity from her aunt, £750 a year for the first three years after her father's death in 1824, and £600 a year thereafter, "according to the price stocks may have been when the money was invested."[59] This inheritance was in the form of a trust, however, over whose investment policy Emily had no control. And, as we have seen with the investments carried out via Joshua Bates, when she could Emily used her independent funds to her advantage.

Despite the fact that financial issues clouded Emily's personal life, she was able to use her connections to the Court and the government to obtain a Civil List pension and a court appointment. Unlike many women in her marital position, that is, she had systems of support that allowed her to act independently of her husband and parents. She was also able to increase her capital and supplement her other income through investments made with the help of her friend, Eliza Caton. Eliza had the security of a wealthy

---

[58] David R. Green and Alastair Owens, "Gentlewomanly Capitalism: Widows and Wealth Holding in England and Wales, c. 1800–1860," *Economic History Review* 56.3 (2003): 528.

[59] Emily Nugent Westmeath, *A Narrative*, 193.

family behind her; Emily was in a much more difficult financial position. But both were not afraid to buy stocks that today would terrify us with their volatility. We can only imagine what Emily's investment strategy would have been if she had been personally able to invest the £12,500 lump sum inherited from her aunt.

In 1857 Emily complained how "a *pauper* every wife is," with unjust treatment not just for her but also for her creditors and defenders. Separated, despite substantial legal costs, she managed to put together a portfolio of incomes and was certainly not a pauper. Emily lived to see the passing of the Matrimonial Causes Act of 1857 but died before the passing of the 1870 and 1882 Married Women's Property Acts, which gave married women the same rights as single women to acquire and keep their own wealth separate from that of their husbands, and of which she would certainly have wholeheartedly approved. Emily's story of marriage and separation reminds us how difficult access to money was for married women before legislation gave them greater financial independence. But it also shows how a separated woman, in legal limbo between being married and divorced, could earn an income and, albeit discreetly, invest her portfolio with success.

CHAPTER 8

Marriage, Celibacy, or Emigration?

DEBATING THE COSTS OF FAMILY LIFE IN
MID-VICTORIAN ENGLAND

ERIKA RAPPAPORT

"How shall men marry in these expensive days, when incomes diminish and outgoings increase?"[1] This was a question on many men and women's minds in the 1860s, or so it would seem to a reader of the liberal newspaper the *Daily Telegraph*. In the summer of 1868, this journal published nearly three hundred letters from readers, which the paper framed as a debate: "Marriage or Celibacy?"[2] For several weeks the correspondence pages became a public forum for discussing the intimate costs of the burgeoning consumer society of mid-Victorian England. While initially correspondents speculated about the causes of growing domestic expenditure, the latter weeks examined solutions, the most popular of which was emigration. Those who contemplated leaving England fantasized about a life where fashionable dress, expensive furnishings, and lavish entertain-

---

[1] "A Single Man," *Daily Telegraph*, 3 July 1868, 2.
[2] John M. Robson, *Marriage or Celibacy: The Daily Telegraph on a Victorian Dilemma* (Toronto: University of Toronto Press, 1995). Robson describes the debate's narrative structure and its relationship to other contemporary discussions of marriage. He also analyzes the correspondents' rhetorical styles and literary influences. Judith Knelman has argued that the debate was the beginning of a trend rejecting marriage. See "She Loves Me, She Loves Me Not: Trends in the Victorian Marriage Market," *Journal of Communication Inquiry* 18.1 (Winter 1994): 80–94.

ments were not necessary to establish one's respectability and middle-class status. Most did not seek to leave England in order to afford a luxurious lifestyle but saw in emigration a way to opt out of England's increasingly consumer-oriented society and thereby afford a family. Collectively, these letters reveal how average middle-class men and women recognized that marriage and parenthood brought a shift in consumer choices and practices as well as new constraints and anxieties.

As personal as these letters were, stories about families devastated by wives' reckless spending or husbands' financial failures ran through much nineteenth-century literature, as did painful scenes of young people balancing the ideal of romance and the reality of economy when choosing a spouse.[3] Such problems were not merely the stuff of fiction. Household guides and women's magazines found a ready market of cash-strapped readers interested in learning how to maintain appearances on limited means. Middle-class diaries, too, exposed the pleasures and struggles of families living in an increasingly commercial age. For example, on the day she married, the middle-class diarist Beryl Lee Booker remembered feeling a new freedom to buy what she wanted and to wander into London's less than respectable shopping streets. Only a few hours after her wedding, she drove to one of London's more famous bookstores and bought "a hitherto forbidden novel." She then walked up and down the notorious Burlington Arcade, because, as she put it, "I was a married woman."[4] Although prostitutes plied their trade and gamblers won and lost vast sums of money in the floors above the Arcade's aristocratic shops, Booker felt that marriage had afforded her access to this consumer culture, which she had not known as a single woman. However, such freedom also became a source of great tension between Booker and her new husband.

The *Daily Telegraph* letters tell essentially the same story as men and women discussed the ethics and consequences of consumerism, the definition of luxuries, the appropriateness of male and female shopping, and its impact on their ability to wed and have children. The debate, however, frequently fell along gender lines, as both sexes blamed the unbridled spending of the other for raising the stakes of bourgeois status. Single women often targeted young men's failure to forgo immature, individualistic, and

---

[3] A classic example is George Eliot's *Middlemarch*, which first appeared in publication just three years after the *Daily Telegraph* debate. George Eliot, *Middlemarch* (1871–72; London: Penguin, 1994). For a recent analysis of some of the themes of marriage, money, and fraud, see Rebecca Stern, *Home Economics: Domestic Fraud in Victorian England* (Columbus: The Ohio State University Press, 2008).

[4] Beryl Lee Booker, *Yesterday's Child, 1890–1909* (London: John Long, 1937), 256.

pleasure-seeking forms of consumption in order to purchase a family. Male correspondents responded that cigars, fine clothing, theater tickets, and prostitutes were but poor substitutes for the family they could not afford in any case. One "Bachelor" who acknowledged himself as an unemployed clerk explained, for example, that though he admired girls' "sweet faces," he could not "afford the luxury of possessing one."[5] Answering a similar charge of extravagance, female correspondents frequently delineated how thrifty housekeeping could stretch modest resources, implying that even in bourgeois homes their domestic labor had financial repercussions.[6] An "English wife," for example, explained how she saved money by not "consigning" her children to the "constant care of a maid," and once they were about nine or ten, she even had them make "some part of their own underclothing" or "dust drawing-rooms and bedrooms."[7] This solution, though, posed a threat to a key fiction of bourgeois culture—that women and children did not engage in the hard work of maintaining a home. As a result, a good many correspondents began to consider how emigration would allow them to marry, have children, and maintain their class position on a small budget. They conceived of the empire as a domestic space that hearkened back to an imagined rural and precapitalist past free from the social and material pressures of the modern age.

In the past few decades, scholars have documented how a spectacular culture of exhibitions and department stores, advertising and mass-market publications, restaurants and theaters addressed women as consumers and encouraged their participation in metropolitan spaces in much of Europe and North America.[8] Such changes transformed material expectations and

---

[5] *Daily Telegraph*, 6 July 1868, 2.

[6] The role of women's domestic labor and class reproduction has primarily been studied among the working classes and not those above them. For the most well-known study, see Ellen Ross, *Love and Toil: Motherhood in Outcast London, 1870–1918* (Oxford and New York: Oxford University Press, 1993).

[7] For an analysis of this correspondent's resources, see Robson, *Marriage or Celibacy*, 73, 131, and 300. Lower-middle- and middle-class men were perceived as not having attained their adulthood or their social station until they married and had children. See Leonore Davidoff and Catherine Hall, *Family Fortunes: Men and Women of the English Middle Class, 1780–1850* (Chicago: University of Chicago Press, 1987), 321–35; John Tosh, *A Man's Place: Masculinity and the Middle-Class Home in Victorian England* (New Haven, CT, and London: Yale University Press, 1999), 108; and Geoffrey Crossick and Heinz-Gerhardt Haupt, *The Petite Bourgeoisie in Europe, 1780–1914: Enterprise, Family, and Independence* (London: Routledge, 1995), 87–99.

[8] This is a large and ever-growing body of literature. For Victorian England, see Erika D. Rappaport, *Shopping for Pleasure: Women in the Making of London's West End* (Princeton, NJ: Princeton University Press, 2000); Margaret Beetham, *A Magazine of Her Own? Domesticity and Desire in the Woman's Magazine, 1800–1914* (London: Routledge, 1996); Rachel Bowlby,

led to a rising cost of living, keenly felt by the British middle classes in the 1860s.[9] They also encouraged this class to delay marriage and to limit the size of their families, but there were other, less measurable domestic reverberations of this emergent consumer culture.[10] Both sexes indulged in new, expensive consumer habits, altering gender dynamics and power relations within the bourgeois family.[11]

The *Telegraph* debate posited that men's and women's excessive consumerism had made the prospects of marriage more expensive and, for men at least, less appealing. Consumerism had in effect produced what became known as the redundant female: single middle-class women who had failed to find a spouse. Feminists, political economists, and popular writers were all invested in the causes of and solutions to the surplus-women problem in these years. After the census of 1851 asked about marital status for the first time, the English discovered that they had approximately half a million more women than men, and the popular press transformed these single

---

Just Looking: Consumer Culture in Dreiser, Gissing, and Zola (London: Methuen, 1985); Deborah Cohen, *Household Gods: The British and Their Possessions* (New Haven, CT: Yale University Press, 2006); Lara Kriegel, *Grand Designs: Labor, Empire and the Museum in Victorian England* (Durham, NC: Duke University Press, 2007); Lori Loeb, *Consuming Angels: Advertising and Victorian Women* (Oxford: Oxford University Press, 1994); Mica Nava, "Modernity's Disavowal: Women, the City, and the Department Store," in *Modern Times: Reflections on a Century of English Modernity,* ed. Mica Nava and Alan O'Shea (London: Routledge, 1996), 38–76; Thomas Richards, *The Commodity Culture of Victorian England: Advertising and Spectacle, 1851–1914* (Stanford, CA: Stanford University Press, 1990); Lise Shapiro Sanders, *Consuming Fantasies: Labor, Leisure, and the London Shop Girl* (Columbus: The Ohio State University Press, 2006); and Krista Lysack, *Come Buy, Come Buy: Shopping and the Culture of Consumption in Victorian Women's Writing* (Athens: Ohio University Press, 2008).

[9] J. A. Banks, *Prosperity and Parenthood: A Study of Family Planning among the Victorian Middle Classes* (London: Routledge and Kegan Paul, 1954).

[10] American historians have done more than the British to consider the relationship between the history of consumer culture and that of the family. See, especially, Elizabeth H. Pleck, *Celebrating the Family: Ethnicity, Consumer Culture, and Family Rituals* (Cambridge, MA: Harvard University Press, 2000); Leigh Eric Schmidt, *Consumer Rites: The Buying and Selling of American Holidays* (Princeton, NJ: Princeton University Press, 1995); and Elaine Tyler May, *Homeward Bound: American Families in the Cold War Era* (New York: Basic Books, 1988), 162–82. For a broad comparative approach to this topic, see John R. Gillis, *A World of Their Own Making: Myth, Ritual, and the Quest for Family Values* (New York: Basic Books, 1996).

[11] This debate thus speaks to a growing concern that focusing on the history of female consumerism has inadvertently neglected how men have been commodified in modern culture. Recently, however, this imbalance has begun to be rectified. See, for example, Justin Bengry, "Courting the Pink Pound: *Men Only* and the Queer Consumer, 1935–39," *History Workshop Journal* 68.1 (2009): 122–48; Christopher Breward, *The Hidden Consumer: Masculinities, Fashion and City Life, 1860–1914* (Manchester and New York: Manchester University Press, 1999); Frank Mort, *Cultures of Consumption: Masculinities and Social Space in Late Twentieth-Century Britain* (London: Routledge, 1996); and Brent A. Shannon, *The Cut of His Coat: Men, Dress, and Consumer Culture in Britain, 1860–1914* (Athens: Ohio University Press, 2006).

women into a pressing social problem. It became an especially compelling issue after William Rathbone Greg asked "Why are Women Redundant?" in an essay he published in the *National Review* in 1862.[12] Thereafter, many tried to rectify this gender imbalance through emigration schemes or by reforming middle-class female education and expanding women's limited labor market.[13]

The mid-Victorians believed that it was harder than ever for a middle-class woman to find a husband, but they also recognized that the nature of middle-class marriage was changing in ways that seemed to be weakening patriarchal authority. As Esther Godfrey's essay in this volume discusses, divorce was being liberalized, and feminists and others were advocating for, but had not yet achieved, the right of married women to retain their property after marriage. Changes in credit and debt law were also rewriting the economic power of husbands and wives in ways that gave women new, if still limited, access to their husband's resources when they went shopping. It seemed ever harder for men to control their family budget.[14]

Correspondents transformed such concerns about single women and powerless men into a critique of unbounded materialism. By the 1880s and 1890s, popular writers such as George Gissing and George Grossmith turned domestic power struggles over money and commodities into social satire and especially targeted the lower middle classes for their degraded tastes and inability to resist the allure of mass culture.[15] The *Telegraph*'s

---

[12] This was also published as a book in 1869. William Rathbone Greg, *Why Are Women Redundant?* (London: Trübner, 1869).

[13] For a recent discussion of this issue, see Kathrin Levitan, "Redundancy, the 'Surplus Woman' Problem and the British Census, 1851–1861," *Women's History Review* 17.3 (July 2008): 359–76. Also see A. James Hammerton, *Emigrant Gentlewomen: Genteel Poverty and Female Emigration, 1830–1914* (London: Croom Helm, 1979), see especially chapters 1, 4, and 5; Rita S. Kranidis, *The Victorian Spinster and Colonial Emigration: Contested Subjects* (New York: St. Martin's Press, 1999); and Diana C. Archibald, *Domesticity, Imperialism, and Emigration in the Victorian Novel* (Columbia: University of Missouri Press, 2002). For an analysis of how unmarried women created communities, see Martha Vicinus, *Independent Women: Work and Community for Single Women, 1850–1920* (Chicago: University of Chicago Press, 1985).

[14] Rappaport, *Shopping for Pleasure*, 48–73.

[15] The "suburban" lower middle classes were key participants in the culture of consumption in late Victorian and Edwardian England. See, for example, A. James Hammerton, Simon Gunn, and Christopher Hosgood's chapters in *Gender, Civic Culture and Consumerism: Middle Class Identity in Britain, 1800–1940*, ed. Alan Kidd and David Nicholls (Manchester and New York: Manchester University Press, 1999). Also see A. James Hammerton, "Pooterism or Partnership? Marriage and Masculine Identity in the Lower Middle Class, 1870–1920," *Journal of British Studies* 38 (July 1999): 291–321; Peter Bailey, "White Collars, Gray Lives? The Lower Middle Class Revisited," *Journal of British Studies* 38 (July 1999): 273–90; and "*Ally Sloper's Half-Holiday:* The Comic Press in the 1880s," *History Workshop Journal* 16 (Autumn 1983): 4–31.

correspondents, however, tell a tragic rather than a satirical story that conveys a pervasive feeling of being "outside" of modern culture.[16] These writers imagined consumerism as engendering loss—of one's social status, of the ability to marry and have children, and of one's national identity.[17] Correspondents saw themselves as falling out of the middle class precisely because others seemed to be rising in prosperity and social expectations.[18]

Whether real, fictional, or the product of the *Telegraph*'s editor, the letters collectively drew upon a similar mixture of romanticism, evangelicalism, and political economy to frame their analysis of consumerism, marriage, and family life.[19] Indeed, the *Telegraph* summarized the series of letters as "CUPID versus PRUDENCE, POLITICAL ECONOMY, and others."[20] Male and female, single and married, nearly all those who wrote to the editor of the *Daily Telegraph* believed that society's growing desire to consume goods and entertainment, coupled with strong support for the male breadwinner as the family's sole earner, had placed tremendous strains on the ability to marry or to manage the family economy after marriage. Nearly all the writers criticized rampant consumerism but maintained the notion of the family as an economic unit, which needed a healthy balance of assets and liabilities.

Three-quarters of the letters were written by married and single men, but this was not only a venue for men to complain about the costs of mar-

---

[16] Fears of falling, a pervasive sense of marginality, and status anxieties seemed almost to be the defining aspect of lower-middle-class identity. Geoffrey Crossick, "The Emergence of the Lower Middle Class in Britain: A Discussion," in *The Lower Middle Class in Britain, 1870–1914*, ed. Geoffrey Crossick (London: Croom Helm, 1977), 23, 30–32.

[17] Hammerton has argued that satirical criticisms of the lower middle class blamed an emasculated lower-middle-class husband and father and a "selfish and consumerist wife" for numerous problems associated with modernity, including national decline. A. James Hammerton, "The English Weakness? Gender, Satire and 'Moral Manliness' in the Lower Middle Class, 1870–1920," *Gender, Civic Culture and Consumerism,* 171. Certainly, the economic and emotional strains discussed by the *Telegraph*'s letter writers contributed to antagonism between couples. Ginger S. Frost, *Promises Broken: Courtship, Class, and Gender in Victorian England* (Charlottesville and London: University of Virginia Press, 1995); Erika D. Rappaport, "A Husband and His Wife's Dresses: Consumer Credit and the Debtor Family in England, 1864–1914," in *The Sex of Things: Gender and Consumption in Historical Perspective,* ed. Victoria de Grazia and Ellen Furlough (Berkeley: University of California Press, 1996), 163–87; and A. James Hammerton, *Cruelty and Companionship: Conflict in Nineteenth-Century Married Life* (London: Routledge, 1992).

[18] Banks, *Prosperity and Parenthood.* A typical example of this type of literature is "Middle-Class Housekeeping," *Tinsley's Magazine* 1 (August 1867–January 1868): 734–42.

[19] Political economy thus shaped both public and private discussions of class identity. On its public influences, see Geoffrey Crossick, "From Gentlemen to the Residuum: Languages of Social Description in Victorian Briton," in *Language, History and Class,* ed. Penelope J. Corfield (Oxford: Basil Blackwell, 1991), 154.

[20] *Daily Telegraph,* 30 July 1868, 4.

riage, since dozens of women responded to men characterizing them as expensive commodities.[21] Women reacted to their commodification in several ways. First they denied the charge that they liked to shop more than men and argued that consumerism was a plague of youth in general. Furthermore, some women insisted that their family's economic stability and comfort depended as much on their private domestic labor—such as doing their own washing or mending—as it did on the size of their husband's income. This debate therefore was a rare moment in which average women spelled out the economics of bourgeois domesticity and rejected the culture's portrayal of them as passionate consumers or leisured ladies.

Participants typically defined themselves by gender, income, age, occupation, marital status, and household size,[22] often using monikers to establish identities and attitudes. So, for example, we have letters from "An English Girl,"[23] "A Matron,"[24] and "A Happy Nine Years' Wife."[25] Some indicated attitudes toward consumerism by calling themselves "A Plain Girl,"[26] "A Simple Country Girl,"[27] or "Home Made Bread."[28] Male correspondents, such as "One Who Looks before He Leaps"[29] and "A Prudent Bachelor,"[30] tended to incorporate their attitude toward marriage when they named themselves. The majority admitted to being—or being supported by—clerks, civil servants, tradesmen, clergymen, accountants, or simply "professionals." A wealthy correspondent labeled this group "lower middle class,"[31] and one even called himself "Nobody in Particular."[32] Most in this vaguely defined group saw themselves as descending from the middle rather than rising out of the working class.

---

[21] About seventy-five percent were from male correspondents. Robson, *Marriage or Celibacy*, 271. Robson identifies the correspondents' gender, age, and occupational background, but he tends to take these as self-evident rather than as sites in which people constructed these identities (269–87).
[22] *Daily Telegraph*, 4 July 1868, 2.
[23] *Daily Telegraph*, 1 July 1868, 8.
[24] *Daily Telegraph*, 3 July 1868, 2.
[25] *Daily Telegraph*, 4 July 1868, 2.
[26] *Daily Telegraph*, 4 July 1868, 2.
[27] *Daily Telegraph*, 6 July 1868, 2.
[28] *Daily Telegraph*, 9 July 1868, 2.
[29] *Daily Telegraph*, 6 July 1868, 2.
[30] *Daily Telegraph*, 11 July 1868, 2.
[31] *Daily Telegraph*, 8 July 1868, 2.
[32] *Daily Telegraph*, 16 July 1868, 2. This sense of being a "nobody" was picked up by one of the most famous portrayals of lower-middle-class life, George Grossmith and Weedon Grossmith, *The Diary of a Nobody*, first published in *Punch* in 1888 (1892; reprint: London, 1965). For the problems associated with labeling such a heterogenous group, see Crossick and Gerhard-Haupt, *The Petite Bourgeoisie in Europe*, 2–8.

PART III. FINANCING THE FAMILY

Key political, economic, and cultural changes had begun to give such "nobodies" a public voice and shaped the issues and assumptions embedded in the debate. The expansion of newspaper publishing, travel by rail, and the emergence of the spectacular culture associated with the Great Exhibition had begun to shape this group into a public of consumers.[33] Politics, too, defined the lower middle class in new ways. The 1867 Reform Act, for example, had just enfranchised many of the male *Telegraph* correspondents. One specifically welcomed his impending franchise, noting that he "shall undoubtedly have a vote under the new lodger franchise."[34] However, as we will see, the right to vote did not necessarily bolster these men's sense of inclusion in the nation, since some felt quite literally priced out of the marriage market. Indeed, their gender privilege was far from secure—especially in the late sixties, a time when women anticipated gaining the vote.[35] The passage of two of the three Contagious Diseases Acts, the liberalization of divorce, and the early stirrings of the Woman's Movement had brought "private" issues such as sexuality and family life into the public sphere of politics and the press. The legal and public wrangling over the CD Acts had further highlighted not only the extent of prostitution but how the bourgeois practice of delayed marriage had turned bachelors into a willing market for this illicit commodity.

The correspondence began in mid-June 1868 after the *Telegraph* published an article exposing the prevalence of prostitution in London's West End.[36] It quickly shifted when "A Barrister" suggested that there were so many prostitutes because there were so many aging middle-class bachelors in need of inexpensive female company. "The principle root of the evil," he surmised, "lies in the exaggerated notions of luxury that pervade our social system, and put an almost impassable bar upon early marriage, in

---

[33] Mary Poovey, *Making a Social Body: British Cultural Formation, 1830–1864* (Chicago: University of Chicago Press, 1995).

[34] *Daily Telegraph*, 26 June 1868, 7.

[35] One female correspondent wondered "while waiting for womanhood suffrage are we to pine away in desolation?" *Daily Telegraph*, 6 July 1868, 2. See Catherine Hall, Keith McClelland, and Jane Rendall, *Defining the Victorian Nation: Class, Race, Gender and the British Reform Act of 1867* (Cambridge: Cambridge University Press, 2000). On the politics of prostitution in the 1860s, see Judith R. Walkowitz, *Prostitution and Victorian Society: Women, Class, and the State* (Cambridge and London: Cambridge University Press, 1980). On the public discussion of marriage and gender surrounding the 1857 Matrimonial Causes Act, see Mary Poovey, *Uneven Developments: The Ideological Work of Gender in Mid-Victorian England* (Chicago: University of Chicago Press, 1988), chap. 3.

[36] The paper's wide circulation had in part been built on sensational reporting. Lord Burnham, *Peterborough Court: The Story of the "Daily Telegraph"* (London: Cassell & Company, 1955), 75–89.

CHAPTER 8. RAPPAPORT, "MARRIAGE, CELIBACY, OR EMIGRATION?"

the middle and wealthier classes." He believed that during the previous half-century a custom had developed that newly married young couples were expected, "if they mean to maintain their social *status,* to live in almost the same style as their parents and the circle in which their parents move." If they married too early, newlyweds could "just keep a modest little cottage in some suburb; but they could not afford to dress for dinner parties and balls, and, if they could, they certainly could not give balls in return." The end result would be social ostracism, as this couple would soon "find that they must drop society of their own class, or that society would drop away from them."[37] Men delayed or avoided matrimony, then, because they feared social decline and a reduction in their material comforts. This "barrister" saw men as sexual beings rationally choosing prostitution as a cheaper means than marriage for satisfying a necessity. This comment was part of the discussion raging in the 1860s surrounding the morality and ethics of prostitution and its regulation. As politicians, reformers, and others considered whether and how the Great Social Evil could and should be regulated, some argued that male sexuality was natural and that unmarried men needed safe and healthy outlets, which the state could ensure through passage of the CD Acts. The entire marriage debate was built upon a similar set of assumptions about the economics of marriage and sexuality. Prostitutes were the quintessential symbol of women's commodification in a capitalist society, but correspondents quickly turned to the perils of the commodified bourgeois family.[38]

The *Telegraph*'s correspondents all felt that social, economic, and cultural changes over the previous decades had turned bourgeois domesticity and respectable sexuality into overpriced commodities. Both male and female correspondents spilled much ink over pinpointing the source of rampant consumerism, blaming "society," women's nature, courtship practices, and youthful offenders of both sexes. Most, but not all, singled out the middle classes for indulging in an extravagant culture of appearances. "A Would be Reformer" complained of the "extravagant style of living and habits of luxury, which prevail amongst the middle and upper class." This reformer blamed parents for bringing up their children "in an expensive lifestyle," and for giving little importance to such attributes as "character, conduct, [and] principles."[39] "A Rural Bachelor" similarly believed that "an expensive style of living has taken the place of the old and charming simplicity," and that "many, very many, of the middle class have got into

---

[37] *Daily Telegraph,* 24 June 1868, 7.
[38] Walter Benjamin, *The Arcades Project* (Cambridge, MA: Belknap Press, 1999).
[39] *Daily Telegraph,* 6 July 1868, 2.

a shamefully expensive way of living."[40] "A Country Girl" also explained that to her "country eyes one cause of the evil appears to lie in the attempt I see everyone around me making to outshine their neighbours. This makes it difficult for young people to live comfortably and enter into any middle class society on so limited income as £200 a year."[41] An "English Girl" complained of "everyone trying to outdo their neighbours in dress and everything" and blamed men for only flirting with "those dressed in the height of fashion; therefore, what can men expect but expensive wives."[42] Others assumed that luxurious tastes were seeping into all ranks, contributing to the volatility of social status. "Plain Truth" bemoaned that "in the present day the great evil is that each grade of society expects to vie with the one above it."[43]

The idea that consumerism was caused by people's attempts to "vie" with the class above their own had already become something of a cliché by the 1860s.[44] However, the *Telegraph*'s correspondents also attacked the young for aping their parents' lifestyle. Modern girls, who apparently spent all their time "dressing themselves up, reading trashy novels, and appearing at every place of amusement,"[45] infected society with their extravagant tastes. A male civil servant opined that modern girls improperly used "amusement, dress, and social intercourse" to show off. "Attendance at concerts, [and] theatres," he suggested, has

> almost ceased to be a matter of hearing, and how many regard it other than as a means of seeing and being seen? The same with what should be the healthful walk, which is taken, not in the healthiest of localities, but in some fashionable promenade. . . . Dress has come to be . . . a mere adjunct to beauty . . . wholly a matter of show . . . and social intercourse is mixed with an unhealthy amount of rivalry which plays the bear with moderate incomes.[46]

This description of modern girls was a direct response to Eliza Lynn Linton's already famous portrait of the pleasure-seeking, consumer-

---

[40] *Daily Telegraph*, 18 July 1868, 2.
[41] *Daily Telegraph*, 10 July 1868, 2.
[42] Quoted in Robson, *Marriage or Celibacy*, 172.
[43] *Daily Telegraph*, 6 July 1868, 2.
[44] This idea dates back at least to the 1690s. See Neil McKendrick, "The Consumer Revolution of Eighteenth-Century England," in *The Birth of a Consumer Society: The Commercialization of Eighteenth-Century England*, Neil McKendrick, John Brewer, and J. H. Plumb (Bloomington: Indiana University Press, 1982).
[45] *Daily Telegraph*, 8 July 1868, 2. Also see "Jane's" comments on the subject, 8 July 1868.
[46] *Daily Telegraph*, 14 July 1868, 2.

oriented "Girl of the Period," which she had published anonymously in the *Saturday Review* in March 1868, just a few months before the *Daily Telegraph* launched its similar discussion of modern girls and their consumer habits.[47] Many writers felt that the modern girl was no hapless victim of fancy window-dressing, advertising, and other retailer seductions.[48] Rather she was a product of family upbringing, male tastes, and misguided notions of domesticity.[49] One young man, for example, surmised that the system of courtship in which parents, especially the much-maligned "Belgravian mamma," purchased "things" and gave "parties or balls, etc . . . to make their daughters more attractive to get them married," created "extravagant ideas in their daughters' minds . . . and render[ed] them unfit wives of men with small incomes."[50] Of course, many also commented that young men adored such showy girls.[51] "A Simple Country Girl" asked why young men did not look for wives "by the domestic hearth" instead of "at balls, parties, [and] concerts."[52] Another concluded that the Girl of the Period "is a creature of the men's own seeking; their folly has called her into existence; she is a deformity and a libel upon her sex."[53] It should be noted that correspondents did not blame retailers for igniting consumer passions. Rather, they all assumed that such desires were driven by misguided family and gender relations.

A good many female writers denied any likeness at all to the Girl of the Period and professed that they were thoroughly domesticated, thrifty helpmeets, not spendthrifts. They wore only simple, dark fabrics, did not go out to the theater or indulge in other public amusements, and did a

---

[47] "The Girl of the Period," *Saturday Review*, 14 March 1868, 339–40. Some correspondents directly took issue with Linton's GOP. See, for example, the letter from "A Few Girls of the Period," *Daily Telegraph*, 6 July 1868; "A London Girl," *Daily Telegraph*, 8 July 1868; and *** *Daily Telegraph*, 11 July 1868. For a discussion of the GOP as a popular icon of female consumerism, see Rappaport, *Shopping for Pleasure*, 32; Knelman, "She Loves Me, She Loves Me Not," 85; and Robson, *Marriage or Celibacy*, 151–54.

[48] This understanding of female consumption was present in the 1860s, but it was by no means a dominant one. In fact, many of the letter writers and the newspaper's readers were retailers who more often portrayed themselves as victims of predatory female consumers than as their seducers. Rappaport, *Shopping for Pleasure*, chaps. 1 and 2. In a later series of letters on marriage in the *Telegraph* in 1888, drapers were sometimes blamed for igniting individuals' desires. For an example, see *Is Marriage a Failure?* ed. Harry Quilter (1888; reprint, New York: Garland, 1984), 220–21.

[49] *Daily Telegraph*, 6 July 1868, 2. The analogy that women were brought up to be expensive household furnishings was quite common. One writer noted that they were like "drawing room ornaments." *Daily Telegraph*, 7 July 1868, 2.

[50] *Daily Telegraph*, 2 July 1868, 8.
[51] *Daily Telegraph*, 8 July 1868, 2.
[52] *Daily Telegraph*, 6 July 1868, 2.
[53] *Daily Telegraph*, 11 July 1868, 2.

good deal of their own housework.⁵⁴ One London girl who was still single advertised herself as being able to "make a pudding, darn my father's hose . . . and play a piece of music or sing a song. I very seldom go to theatres or operas. . . . I think a good wife finds her pleasure and amusement in the well ordering of her husband's house."⁵⁵ "A Happy Nine Years' Wife" who had been "brought up in absolute luxury" but had married an Irishman earning only £100 a year preached that "if a girl is happy in the man she marries, love makes up for all such necessaries as bouquets, silk dresses, rides in the Park, [and] eau-de-cologne."⁵⁶

"Charlie's Wife" only learned this self-denying lesson over time. This once-wealthy girl had married a music teacher with an income of £120 a year. Early in their marriage the couple had indulged in "wine and servants" and had even "put their clothes out to wash." The bills and babies came fast, and so did the "bitterness of poverty." Charlie's wife admitted that she had not been "taught to work," and would "have blushed had any of my lady friends caught me with a duster in my white hand." The family was, of course, plunged into debt as they struggled to keep "up appearances." They were not only poor but also lonely since, as Charlie's wife explained, "not even finally my own parents suspected how terribly poor we were." Eventually, however, this family's fortunes turned when they "got rid of their servants," and Charlie's wife was transformed into "the happiest wife and mother in England."⁵⁷ Like many of the correspondents, this wife had initially seen domestic servants as necessities but soon found them unaffordable luxuries. By agreeing to perform their own household labor, such women were redefining prevailing ideals of middle-class womanhood. In a sense they were interpreting domesticity in ways that would make themselves desirable to men with modest incomes.⁵⁸ Even as separate-spheres ideologues rendered women's labor invisible in bourgeois homes, "Charlie's Wife" hearkened back to a time when female domestic labor was valued. In the twentieth century, the needs of wartime and postwar economies would make the servantless home a reality for much of the lower middle and middle classes, but in the 1860s this idea was decidedly out of step with the cultural and social norms of the English middle

---

⁵⁴ See, for example, "Matrafamilias," *Daily Telegraph,* 30 June 1868, 8; and the letter from "An English Wife," 6 July 1868, 2.
⁵⁵ *Daily Telegraph,* 9 July 1868, 2.
⁵⁶ *Daily Telegraph,* 4 July 1868, 2.
⁵⁷ *Daily Telegraph,* 6 July 1868, 2.
⁵⁸ These women's self-presentation as "cheap" and domestic may have also been a result of the prevailing perception that women outnumbered men. See Knelman, "She Loves Me, She Loves Me Not," 81–83.

classes. Servants were very much a part of the paraphernalia of bourgeois domesticity in the mid-Victorian years, though some women openly admitted that they would rather live without them than give up their chances of marriage altogether.

This fantasy wife who did her own housework, shopped little, and expected to find her pleasures at home was invented, or at least gained force, as a kind of foil to the Girl of the Period. The Angel in the House thus took on a particular meaning in the mid-Victorian era in opposition to a new image of public, self-indulgent womanhood. Separate spheres ideology had played havoc with the lower-middle-class domestic economy, since this group could not afford both leisured wives and domestic servants. Yet some correspondents hoped that a kind of authentic domesticity in which women still did housework and domesticated men would solve their class's economic difficulties.[59] Several of the *Telegraph*'s unmarried female correspondents were engaged in paid labor, but they implied that they would quit their jobs upon marriage. One married lady who called herself "Matrafamilias" explained how she had given up her £80 income upon marriage because her "husband considered it a wife's province to stay at home." She saw it as her Christian duty to stay at home and thereby show her "trust in God, our love, and his [her husband's] manliness."[60]

Quite a few correspondents insisted that the young of both sexes had acquired expensive habits and that young men indulged in fine fashions as much as their sisters and would-be wives did.[61] "A Draper" observed that Britain's "sons and daughters" equally launched into "a great deal of unnecessary extravagance . . . [and would] squander any amount of money which, if saved, would be very valuable in establishing for them a comfortable home."[62] Another believed that consumerism was part and parcel of youthful rebellion or, as he put it, "children . . . anxious to throw aside the yoke of their parents." In particular, "young men entering banks [and] counting-houses" seemed to have contracted "fast habits."[63] The so-called Young Men of the Period gambled "away money enough to keep

---

[59] Crossick and Gerhard-Haupt, *The Petite Bourgeoisie*, 87–99. It is possible that the next generation attempted to solve this problem by maintaining a dual-income family. Dina Copelman examined this sort of lower-middle-class family in her study *London's Women Teachers: Gender, Class and Feminism, 1870–1930* (London and New York: Routledge, 1996), 176–95.

[60] *Daily Telegraph*, 30 June 1868, 8.
[61] *Daily Telegraph*, 10 July 1868, 2; Robson, *Marriage or Celibacy*, 154–58.
[62] *Daily Telegraph*, 17 July 1868, 2.
[63] *Daily Telegraph*, 8 July 1868, 2.

even an expensive wife" and were "too selfish to give up such amusements, and appropriate their surplus money in establishing a comfortable home."[64] "Two Plain English Girls" asked the British Bachelor, "Is it at the billiard table, the gambling house, [and] the theater, &c that you find 'happiness?'"[65] "A Wife and Mother" also believed that "drink, pleasure (so-called), [and] dice" were the "temptations" that led "young men away from home circles."[66] A consensus had developed that bachelors spent a great deal on the wrong things: wine, loose women, and expensive clothes. Though many bachelors pleaded that they simply could not afford to marry at all, both male and female correspondents emphasized that bachelors in fact spent a great deal, but on prostitutes and other indulgences. The problem was that young men spent on themselves rather than saving for a family. Especially those who lived at home seemed to have "plenty of money to spend on their individual pleasures" such as "a good coat, fashionable gloves; a decent cigar, dinners out at Richmond and other pleasure resorts, and an occasional stall in the theatre."[67] Men of the Period evidently had a particular liking for lavender kid gloves, patent-leather shoes, and silk stockings.[68]

Men, many assumed, delayed marriage not because they feared their young wives would overspend but because they treasured the material goods and amusements they could afford only as bachelors.[69] A bachelor clergyman counseled others, and reminded himself, that upon marriage one must "cease to think so much of our own comfort and ease." Giving up such things as cigars and new suits, he suggested, will "no longer [be] painful; and the seducing and debasing exhibition of ballet girls dressed in tights will give place to the pure and hallowed joy of intellectual conversation with a loving, if not lovely wife." Though he favored early marriage, this clergyman also implied that it entailed a material and social loss in which young men were cut off from a well-established bachelor consumer subculture.[70] Though condemning his single friends' behavior, this young clergyman was clearly reluctant to depart from the company of his old "college chums," whom he described as "exhaling the fumes of the weed," "running up a heavy bill in New Bond-Street," and "leering at every well-dressed girl in the boxes."[71]

---

[64] *Daily Telegraph,* 4 July 1868, 2.
[65] *Daily Telegraph,* 8 July 1868, 2.
[66] *Daily Telegraph,* 16 July 1868, 2.
[67] *Daily Telegraph,* 8 July 1868, 2.
[68] *Daily Telegraph,* 8 July 1868, 2.
[69] *Daily Telegraph,* 6 and 10 July 1868, 2.
[70] Tosh, *A Man's Place,* 108–10 mentions certain aspects of bachelor subculture. Also see Breward, *The Hidden Consumer,* 170–85.
[71] *Daily Telegraph,* 14 July 1868, 2.

CHAPTER 8. RAPPAPORT, "MARRIAGE, CELIBACY, OR EMIGRATION?"

Just as thrifty, domesticated girls and wives were constructed in opposition to the Girl of the Period, a sober, prudent man was also called up in response to the Young Man of the Period. Prudence was a highly debatable term, however. For some, a watchful control over one's domestic economy was the wise choice, while for others, delayed marriage was rational and prudent. Several patriarchs published detailed domestic budgets, implying that precise knowledge of their family's expenses had kept them above water.[72] Others narrated their domestic spending and proudly economized by walking to work, eating plainly, and finding their amusements "at home."[73] Such economies allowed these men to marry early and beget large families. Indeed, many appeared to be religiously inspired to procreate. One, for example, concluded his letter with this advice for unmarried men: "It is better to marry than burn; don't be afraid—trust in God."[74]

Not everyone, however, felt that penny-pinching and careful budgeting would protect a family from debt and unhappiness. Perhaps the most convincing exposure of this fiction was a letter written by a middle-aged clergyman. He, too, published his detailed budgets, but he did so to show that with four children and two servants, his salary of two hundred a year was never enough to cover his expenses. He survived only by taking on extra employment and borrowing and receiving gifts from "kind-hearted relatives."[75] No doubt, a letter such as this would have had added currency for the readership of the *Telegraph,* since the newspaper routinely published letters from concerned citizens pleading for financial aid for respectable families that had fallen into "distress." Indeed, the "Marriage or Celibacy?" debate only crystallized themes already present throughout the newspaper. Bankruptcy, illness, marital infidelity, and other problems were daily reading in the correspondence pages and the legal sections of the paper long before readers began to talk directly to one another about these issues in June and July of 1868.[76]

A good many correspondents, most of whom identified themselves as followers of political economy, responded to the portrait of prudent patriarchy by charging that procreation itself was a form of conspicuous consumption. "Solon Smiff," for example, humorously remarked, "I never go

---

[72] Robson has republished these budgets in his appendix. See Robson, *Marriage or Celibacy,* 293–98.
[73] *Daily Telegraph,* 4 July 1868, 2.
[74] *Daily Telegraph,* 4 July 1868, 2.
[75] *Daily Telegraph,* 15 July 1868, 2.
[76] See, for example, the stories of infidelity among the lower middle class reported in the divorce proceedings of *Lloyd v. Lloyd* and *Everard v. Everard and Hardy, Daily Telegraph,* 20 June 1868, 3. See also the narrative of lower-middle-class domestic failure documented in the letter "A Family in Distress," *Daily Telegraph,* 25 June 1868, 5.

without his [Mill's] 'Principles of Political Economy' in my pocket." Mill's text had convinced this thirty-two-year-old bachelor that "in a highly-civilized State, a happy marriage—that is, a marriage free from the mean dread of absolute want—is an impossibility for all but the rich." Poor Smiff, however, had recently fallen in love, and his determination was rapidly fading, though he made "frantic efforts" to steady himself by "the light of cool reason."[77] Several others mentioned "Parson Malthus," believing that his equation of population with poverty adequately described their own and the nation's condition.[78] Still others employed a Darwinian vision of society as overcrowded and competitive, arguing that men with modest incomes were losing out to wealthier men in a kind of Darwinian struggle.[79] "Society is fiercely competitive, and every child born is a new competitor," wrote Benedick, a prolific writer but firm believer in small families. Later in the same letter he took a swipe at the Reformation for convincing English men that a large family was "something truly Protestant." As he saw it, "If every Englishman in England . . . married early and begot six or perhaps sixteen children, England in the next generation would be a poorer country than it is now."[80]

Benedick and others who shared his views thus drew upon Malthus, Mill, and Darwin to assert an intimate connection between sexuality, family, class, and national health. These correspondents steered the discussion from issues related to consumption, vanity, the costs of living, and the ideals of domesticity toward an assessment of the middle- and lower-middle-class labor market and emigration. They hoped that emigration to Australia, Canada, South America, and the western United States could solve their personal, as well as national, problems. Such ideas had been popular since at least the 1830s, when pro-empire propagandists had promised men that by leaving England they might make enough money to afford a wife and family. In fact, men had found nonwhite or mixed-race families in the empire, but the practice was increasingly frowned upon, and socially it became necessary to find a legal "European" wife.[81] This

---

[77] *Daily Telegraph,* 30 June 1868, 8. Also see E.F.G.'s letter on 4 July 1868, 2, and "A Plain Man," 11 July 1868, 2.

[78] *Daily Telegraph,* 17 July 1868, 2. Also see the letter by J.A.C.V. the same day.

[79] *Daily Telegraph,* 14 July 1868, 2.

[80] *Daily Telegraph,* 9 July 1868, 2.

[81] For an excellent analysis of race and changing colonial family structures, see Durba Ghosh, *Sex and the Family in Colonial India: The Making of Empire* (Cambridge: Cambridge University Press, 2006). Also see Elizabeth Buettner, *Empire Families: Britons and Late Imperial India* (Oxford: Oxford University Press, 2004). For imperial family economies, see Erika Rappaport, "'The Bombay Debt': Letter Writing, Domestic Economies and Family Conflict

may have been difficult in practice since there were as yet a limited number of single white women on the frontier, but the Victorians imagined this as simply a problem of supply and demand and thus set up various schemes to send single women to the empire to find husbands. For these correspondents, the desire to set up house on the frontier seemed less a flight from domesticity, as John Tosh has recently suggested, than a flight to domesticity.[82] Over the long run emigration created new consumer cultures on the frontier.[83] However, many settlers were trying to escape the costs of consumerism. The *Telegraph*'s readers imagined that if they left England they would find work, marry, and set up a cozy if not extravagant home. Some writers urged others to "go to the far West or to some parts of South America, where land can be had for asking almost."[84]

Promises of free land excited readers, to be sure. However, many were simply looking for a place where they could escape England's materialistic social requirements; as Gordon Bigelow argues in this volume, consumer tastes were often produced by the very markets they were thought to drive. "Colonista," for example, had enjoyed living in British Columbia because, she claimed, "you may, if your income be small, live in a tiny house without scandalizing your nearest and dearest; and . . . should you answer your own door with a broom in your hand, society will actually survive the blow." "In England," she concluded, "half your income at least is spent upon that dreadful bugbear 'society'; you have to go through that dreary grind of 'keeping up appearances.'"[85] "A Minister of Religion" who was about to emigrate to Canada with his family similarly believed that by leaving England and turning back to the land he would find, as he put it, "a remedy for our modern ills."[86]

Colonial domesticity was an especially compelling issue during the midcentury, a time when popular writers, philanthropists, and domestic economists reached out to the "genteel female emigrant" by describing the simpler pleasures of colonial domesticity. The *Colonial Magazine and East*

---

in Colonial India," *Gender and History* 16.2 (August 2004): 233–60.

[82] Tosh, *A Man's Place*, 170–94.

[83] James Belich, *Replenishing the Earth: The Settler Revolution and the Rise of the Anglo-World, 1783–1939* (Oxford: Oxford University Press, 2009) and Gary B. Magee and Andrew Thompson, *Empire and Globalisation: Networks of People, Goods and Capital in the British World, c. 1850–1914* (Cambridge: Cambridge University Press 2010).

[84] *Daily Telegraph*, 9 July 1868, 2. Several mentioned the western United States, and one in particular noted the recent United States Homestead Act, which he believed would give 160 acres of land to settler families in the west. "An Anxious Father," 14 July 1868.

[85] *Daily Telegraph*, 4 July 1868, 2.

[86] *Daily Telegraph*, 21 July 1868, 2.

PART III. FINANCING THE FAMILY

India Review, for example, explained how "hundreds of young ladies who once figured as belles in crowded ball-rooms, are now the happy, industrious and prosperous wives of Colonists, and mothers of healthy children."[87] A similar story appeared in nearly every issue of the weekly periodical the *Domestic Economist Advisor,* a journal that also linked domestic economy to themes of emigration and empire. Like many similar texts, this journal had countless articles about how to live a modest and respectable middle-class lifestyle that was in "good taste" but that "eschewed extravagance" and "expensive habits."[88] It also frequently included letters from colonists who described how they had achieved this balance by leaving England. Emigration did not imply abandoning one's Britishness, since establishing a home and family was cast as a key pillar of national identity. In an article published in January 1850, the author made this point explicitly:

> Our homes! Our British homes! What simple words these are. . . . How truly English is the name—the bare idea of home! It is a word no other language can express, and few other nations understand—none, perhaps as we understand it. . . . "Home" . . . it is one of the foundation-stones of our happiness as a people; and whatever tends to increase the comfort—the peace—the enjoyment of our homes . . . strengthens our national framework—adds stability to the beautiful structure of our constitution—and tends to purify the moral atmosphere we breathe.[89]

Emigrants thus had to consider whether moving abroad to build a home and family was more in keeping with their national character than was staying single in England. Numerous failure narratives written by former emigrants went some way, however, toward shattering this fantasy of colonial domesticity. These letters warned other clerks that they were as redundant overseas as they were at home.[90] "A Mariner," for example, explained that "the colonies, like England, are overrun with clerks."[91] Others implied that urban clerks were not manly or strong enough to endure colonial life. "N.Z." bluntly stated that for "a man who has been brought up to the desk, unaccustomed to, and perhaps incapable of, severe manual

---

[87] *Colonial Magazine and East India Review* 21 (April 1851): 344, quoted in A. James Hammerton, *Emigrant Gentlewomen,* 93.
[88] "Thoughts upon Dress and Good Taste," *Domestic Economist and Advisor in Every Branch of the Family Establishment,* 10 January 1850, 14.
[89] "Our Homes," *Domestic Economist,* 3 January 1850, 2.
[90] *Daily Telegraph,* 22 July 1868, 2.
[91] *Daily Telegraph,* 24 July 1868, 2.

· 160 ·

labour, to emigrate is simply an absurdity."[92] Though many promoted emigration and imperialism as a remedy to the problems of bourgeois society, letters such as these told male and female readers alike that there was no escaping their problems.

In the end, the "Marriage or Celibacy?" debate became an expression of bourgeois dislocation and displacement in which neither England nor frontier spaces provided a place for the lower middle classes to achieve their domestic ideals. Correspondents imagined that poor parenting, the demands of the marriage market, and youthful rebellion all contributed to a competitive and materialistic social system and helped create a self-indulgent culture that infected both men and women. The private sphere was both cause and victim, then, of the Victorian culture of consumption. The nearly three hundred men and women who felt compelled to expose their domestic struggles in a letter to the editor of the *Daily Telegraph* were all anxious about what they perceived as a new, competitive, and unhealthy culture. They sought shelter in an imagined past of material simplicity, in vigilance over personal and familial spending, and, most tellingly, in far-away places in which they could be productive and free from consumer and social pressures. Of course, the very terms of debate in which family and marriage were discussed as commodities suggest that whether they liked it or not, the participants in this debate were already deeply embedded in a consumer society.

---

[92] *Daily Telegraph*, 22 July 1868, 2.

CHAPTER 9

"Absolutely Miss Fairlie's own"

EMASCULATING ECONOMICS IN *THE WOMAN IN WHITE*

ESTHER GODFREY

> "My good friend, you are on the edge of your domestic precipice; and if I let you give the women one other chance, on my sacred word of honour, they will push you over it!"
>
> —Count Fosco to Sir Percival, *The Woman in White*[1]

*N*ineteenth-century literature abounds with stories of women's struggle to secure their futures through fortunate marriages to wealthy husbands. Throughout the period, women lacked equal access to the law, education, or the workforce, and, unless women were independently wealthy, marriage often proved essential to their economic stability even as it deprived them of economic autonomy. This sexual economy largely benefited middle- and upper-class men, who could capitalize on gender inequities to exchange their wealth for youth and beauty. Thus, the logic of the marriage between Marianne Dashwood and Colonel Brandon in Jane Austen's *Sense and Sensibility* (1811)[2] makes perfect sense to Mrs. Jennings, who assumes the match settled equitably: "For *he* is rich and *she* is handsome." Fictional accounts of the nineteenth-century traffic in women are commonplace and, by the end of the century, lead to direct

---

[1] Wilkie Collins, *The Woman in White* (1860; Ontario: Broadview, 2006), 334. All subsequent parenthetical citations refer to this text.

[2] Jane Austen, *Sense and Sensibility* (1811; Oxford: Oxford University Press, 1988), 36.

CHAPTER 9. GODFREY, "'ABSOLUTELY MISS FAIRLIE'S OWN'"

attacks on marriage as socially sanctioned prostitution in works such as George Bernard Shaw's *Mrs. Warren's Profession* (1893) and George Gissing's *The Odd Women* (1893). As conventional (and disturbing) as this trope is, however, it fails to present a sufficient picture of mercenary marriages in which women, instead of men, possess fortunes. Focusing on the possible marriage between Marianne and Colonel Brandon, for example, directs attention away from Marianne's other suitor, Willoughby, and his eventual marriage to Sophia Grey—a marriage he enters not for love, youth, or beauty, but for her £50,000. Such a marriage serves as a counterpoint to the recent argument put forth by Elsie Michie; tracing the development of the heiress in the nineteenth-century marriage plot, Michie argues that a hero's overwhelming preference for the "poor woman" over the "rich woman" demonstrates the cultural anxiety that rapid economic development and increasing materialism might corrupt moral sentiments.[3] Ultimately an antihero, Willoughby makes the wrong decision, teaching by example the negative consequences of privileging fortune over feeling.

Yet, as Michie acknowledges, the ramifications of the heiress's wealth change when she is sought by two men. Although Michie is certainly right to suggest that in Victorian fiction women must "choose the man who represents love rather than the love of money" (5), I'm most interested here in an heiress's relationship to her own wealth, both before and after marriage. Though the ability for women, and especially married women, to control their finances remained limited for much of the century, women did wield capital, and their wealth not only made them consumers (as well as objects) in the sexual market but also made masculinity itself—even that of their chosen husbands—vulnerable. In Wilkie Collins's *The Woman in White* (1860), the anxieties that arise after Laura Fairlie's marriage center less on materialism than on the way that money had the potential to trouble gender. While studies of nineteenth-century marriages often run the risk of promoting compulsory heterosexuality, this essay suggests that gender identities are both fluid and economically driven and that marriage is unavoidably queer.[4] As Kathy Psomiades[5] points out, myths of compulsory

---

[3] Elsie Michie, *The Vulgar Question of Money: Heiresses, Materialism, and the Novel of Manners from Jane Austen to Henry James* (Baltimore: The Johns Hopkins University Press, 2011), 7, 24.

[4] See Sharon Marcus's *Between Women: Friendship, Desire, and Marriage in Victorian England* (Princeton, NJ: Princeton University Press, 2007) for a parallel argument that women's homosocial relationships actually helped to produce many of the heterosexual marriages of Victorian literature.

[5] Kathy Alexis Psomiades, "Heterosexual Exchange and Other Victorian Fictions: 'The Eustace Diamonds' and Victorian Anthropology," *Novel: A Forum on Fiction* 33 (1999): 93–118, 116–17.

heterosexuality and the traffic in women emerge in periods of increased male anxiety, and they resurface as comfortable and familiar narratives to reify gender roles. The idea of a traffic in women is critically expedient but reduces the complexities of sexual economies to the foregone conclusion of women's victimization by men. Instead of looking solely at women's mercenary marriages, we need to consider the ways in which fiction presents the desire for male financial security, while also suggesting how independent wealth could both empower and imperil women. Examining this dynamic in fiction reveals a multiplicity of evolving and varied economic scenarios. Within these sexual economies, men are not always the agents nor are women always the victims; in fact, the process of valuation and exchange destabilizes gender so fundamentally that critics must recognize such identities as intrinsically flawed. Although, as Eli Zaretsky[6] and other feminist scholars emphasize, sexism predates capitalism, fictional representations of nineteenth-century economic conditions point to weaknesses in a seemingly monolithic and insurmountable gender system rather than just stabilizing or simplifying a patriarchal order. Wealth offers one avenue to power, and, because gender remains inextricably linked to power, wealth—or the lack of wealth—has the potential to rewrite gender identities.

I. THE THREAT OF *FEME SOLE*

The Woman in White appears to follow a familiar master narrative: Sir Percival Glyde, a forty-five-year-old baronet, marries twenty-year-old Laura Fairlie, and the storyline of a woman's advantageous yet troubled marriage seems understood—even trite. Laura is sweet, fair, delicate, dutiful, and not as smart as her darker, stronger, and mustached half-sister Marian.[7] Laura quickly suppresses her emerging feelings for Walter Hartright to fulfill the desires of the men in her life who have more immediate claims: her deceased father, her effeminate uncle, and her prospective husband. Following the advice of conduct-book writer Sarah Stickney Ellis and other midcentury women, Laura tries to "suffer, and be still" in a loveless marriage, and she explains to her sister, "Whenever you and I are together,

---

[6] Eli Zaretsky, *Capitalism, The Family, and Personal Life* (New York: Harper and Row, 1976).

[7] See Cindy LaCom's essay "Ideological Aporia: When Victorian England's Hairy Woman Met God and Darwin," in *Nineteenth-Century Gender Studies* 4.2 (2008), for further discussion of Marian's moustache and its gendering effects.

CHAPTER 9. GODFREY, "'ABSOLUTELY MISS FAIRLIE'S OWN'"

Marian, we shall both be happier and easier with one another, if we accept my married life for what it is, and say and think as little about it as possible" (235).[8] In becoming Lady Glyde, Laura gains a title but loses much more. Yet the novel's titillating sensationalism comes not from its ability to replicate the trope of women's victimization and economic disadvantage, but from problematizing that pattern by emphasizing men's precarious hold on wealth and women's economic agency. *The Woman in White* reveals that Sir Percival has no fortune and that he marries Laura not because she is pretty, well-bred, and half his age, but because she is rich and he is poor. Sir Percival's title seems to promise a good return on Laura's investment, and, though the choice to marry Sir Percival is not entirely her own, Laura is an active participant in the transaction. Her marriage into the ranks of nobility increases the value of her family, and, as such, her acceptance of Sir Percival is "an engagement of honour, not of love" (111). As the novel explains, Laura is not especially excited about her acquisition, but, since she has not met Walter at the time of the engagement, she considers it a fair deal: "she herself neither welcomed it, nor shrank from it—she was content to make it" (111). Thus, while the novel emphasizes the continued abuse of women within a male-centered Victorian economy, it also reveals the anxiety produced by the transitory nature of wealth. If power is economic and tied to material wealth, rather than to masculinity, then financial fictions provide the potential to trouble gender relations. I do not claim that *The Woman in White* pretends to court such trouble; in fact, the novel teems with gender essentialism, from its opening line, "This is the story of what a Woman's patience can endure, and what a Man's resolution can achieve" (49), to its conservative conclusion that presents Laura's son as the heir to her estate. I also grant that Laura's purchase of a title benefits her father and uncle at least as much as it does her. But these conventional renderings of gender compensate for anxieties raised by debates over married women's property and by the destabilizing effects that women's separate property enabled.

Ultimately, the novel recognizes that even women's limited exercise of financial freedom threatens the conventional marriage plot in sensational ways. Despite her solicitor's unease that faulty provisions in her settlement could award all of Laura's wealth to Sir Percival upon her death without children, prenuptial arrangements keep her property from falling into his

---

[8] See Sarah Stickney Ellis's *The Daughters of England, Their Position in Society, Character, and Responsibilities* (London: Fisher, 1842), microfilm, 94. In *The Spectacle of Intimacy: A Public Life for the Victorian Family* (Princeton, NJ: Princeton University Press, 2000), 65–85, Karen Chase and Michael Levenson expose irony and resistance in Ellis's life.

PART III. FINANCING THE FAMILY

hands during the marriage and place the traditional angel in the house in an unlikely position of economic authority.[9] Sir Percival's gambling debts have led him to take desperate measures, but he attempts to gain control despite his economic weakness. Trying to lay claim to Laura's separate assets and satisfy his creditors, he commands her to sign a document without informing her that it will relinquish her rights:

"What is it I am to sign?" she asked, quietly.

"I have no time to explain," he answered. "The dog-cart is at the door; and I must go directly. Besides, if I had time, you wouldn't understand. It is a purely formal document—full of legal technicalities, and all that sort of thing. Come! come! sign your name, and let us have done with it as soon as possible."

"I ought surely to know what I am signing, Sir Percival, before I write my name?"

"Nonsense! What have women to do with business? I tell you again, you can't understand it."

"At any rate, let me try to understand it. Whenever Mr. Gilmore had any business for me to do, he always explained it, first; and I always understood him."

"I dare say he did. He was your servant, and was obliged to explain. I am your husband, and am *not* obliged. How much longer do you mean to keep me here? I tell you again, there is no time for reading anything: the dog-cart is waiting at the door. Once for all, will you sign, or will you not?" (267)

Sir Percival's desperation and Laura's power are evident; he assumes the role of pushy salesman—"How much longer? . . . there is no time . . . the dog-cart is waiting"—and she of reluctant buyer. And, although he openly demeans her ability as a woman to negotiate finances and misrepresents his power as husband, he all too clearly concedes that Laura remains in control of their resources. His repeated commands, while oppressive in their insistence, nevertheless recognize her authority and economic understanding

---

[9] Settlements in a court of equity provided an alternative to the coverture of common law. See Mary Lyndon Shanley, *Feminism, Marriage, and the Law in Victorian England* (Princeton, NJ: Princeton University Press, 1989), 25–26. Laura remains passive throughout the settlement process, but her lack of savvy here is indicative more of her youth than of her gender. Later in the novel, she becomes more interested in her finances. For a somewhat earlier treatment, but one that also discusses alternatives to coverture, see Amy Louise Erickson's *Women and Property in Early Modern England* (London: Routledge, 1993), which argues that ordinary women were more likely than the common law suggests to have settlements (130).

and belie his threat that he is *"not* obliged to explain." It is Laura's choice whether to sign or not, and the legal necessity for witnesses to the signature limits the duress she faces. Because he must have witnesses, he also cannot forge her signature and assume control of her property. Laura refuses to allow her writing to be used against her; she does not sign.

The complex laws surrounding coverture and the intermingled Parliamentary debates concerning married women's property and divorce during the 1850s increase the significance of Laura's refusal and emphasize the impact of women's economic independence on contemporary debates about gender. According to the courts of common law, a married woman was "covered" by her husband, and therefore had no need for rights as a separate individual. Her property, earnings, and body were under the control and protection of her husband.[10] While Lenora Ledwon reads *The Woman in White* as initially "a radical critique of women's loss of identity under coverture," she finds that it ultimately "reinforce[es] the ideological assumption that law should work differently for men than for women."[11] While Collins certainly exposes men's abuse of law and gender roles only to uphold a masculine hierarchy, the inequities in Laura's marriage to Sir Percival do not stem from coverture. Most women in England did lose their property under the laws of coverture; however, Laura—as made clear in the preceding exchange with Sir Percival—did not.[12] Mr.

---

[10] See Barbara Leigh Smith, *A Brief Summary, in Plain Language, of the Most Important Laws Concerning Women* (London: John Chapman, 1854), microfilm, 6: "A man and wife are one person in law; the wife loses all her rights as a single woman, and her existence is entirely absorbed in that of her husband. He is civilly responsible for her acts; she lives under his protection or cover, and her condition is called coverture. . . . What was her personal property before marriage, such as money in hand, money at the bank, jewels, household goods, clothes, etc., becomes absolutely her husband's, and he may assign or dispose of them at his pleasure whether he and his wife live together or not." Coverture was not without possibilities. Margot Finn ("Women, Consumption and Coverture in England, c. 1760–1860," *Historical Journal* 39.3 [1996]: 703–22) thoughtfully investigates several methods used by women to subvert their husbands' power within coverture, including wives' ability to amass debt in their husbands' names. Finn argues that "the purchase of coverture in the sphere of consumption was partial and contested, rather than monolithic" (703). See also 168–90 in Erika Rappaport's "A Husband and His Wife's Dresses" in *The Sex of Things: Gender and Consumption in Historical Perspective,* ed. Victoria de Grazia with Ellen Furlough (London: University of California Press, 1996), 163–77. For more on the possibilities of coverture, see Janette Rutterford's essay in this volume.

[11] Lenora Ledwon, "Veiled Women, the Law of Coverture, and Wilkie Collins's *The Woman in White,*" *Victorian Literature and Culture* 22 (1994): 1–22, 1.

[12] As I state earlier, Laura does lose other rights upon marriage (under English law, Sir Percival has conjugal rights as well as the right to commit her to an asylum), and Marian compares Laura's marriage to her death (211). Nevertheless, Marian is aware that married women are not entirely unprotected; she demands to see bruises on Laura's arm to use in court as a

PART III. FINANCING THE FAMILY

Gilmore, Laura's family's solicitor, goes into painstaking detail about protecting her separate assets, which include a life interest in an estate worth over £3,000 a year and an inheritance of £20,000. Gilmore does not receive all the stipulations he wants in "a proper settlement"—it is crucial to the plot that Sir Percival is to be the sole beneficiary of the £20,000—but there is no question of Laura losing her assets during marriage through common law (179). Women like Laura with substantial property and male protectors were able to evade common law through the courts of equity. As Gilmore explains, "This sum was absolutely Miss Fairlie's own, on her completing her twenty-first year; and the whole future disposition of it depended, in the first instance, on the conditions I could obtain for her in her marriage settlement. . . . The whole amount was to be settled so as to give the income [the interest] to the lady for her life; afterwards to Sir Percival for his life; and the principal to the children of the marriage" (180). Not only is the principal "absolutely Miss Fairlie's own" and, even after marriage, absolutely Lady Glyde's own, but so is the yearly interest earned by the principal. Some of the novel's sensationalism does stem from the abusive powers of men, but in Collins's fiction, Laura is also made vulnerable through her own wealth, which leaves her open to Sir Percival's plotting and, at least initially, prevents her from achieving traditional domestic happiness. Thus, what Ledwon deems "a radical critique of women's loss of identity" could more aptly be hailed as Collins's conservative response to what he perceived as women's rising economic independence.

Collins notably places the beginning of the novel in 1849—before the well-publicized agitation for married women's property reform in the 1850s—but *The Woman in White*'s concern over men's potential disenfranchisement reflects growing gender unrest that was evidenced in and caused by contemporary reform literature and Parliamentary debates. As Harriet Martineau acknowledges in her 1859 essay "Independent Industry for Women,"[13] the very idea of women's economic dependency had "been out at elbows" since Waterloo (301). Martineau clarifies that by 1851 over half of Britain's women were employed and one-third were "independent in their industry . . . self-supporting, like men" (301). Thus, by

---

"weapon" against Sir Percival (317). See Marlene Tromp's discussion of *The Woman in White*'s treatment of marital violence in *The Private Rod: Marital Violence, Sensation, and the Law in Victorian Britain* (Charlottesville: University Press of Virginia, 2000), 69–102.

[13] Harriet Martineau, "Independent Industry for Women" (1859), in *The Voice of Toil: 19th-Century British Writings about Work*, ed. David J. Bradshaw and Suzanne Ozment (Athens: Ohio University Press, 2000), 300–304.

CHAPTER 9. GODFREY, "'ABSOLUTELY MISS FAIRLIE'S OWN'"

midcentury, a significant number of women were responsible for the economic vitality of households, but, in most marriages, coverture deprived them of their right to control their resources. Real-life accounts of women suffering under coverture, such as the case of Caroline Norton, led to open agitation for reform of married women's property rights. Harriet Taylor Mill's "Enfranchisement of Women" (1851),[14] Barbara Leigh Smith (later Bodichon)'s *A Brief Summary in Plain English of the Most Important Laws of England Concerning Women* (1854), and Norton's *English Laws for Women in the Nineteenth Century* (1854)[15] condemned the illogic and injustice of wives' economic inequality. Simultaneously, calls for expanded access to divorce were separate from, but paralleled, the demands for equal access to property. Before 1857 divorce was an option only for the elite, as it actually required Parliamentary approval.

Both the 1856 Married Women's Property Act (which failed) and the 1857 Matrimonial Causes Act (which passed) influenced the 1860 novel, since they both brought substantial challenges to entrenched systems of male entitlement.[16] Stories of abusive and adulterous husbands (many of the same stories made public in the debate over property) shattered myths of men as women's protectors, and, whereas Parliament rejected measures to legislate gender equality within marriage, it did decide to provide more women with a way out.[17] The years preceding the novel's publication reflect the deep social ambivalence regarding gender, marriage, and economics. Something was wrong with marriage; examples of the failure of husbands to provide for their families were too numerous and too egregious to ignore, but Parliament was not ready for full reform. Referring to the 1857 Act by its more common name, Shanley explains, "[The] Divorce [Act] simply gave legal recognition to de facto marital breakdown. A married women's property law, on the other hand, would have recognized the existence of two separate wills within an *ongoing* marriage" (46). Passing the Divorce Act allowed some women a path back to the economic

---

[14] Harriet Taylor Mill, "Enfranchisement of Women" (1851), in *The Complete Works of Harriet Taylor Mill*, ed. Jo Ellen Jacobs (Bloomington: Indiana University Press, 1998), 51–73.

[15] Caroline Sheridan Norton, *English Laws for Women in the Nineteenth Century* (1854; Westport, CT: Hyperion Press, 1981).

[16] Agitation continued, resulting in the 1882 Married Women's Property Act, which dramatically increased married women's access to their property.

[17] Because the novel is set before 1857, Laura would have needed to apply directly to Parliament if she wanted a divorce, but she had no legal grounds for such an action. Even the new divorce law perpetuated male privilege; for example, a man could divorce his wife for adultery, whereas a woman would have to prove her husband's adultery, plus another grievance such as sodomy, bestiality, or gross cruelty.

independence of unmarried women, but the failure of the Married Women's Property Act denied women's individualism within marriage.

In its evasion of common law and coverture through equity, *The Woman in White* engages contemporary calls for reform by giving Laura her separate estate. Equity law allows the sexual economies within their marriage to work as if the Act had passed, and the novel thus explores the anxiety and even dangers that women's economic independence and men's economic dependence might engender.[18]

Sir Percival's relative poverty unmans him. His rank and estate, rather than signifying elite masculinity, are both fraudulently maintained by hiding his illegitimate birth and enormous debt. Sir Percival resents the uneven distribution of wealth in their marriage and the fact that he knows himself to be an unwanted husband; Laura loves a man almost twenty years younger than himself.[19] When Laura asks if he will build her a tomb like Marcus Crassus erected for his wife Cecilia Metella on the Appian Way, he responds bitterly: "If I do build you a tomb, it will be done with your own money. I wonder whether Cecilia Metella had a fortune, and paid for hers" (280). Even what would have been considered the most basic conjugal rights of any Victorian husband to his wife's body are denied to him because of his financial straits.[20] He cannot risk sex with Laura because producing an heir would immediately curtail his access to the £20,000. Thus, when Count Fosco questions him about the possibility of Laura being pregnant, Sir Percival admits that "she is not in the least likely" to conceive (342). His age, his secret, and his debts further devalue his already dwindling stock in masculinity and spawn his sensational attempts to recoup his losses.

While Collins clearly intends Sir Percival to be a villain, Laura's economic independence instigates much of the novel's mischief. Knowing that Sir Percival cannot obtain Laura's signature, Fosco suggests her "death" as an alternate solution: "Here is your position. If your wife lives, you pay

---

[18] Even progressive reformers such as Charlotte Tonna, Edith Hogg, and Friedrich Engels lamented capitalism's ability to complicate traditional gender roles. Women in the factories, for example, undercut men's wages and led to women being the primary breadwinners in many working-class homes. In *The Condition of the Working Class in England* (1845; Moscow: Progress, 1973), Engels complains of seeing a husband mending garments by the fire at home, while his wife worked at a factory (184). See selections from Tonna (434–45) and Hogg (598–608) in Bradshaw and Ozment, *The Voice of Toil: 19th-Century Writings about Work*.

[19] Percival is forty-five, Walter twenty-eight.

[20] See Shanley, *Feminism, Marriage, and the Law in Victorian England,* chap. 6: "A Husband's Right to His Wife's Body: Wife Abuse, the Restitution of Conjugal Rights, and Marital Rape" (156–88).

those bills with her signature to the parchment. If your wife dies, you pay them with her death" (343). Collins suggests that under coverture the drastic steps of placing Laura in a madhouse and faking her death would have been unnecessary: women would not have equal rights, but they would not provoke such extreme actions from men. Under this faulty logic, Collins depicts Laura longing for her wealth to disappear, as if poverty promised the resolution, rather than the intensification, of wealth's power dynamics. She tells her sister, "How often . . . I have heard you laughing over what you used to call your 'poverty'! how often you have made me mocking speeches of congratulation on my wealth! Oh, Marian, never laugh again. Thank God for your poverty—it has made you your own mistress, and has saved you from the lot that has fallen on *me*" (279). Poverty and spinsterhood do allow Marian certain gendered liberties, but it does not follow that women's wealth is responsible for male tyranny.[21] Indeed, as the existence of Laura's illegitimate half-sister Anne Catherick suggests, poor women were frequently depicted as the prey of wealthy men, rather than as their contented wives, so the romance plot often failed to offer security to the poor as well as to the wealthy.[22] Blaming women's abuse on married women's property rights misdirects the source of the crisis. In the sensational upending of the traditional marriage plot, we see the dramatic stakes of male disempowerment.

II. "TREASURES BEYOND PRICE": GENDER AND VALUE

The presumably happy love affair and eventual marriage between Laura and Walter also highlight men's increasingly precarious value in mid-nineteenth-century England, and the novel compensates for this state of affairs through the hyperfeminization of its heroine. Walter is below Sir Percival on the economic ladder; although Walter does not have Sir Percival's debts, he does not have his title or estate either. When Anne Catherick questions if Walter is a man "of rank and title," he responds "a little bitterly"

---

[21] My article *"Jane Eyre,* from Governess to Girl Bride" (*Studies in English Literature 1500–1900* 45 [2005]: 853–71) explains how Jane's economic disadvantages encourage her gender ambiguity (853–60). Like Jane, Marian is free from many class-based gendered conventions.

[22] See, for instance, Deborah Epstein Nord, *Walking the Victorian Streets: Women, Representation, and the City* (Ithaca, NY: Cornell University Press, 1995), 151: "We need only think of fictional heroines from Richardson's Pamela to Brontë's Jane Eyre to Disraeli's Sybil to appreciate the cultural power of the competing idea of marriage as the route to upward mobility for 'women of the people.'"

that he is "far from it" (67). Walter must work as a drawing master for his money—like a governess, an employee of the wealthy—and Walter opens his narrative by confessing that "the fading summer left me out of health, out of spirits, and, if the truth must be told, out of money as well" (50). He eagerly accepts a salary and accommodations for teaching Laura and Marian to paint; he betrays his class difference when he gushes about his private sitting room to the servant (80). On the surface, Walter is "masculine." He is young, chivalrous, and handsome. At least initially, however, his lack of wealth and title overrides his claim to masculine power, offering another example of how economics can trouble gender.[23]

Throughout the novel, Walter struggles with his economic disadvantages and repeatedly reassures himself that he is not in a weaker position than Laura, despite her enormous wealth. When he considers the offer of employment, he welcomes the promise that "he was to be treated there on the footing of a gentleman" as much as he looks forward to the generous compensation (59). His sister bolsters his delusion: "Such distinguished people to know . . . and on such gratifying terms of equality, too!" (60). At Limmeridge, eating Limmeridge food, enjoying the Limmeridge grounds, and being cared for by Limmeridge servants, Walter can pretend that he is a guest of the house rather than its employee. This fantasy of economic equality with Laura facilitates his attachment to her, but it is the possibility of a relationship with her that tears down this façade. When he realizes he is in love, he can no longer play that he is the gentleman he pretends to be. Begging the reader's forgiveness for overstepping the "conditions" of his "term" of "hired service," he admits, "I should have remembered my position, and have put myself secretly on my guard" (101, 102). No longer "on equal footing," Walter reveals the unstated conditions of his business contract:

> It had been my profession, for years past, to be in this close contact with young girls of all ages, and of all orders of beauty. I had accepted the position as part of my calling in life; I had trained myself to leave all the sympathies natural to my age in my employer's outer hall, as coolly as I left my umbrella there before I went up-stairs. . . . I was admitted among beautiful and captivating women, much as a harmless domestic animal is admitted among them. (102–3)

---

[23] Charles Kingsley's revival of muscular Christianity, beginning in the mid-1850s, is one testament that respect for physical prowess as a measure of masculinity had declined and was in need of reviving. See, for instance, the sustained emphasis on physicality in Kingsley's *Two Years Ago* (1857) and Thomas Hughes's *Tom Brown at Oxford* (1861).

CHAPTER 9. GODFREY, "'ABSOLUTELY MISS FAIRLIE'S OWN'"

Here, Walter seems aware of not only the emasculating effects of class hierarchy, but the dehumanizing ones as well. Heretofore, his position has unsexed him like a neutered dog, and, even more powerless than Sir Percival, he is not even allowed to enter into the marriage market.[24]

When Marian asks Walter to leave Limmeridge, she claims that her request is not based on "social inequalities" (109). Marian, economically disadvantaged like Walter, means to avoid "humiliating reference to matters of rank and station" in rejecting the possibility of a relationship between Walter and Laura, yet ultimately "blame[s] the misfortune of [his] years and [his] position" (109). Laura's engagement to Sir Percival is never the real obstacle to Walter marrying Laura; even with Sir Percival out of the picture, the taint of class difference is too much. Giving Sir Percival an opportunity to break their engagement, Laura clarifies her intentions that "you do not leave me to marry another man—you only allow me to remain a single woman for the rest of my life" (198). Laura's fortunes soon turn, however, and Collins intentionally balances Walter's lower value with her new lack of wealth. Sir Percival fakes her death and places her in a madhouse; she escapes, but, until she can prove her identity, Laura cannot claim her name or wealth. Poor and living secretly with Marian and Walter, she is unsexed and dehumanized like Walter, the female equivalent of a "harmless domestic animal." "Sorrow and suffering" traced "profaning marks on the youth and beauty of her face" and left her with "weakened, shaken faculties" (441). Doggish, Laura looks now with "poor weary pining eyes" (441) instead of with the "lovely eyes in colour, lovely eyes in form" (89) she formerly possessed, and Walter and Marian entertain their pet by taking her on walks and giving her treats (442). Though the abrupt cessation of sexual desire between Walter and Laura seems unlikely, Walter now swears, "God knows," that he regards Laura only as a "father or brother might have felt" (459).[25] His disclaimer soothes Victorian unease with their cohabitation—though she is legally dead, she is technically still married to Sir Percival—but also emphasizes the interwoven status of

---

[24] Middle-class men could not responsibly marry until they could financially afford a wife and family and often had to delay marriage until midlife (see Erika Rappaport's essay in this volume). With Laura out of reach because of her wealth, Walter muses ironically that he also cannot marry within his rank and "innocently wondered whether I should ever leave my lonely chambers and have a wife and a house of my own" (150).

[25] Scholars have recently given more attention to incestuous desire in nineteenth-century literature. Both Robert Polhemus in *Lot's Daughters: Sex, Redemption, and Women's Quest for Authority* (Stanford, CA: Stanford University Press, 2005) and Mary Jean Corbett in *Family Likeness: Sex, Marriage, and Incest from Jane Austen to Virginia Woolf* (Ithaca, NY: Cornell University Press, 2008) show that familial ties did not necessitate lack of sexual desire.

their gendered, sexed, and classed identities. Laura's poverty additionally allows for the restoration of Walter's masculinity. Walter can now be the breadwinner for Laura that he never could be before. Just as the unequal distribution of wealth was the means of Walter's disempowerment, it also proves to be the means of the novel's reestablishment of traditional gender roles. Poor, Laura again falls under coverture. Though she is not legally married to Walter or technically restricted by coverture, the novel reasserts a distinctly conservative position by imaginatively extending the law's reach. Walter now controls her finances—indeed, he kindly ensures that she has little.

In this new "marriage," Laura objects to the altered economic realities. Walter supports their meager lifestyle through his artwork, and Laura wants to contribute: "You work and get money, Walter. . . . Why is there nothing I can do? . . . don't, don't, don't treat me like a child!" (480). Laura displays a "breathless interest" in the household economy and a "feverish eagerness" to work, so Walter constructs an elaborate ruse. "You know that I work and get money by drawing," he explains as he places a sketch in front of her, so "finish this little sketch . . . when it is done, I will take it away with me; and the same person will buy it who buys all that I do" (480). Walter promises she will keep her profits "in her own purse" and that Marian will ask for her money for household expenses (480). Thus, Walter reconstructs the separate "estate" that Laura enjoyed under equity law, and Laura is thrilled, in Walter's words, "longing to assume her own little position of importance" (481). The critical difference is that now Laura's financial independence is an illusion, an "innocent deception" (481). Walter can speak patronizingly of her pride as a wage earner because he controls the means of both production and distribution. In truth, he never sells Laura's art; he never even attempts to sell it. Instead, he explains, "I set aside a little weekly tribute from my earnings, to be offered to her as the price paid by strangers for the poor, faint, valueless sketches, of which I was the only purchaser" (481). Laura's drawings never enter the open market, and Walter makes any chance of her resuming the economic authority that she once held impossible. Her pen was valuable for her signature as Glyde's wife, but worthless now, except in its symbolic register of her domestic infantilization and her new dependence upon a man. Walter can enjoy the restoration of accepted gender roles and claim financial and masculine privilege. Laura's attempts to participate in the household economy—when she "proudly brought out her purse to contribute her share towards the expenses" and when she "wondered, with serious interest, whether [Walter] or she had earned the most that week"—are intended to be laughable moments (481). They are endearing to Collins and his hero Walter because they are ridiculous, drawing attention away from the power her pen has held, from the midcentury reality of women in the workplace, and also from the capital that Collins's own competition—middle- and upper-class women—were earning through writing and drawing. As these moments of "innocent deception" reinforce masculine identity, Walter keeps Laura's drawings "hidden" after they are married so that he may refer to them when he desires. Thus they are not "valueless," as Walter first suggests, but admittedly "treasures beyond price" because they increase his false sense of superiority within their marital economy (481).

These restorative moments attempt to reassert male control, but Laura's first marriage to Sir Percival, and her second marriage to Walter Hartright, represent the larger unraveling of the fabric of gendered power because of the threat of women's financial independence. The novel applauds man's traditional role as the breadwinner; Walter is rewarded for financially supporting Laura throughout Sir Percival's conspiracy by finally gaining her hand in marriage, producing a son who legitimates his own sexual prerogative, and thereby restoring masculine control of wealth. But this control is tenuous at best. In the previous generation, men held traditionally empowered positions: Laura's father's financial superiority to Laura's mother affords him access to his mistress Mrs. Catherick, and Sir Percival's estate, however illegitimate, comes from his father, not his mother. But even primogeniture fails to preserve male dominance. The younger generation of men—Sir Percival, Walter, and even Count Fosco—all need their wives' money. Laura's position as a wealthy woman has threatened the all-male hold on power so fundamentally that such superficial coverings as the novel's pat conclusion fail to hide underlying anxieties about women's ability to assume power, and transcend gender, through wealth.

PART IV

Women's Business

CHAPTER 10

"She'd give her two ears to know"

THE GOSSIP ECONOMY IN ELLEN WOOD'S *ST. MARTIN'S EVE*

TARA MacDONALD

> By some defect of organization, the English, taken as a mass, are gossips—decided gossips. Is it not written in the book of the chronicles of their public journals—those bulletins of the national mind? Is it not attested by the avidity with which the most trivial anecdotes of domestic life are circulated and eagerly swallowed, by that yawning gulf, the reading public?
>
> —Catherine Gore, *New Monthly Magazine,* November 1840[1]

In the above quotation, nineteenth-century author Catherine Gore bemoans the English public's love of gossip, suggesting that what occurs in the privacy of Victorian households has overflowed into public journals and novels. The piece playfully chides the agents of gossip, but it is also an attempt, in the early years of the Victorian period, to come to terms with the nature of the act itself, its connections to other forms of information, and its manner of circulation. Gore goes on to point out that the constant demand for gossip is even more alarming than its actual pres-

---

[1] Catherine Gore, "Sketches of Modern Character (No. III): The Gossip," *New Monthly Magazine* 60 (1840): 382–6, 383. Gore (1799/1800–1861) was a novelist and playwright who wrote popular "silver fork" novels in the 1830s, 1840s, and 1850s (Winifred Hughes, "Gore, Catherine Grace Frances [1799/1800–1861]," *Oxford Dictionary of National Biography,* online ed. [Oxford: Oxford University Press, 2004], accessed 1 June 2010).

ence: "it is the appetite for gossip, and not the food which the yearnings of that appetite bring into the market, with which we have to deal."[2] In this essay, I take up Gore's association of gossip with "the reading public" and "the market" in an attempt to consider how gossip, in the Victorian novel, functions as an alternative economic system, but one that nonetheless influences and is affected by other economies. In the analogy above, gossip is linked to consumerism and consumption: it is a kind of food swallowed by a public hungry for "trivial anecdotes of domestic life." In order to be served up, these anecdotes must be "circulated" and brought "into the market." Using Ellen Wood's sensational *St. Martin's Eve* (1866),[3] a text obsessed with gossip and economics, I argue that gossip in the novel, and in Victorian society more generally, constitutes its own economy wherein private information functions as treasured currency.

Like much sensation fiction, Wood's plots frequently turn on women's financial insecurity. As Lyn Pykett writes, Wood was highly aware of the "fragility of prosperity and social position."[4] Her family suffered at least two reversals of fortune: in the 1830s, her father's glove manufactory failed; and in 1856 Wood's husband, the overseas manager of a banking and shipping firm, was forced to retire, an episode that altered the family's financial and domestic life.[5] A year after her husband lost his post, Wood published her first novel, *Danesbury House* (1857), and began a period of high productivity and financial success, providing for her family when her husband could no longer do so. After his death in 1865, she not only continued to write fiction but later bought and edited her own magazine, *Argosy*. Wood was able to engage with the market economy very effectively while still retaining her image as a conventional Victorian woman, wife, and mother.[6] A 1904 survey for *Economic Review*, "What Do the Masses Read?" recorded that Wood was "easily first favourite,"[7] and Lucy Sussex has found that in

---

[2] Gore, "Sketches," 383.

[3] Ellen Wood, *St. Martin's Eve*, ed. Lyn Pykett, in vol. 3 of *Varieties of Women's Sensation Fiction, 1855–1890*, 6 vols., gen. ed. Andrew Maunder (London: Pickering & Chatto, 2004). Further references are cited parenthetically.

[4] Lyn Pykett, "Introduction to *St. Martin's Eve*," in *Varieties of Women's Sensation Fiction: 1855–1890*, 3: vii–xxii, ix.

[5] Pykett, "Introduction to *St. Martin's Eve*," 3: ix–x.

[6] In "'Dangerous and Foolish Work': Evangelicalism and Sensationalism in Ellen Wood's *Argosy* Magazine," *Women's Writing* 15.2 (2008): 187–98, Beth Palmer argues that Wood's "perceived conventionality was carefully constructed and complexly shifting" (189). Specifically, she suggests that Wood "cultivated a Christian and conservative reputation in order to distance herself from the more dangerous facets of sensationalism" (187).

[7] Quoted in Emma Liggins and Andrew Maunder, "Introduction: Ellen Wood, Writer," *Women's Writing* 15.2 (2008): 149–56, 150.

Wood's letters to publisher Richard Bentley, she "haggl[ed] mercilessly on contract and payment detail."[8] Despite her own success, Wood understood that those members of Victorian society who were frequently marginalized by the market economy, namely women and servants, could develop alternative economies, which gave them opportunities to acquire greater agency and control their domestic lives. One of these economies, I argue, revolved around the circulation of gossip, the exchange of information that could prove vital to social status, community regulation, and the marriage market.

Gossip is an important element of virtually all sensation novels, but Wood, whose novels straddle the genres of sensation fiction and domestic fiction, uses gossip both as a sensational plot device and as the everyday exchange of information between servants and their employers. Gossip can be understood politically as the refuge of the disenfranchised: Wood shows how both middle-class women and servants are disenfranchised by the patriarchal structures of the Victorian market economy and how they, in turn, rely on gossip to assess character and achieve domestic security. Gossip therefore emerges as a "feminine" economy, in contrast to the masculine dominion over commerce, employment, and trade (though there are, of course, exceptions to this patriarchal rule, as many of the essays in this volume show). Through their possession and informal exchange of personal information, Wood's women and servants achieve a degree of control over their own destinies and the connected lives of others. By offering pieces of gossip, they can participate in and benefit from "the circulation of meanings, ideas, and identities."[9] In this gossip economy, personal information thus becomes a kind of currency, which is traded and assigned value by others within the economy. Yet men are not absent from this economy, as they, too, can benefit from exchanges of gossip. While men in Wood's novels cannot circulate gossip in the same way as women, they can nonetheless profit from the gossip economy via strategic exchanges with women and servants. Indeed, as I show, male characters frequently supply the motivation for gossiping in the first place.

In her novels Wood frequently emphasizes the power of gossip to influence communities. The narrator in *East Lynne* (1861) emphasizes the

---

[8] Lucy Sussex, "Mrs Henry Wood and Her Memorials," *Women's Writing* 15.2 (2008): 157–68, 159.

[9] Margaret Beetham, "Women and the Consumption of Print," in *Women and Literature in Britain, 1800–1900*, ed. Joanne Shattock (Cambridge: Cambridge University Press, 2001), 55–77, 63.

town's widespread dependence on gossip: "How the world would get on without gossip, I will leave the world to judge. That West Lynne could not have got on without it, and without interfering in everybody's business but its own, is enough for me."[10] While Wood shows how gossip can give individuals and social groups the power to shape communities, she does not depict gossip as a utopian form of exchange; in her fiction, it is just as unstable as the market economy.[11] Like the market economy, gossip creates identities and communities, and unfolds on multiple social planes. It is also unreliable in its movement: like money, gossip circulates, changes hands, and fluctuates in value. Though she maps its movement and potential, Wood is finally ambivalent about the effects of gossip. For faithful servants and flirtatious ladies, gossip figures as an alternative to the market economy and poses a degree of resistance to patriarchal structures. However, it is ultimately a limited refuge for Wood's characters.

On the other hand, gossip as a narrative strategy becomes a vehicle for the sensation novelist to not only survive but excel in the male-dominated literary marketplace. As I later explain, Wood incorporates gossip into her writing style and, in doing so, enters into a gossip economy with her readers. Sensation fiction was frequently linked to gossip in the 1860s and 1870s: in 1870 Alfred Austin writes that "the modern sensational novel gratifies the same petty taste that hungers for depreciatory tittle-tattle and scandalous gossip."[12] Rather than avoiding such comparisons between sensation fiction and depreciatory gossip, Wood embraced them, and cannily created alliances with her readership, made up largely of women and servants.[13] By also receiving direct financial benefit from this exchange, Wood found success in the market economy as well.

---

[10] Ellen Wood, *East Lynne* (Oxford: Oxford University Press, 2005), 311.

[11] In *Financial Speculation in Victorian Fiction: Plotting Money and the Novel* (Columbus: The Ohio State University Press, 2010), Tamara Wagner explains that in the Victorian period, "financial instability was a widespread experience and, in connecting personal losses to a broadening spectrum of interlinked economic struggles, a pervasive cultural preoccupation" (24).

[12] Alfred Austin, "Our Novels: The Sensational School," *Temple Bar* 19 (July 1870): 410–24, 424.

[13] This, at least, is what the Victorian popular press insisted. Mary Elizabeth Braddon, for instance, was credited with "making the literature of the kitchen the favourite reading of the Drawing-room" ([W. Fraser Rae], "Sensation Novelists: Miss Braddon," *North British Review* 43 [1865]: 180–204, 204). Emma Liggins and Andrew Maunder argue that Wood's "middle-brow" status was helpful to her sales but tarnished her subsequent reputation ("Introduction: Ellen Wood, Writer," 151).

I. *ST. MARTIN'S EVE* AND THE CIRCULATION OF GOSSIP

In *St. Martin's Eve,* the gossip economy is set up against legal systems that favor traditionally masculine economies such as primogeniture. After her husband dies, Charlotte St. John becomes consumed by jealousy over the disparate futures of her son and stepson: her son, Georgy, is left with little, while Benja, her stepson, inherits his father's title, estate, and social rank, and Charlotte, despite her healthy allowance, resides at Alnwick Hall simply as the guardian of the heir.[14] When Benja dies mysteriously, Charlotte's oddly guilty behavior betrays her role in the child's death. We later learn that she locked the boy in his room after he caught fire, thus ensuring her own son's inheritance, and freeing her from the guardianship of a child she despised. Yet this dramatic turn of events does not bring about happiness or financial security for the heroine-villainess. Charlotte's beloved child Georgy also dies: she then loses Alnwick and is left with "just a pittance" as her husband's money passes along the male line (310). Although she attempts to remarry his next heir, her hereditary madness can no longer be disguised, and she, like Lucy Audley before her, is tidily disposed of in a mental institution. The novel has been read as a warning against maternal indulgence and as a condemnation of patriarchal inheritance laws, readings that vary in the sympathy afforded to Charlotte.[15] But gossip, as this paper will show, is crucial both to undermining these patriarchal hierarchies and to Charlotte's eventual undoing.

Within the novel, the value of gossip to Wood's characters cannot be overstated: "For ten minutes' conversation with the serving-woman, Mrs. Darling would have given an earldom" (226); "Madame Baret said she'd give her two ears to know" (277); "Those words were worth a king's ransom" (294); "It seemed he would give half his own undoubted inheritance to set the question at rest" (367). Gossip may be worth aristocratic

---

[14] As Benja's guardian, Charlotte has an allowance of £4,000 a year, an amount that is reduced to £2,000 if she is found unfit to care for her stepson.

[15] For instance, in "Demonic Mothers: Ideologies of Bourgeois Motherhood in the Mid-Victorian Era," in *Rewriting the Victorians: Theory, History, and the Politics of Gender,* ed. Linda M. Shires (London: Routledge, 1992), 31–51, Sally Shuttleworth suggests that "Charlotte is not the kind of demonic mother who rejects her child, but one who loves to excess" (45). As I later explain, she also notes that Charlotte's instability is a result of living under a strict "patrilineal legal and economic system" (47). Lyn Pykett, too, argues that St. John's will "emphasizes the disadvantages for women of the operations of a patrilineal system of inheritance, and the extent to which they are dependent on their male relatives" ("Introduction to *St. Martin's Eve,*" xiv).

titles, large sums of money, and even body parts in this novel, but such an exaggerated price on language only ensures its continued circulation, since gossip can't actually be exchanged for ears or an earldom. Yet Wood's heroine is noticeably excluded from this system of exchange. The narrator describes Charlotte as "haughty," "quiet," and "proud" (16), and the other characters in the novel are no less forthcoming in their criticisms of her. These aspects of Charlotte's personality keep her at a distance from other women in the novel and make her an object, rather than an agent, of the gossip economy, a position that dually marginalizes her. Charlotte's isolation means that she is shut out from the market of information circulating around her and also turns gossip about her into a valuable commodity. Female readers are thus subtly encouraged to engage in such exchanges, as Wood shows what happens to women who evade them. Furthermore, Charlotte's economic viability is contingent upon gossip, and in this way Wood shows how gossip, through the formation or destruction of character, influences the marriage market and the distribution of wealth in the novel.

As soon as Charlotte moves into Alnwick Hall, as the new bride of George St. John, the servants begin gossiping about her in an effort to understand and evaluate their employer's wife. In Victorian fiction, servants were often represented as gossiping about their middle-class employers. Anthea Trodd argues that Victorians worried that servants might manipulate their "knowledge of the family for their own ends, or at least involuntarily expose and misrepresent it to the outside world."[16] Such exposure could challenge the class hierarchy of the domestic sphere and the notion of the domestic realm as safe and secure. An 1853 *North British Review* article warns, "Everything that you do, and very much that you say at home, is related in your servants' families, and by them retailed to other gossips in the neighborhood, with appropriate exaggerations, until you almost feel that you might as well live in a glass house or a whispering gallery."[17] *St. Martin's Eve* emphasizes the pervasiveness of gossip to the point that the "hushed," "noiseless" gathering of servants in the novel's opening chapter is perceived as so "unusual" that it is "unnatural" (5). A key figure in Wood's representation of the gossip economy is Benja's nursemaid, Honour, as her gossip about her mistress has a material effect on George St. John's will and Charlotte's financial future. Honour's role

---

[16] Anthea Trodd, *Domestic Crime in the Victorian Novel* (New York: St. Martin's Press, 1989), 53.

[17] Review of *Nelly Armstrong: A Story of the Day, North British Review* 20 (1853): 179–208, 183.

CHAPTER 10. MACDONALD, "'SHE'D GIVE HER TWO EARS TO KNOW'"

as a gossip is emphasized throughout the novel, and in an early, dramatic instance, she leaves her young charge alone to gossip with the other servants in the kitchen: "Never had Honour so relished a gossip more than the one she now entered on with the servants" (140). Left alone with a candle and a murderous stepmother, young Benja burns to death. While this is a rather extreme case of the price of rebellious gossip and the sympathetic connections it affords servants, Honour's gossip is largely encouraged by her employers in exchanges that are mutually beneficial.

When Charlotte enters Alnwick as George's second wife, Honour is predisposed to distrust her. Honour adores her young charge, Benja, and views Charlotte "in the light of a usurper" (30). As the narrator explains, "A new mistress suddenly brought to an established home, rarely gives pleasure to its inmates. This applies, in an especial degree, to its female servants" (30). Furthermore, Honour senses that Charlotte dislikes the future heir. When George St. John suggests to Honour that he is worried about his health, she exclaims, "If you fear that you will be taken from us, *don't* leave this child in the power of Mrs. St. John" (61). She insists that Charlotte "might become cruel to [Benja] in time" (62). George is shocked by the nurse's words but does not ignore them. Honour's advice, coupled with that of the family doctor, who similarly warns, "Don't leave Benja under your wife's charge" (64), encourages George to introduce a codicil to his will. The codicil allows George's cousin Isaac St. John to remove Charlotte from Benja's guardianship, and from Alnwick, should he deem her unfit. George also arranges for all of the servants to hear the reading of the will, which angers Charlotte, who sees this disclosure of her personal affairs as giving the servants license to gossip. She complains, "That will was read out to the servants on purpose that they might know they have it in their power to carry tales to Isaac St. John" (77). And this, in fact, is precisely what occurs after George's death when Isaac asks Honour if she knows any reason why Charlotte's guardianship should be terminated.

The nursemaid is given unusual legal and financial power as Isaac interviews her in order to ascertain Charlotte's fitness as a parent. He explains to Honour, "you were named to me by your last master as one in whom every confidence might be placed" (123). In exchange for this information, Honour ensures her status as a faithful, confidential servant. Yet Honour receives more than just symbolic remuneration: Isaac "pressed a very handsome present into her hand as he concluded, saying it was in recompense of her trouble and attention to the child" (123). Though the narrator implies that Honour offers this valuable information to Isaac out of her love for Benja and her desire to be a useful servant, she nonetheless takes the money Isaac offers. And she is aware of the power of her words. Later, when Charlotte threatens to fire her, Honour tells Benja, "If she does turn me away, I'll go every step of the way to Castle Wafer and tell all I know to [Isaac]" (138). Furthermore, by aligning herself with the future heir of Alnwick, Honour ensures her own financial and domestic security. Honour's rival nursemaid, Prance, complains that Honour "thinks she's fixed at the Hall," explaining that when George was dying, "he told my mistress that he should wish Honour to remain with Benja so long as he required a woman attendant" (74). And Honour seems to imagine a future with Benja at Alnwick, without Charlotte and her son. She tells the boy, "when you are of age, my darling, all Alnwick will be yours, and she and Master Georgy must turn out of it. . . . Nobody can live here unless you choose to let them" (139). Benja continues this fantasy, telling her that when he is master of Alnwick, "You shall be mistress, and give all the orders, and we'll have a great wall built up, so that mamma can't come near us" (416). After Benja's death, Honour abandons such fantasies, but notably, she continues to reside with the heir of George St. John's estate and fortune. That is, Honour is rewarded for her exchanges with Isaac St. John, to whom she also supplies information about Benja's death, with a position in his home. Unlike Charlotte, she ends the novel by residing comfortably with the heir of Alnwick. Thus, in addition to her exchanges with other servants in the house, Honour's exchanges with her employers provide her with both symbolic and material economic rewards.

Not all servants in Wood's novels are so forthcoming: some servants keep important information "off the market" and thus ensure their employers' privacy. Yet this withholding of information still contributes to the gossip economy. Annette Weiner emphasizes that reciprocity is only one aspect of exchange, obscuring what she terms "keeping-while-giving." For Weiner, "inalienable possessions" are kept off the market but nonetheless affect other transactions "as a possible future claim and potential source of power."[18] Gossip that is withheld from the market also figures as a "potential source of power" for others, and can likewise affect other transactions. In *East Lynne,* the maid Joyce withholds the key information that Isabel Carlyle has returned to her former household in disguise, and in *St. Martin's Eve,* the nursemaid Prance withholds information that implicates Charlotte in Benja's murder. Prance, who protects Charlotte and Mrs. Darling with her silence, "gratefully liked" them because Mrs. Darling was

---

[18] Annette Weiner, *Inalienable Possessions: The Paradox of Keeping-While-Giving* (Berkeley: University of California Press, 1992), 10.

CHAPTER 10. MACDONALD, "'SHE'D GIVE HER TWO EARS TO KNOW'"

kind to her (22). Her silence can be read, then, as a kind of repayment. Because Prance keeps silent, Charlotte's culpability takes much longer to unfold; yet, in turn, the mystery surrounding the murder and Charlotte's possible role in it makes gossip about her a valued commodity. Prance's silence allows for her mistress's (temporary) domestic security and also secures her own position. Withheld gossip is ultimately different from an inalienable possession, however, since it is always potentially alienable.

In addition to servants, bourgeois women drive the gossip economy, and one of the novel's most inveterate gossips is Charlotte's youngest half-sister, Rose. The narrator explains that Charlotte's mother, Mrs. Darling, exhibits a marked preference for Charlotte, her first child. Mrs. Darling, we later learn, worries about Charlotte's sanity, and so indulges Charlotte's bold behavior. Rose freely admits to Frederick St. John, Isaac's brother, that she does not regard her sister "with any great degree of affection" (185). "If you only knew how mamma has made us bend to Charlotte and her imperious will all our lives, you'd not wonder at me," she insists (186). More than once, Rose's dislike of her sister encourages her to gossip about Charlotte. In an instance in which gossip circulates across class and even national boundaries, Rose encounters a woman recently employed as Charlotte's nurse and insists that she relate her experiences. Mrs. Brayford is happy to oblige, and she explains that Charlotte, overwhelmed by visions of Benja's ghost, collapsed in a hotel in France. Mrs. Brayford insists, "She was mad that night, Miss Darling, as anybody ever was" (312).

Wood shows how gossip circulates in the novel as, soon after, Rose retails the story to Frederick St. John. Rose "disclosed to Mr. St. John all she had heard from Nurse Brayford. It was lamentably imprudent of her, without doubt; but she meant no harm" (344). The narrative seems to exceed the bounds placed by the implied author here, as Rose is no doubt aware that her comments may "harm" her sister's character. In this instance, Rose benefits from a flirtation with Frederick and from insulting her proud sister. Following Rose's imprudence, the story becomes implanted in Frederick's mind, and the possibility of a madwoman marrying his brother haunts him, just as Honour's advice worries George. And just as that earlier gossip diminished Charlotte's authority over her sons' inheritance, in this instance gossip has the power to devalue Charlotte in the marriage market. Again like George, however, Frederick requires further (male, medical) evidence to validate a woman's claims. Fearing that Charlotte hopes to marry Isaac, Frederick attempts to warn his older brother of Charlotte's instability. Yet he is challenged by Isaac, who asks "what grounds you have for saying this" (376). The narrator relates, "Here was Frederick's dilemma:

the stumbling block he had foreseen from the first, if he spoke to Isaac. What grounds had he? None. The reasons that seemed weighty enough in his own mind, were as nothing when spoken of; and it suddenly struck him that he was not justified in repeating the gossip of a careless girl like Rose" (376). Upper-class men can receive and benefit from gossip but they cannot retail it in the same manner as women. Frederick calls in the family doctor, Mr. Pym, who confirms, in writing, that Charlotte's father "had died *mad*" (383). Though this is not in fact evidence that Charlotte herself is mad, it proves that madness runs within her family. So while Frederick benefits from the gossip economy, having received information that has travelled from Mrs. Brayford to Rose, he must recontextualize Charlotte's madness as a medical likelihood in order for it to have value in his own exchange. In a novel where inheritance, of both the financial and blood variety, cannot be underestimated, this taint of madness devalues Charlotte as a marriageable woman.[19] Through the gossip he gains from these women, Frederick works to thwart Charlotte's *second* attempt to gain access to her husband's fortune. Charlotte is again undone by the gossip economy.

Rose, however, is rewarded for her efforts negotiating and exchanging within the gossip economy: her troublesome sister is locked away, and she marries a man who, she says, "heaps such luxuries upon me" (424). Charlotte, the transgressive female figure whose history is exchanged among many characters, is made an object rather than agent of this gossip economy by her silence and solitude. Moreover, her madness, the most frequent topic of gossip in the novel, is exacerbated by her economic marginalization. Though Charlotte's financial and social value increase upon marriage, she is left vulnerable to patrilineal economic systems after her husband dies. Further, as a guest in someone else's home, she is peculiarly open to scrutiny and, consequently, to gossip—making her vulnerable within *both* economies. Sally Shuttleworth suggests that Charlotte's mental instability is intensified by "the very obvious injustices of a patriarchal legal and economic system which insistently disinherits women, a fact which suggests justifiable rage rather than madness as the cause of her behaviour."[20] Wood seems intent on establishing Charlotte's madness, but Shuttleworth

---

[19] The novel's eugenic thread implies that those who are physically or mentally unfit should not marry or have children. Frederick St. John narrowly misses marrying a woman who dies after bursting a blood vessel. He later muses that it is all for the best, since had "she lived to bear him children" she likely would have "entail[ed] upon them her fragility of constitution" (346). And he later worries about Isaac marrying Charlotte "with that possibility of taint in her blood" (352).

[20] Sally Shuttleworth, "Demonic Mothers," 47.

is certainly right to suggest that the novel is critical of women's economic dependence upon men. Here, the gossip economy offers no refuge from traditionally masculine economies, and Wood shows how women can just as easily be exposed as protected by its circulation.

Charlotte's example shows that while gossip has potentially positive outcomes (social status, community regulation, domestic security), gossip could also be alienating or malevolent, since it was not—and is not—a strictly regulated economy: gossip constantly moves outward from its source. For women who exhibit signs of madness or who attempt to aggressively surmount class boundaries in the manner of the sensation heroine, gossip can drive one's "price" down. Wood portrays these contradictory aspects of the gossip economy in *St. Martin's Eve,* showing how for faithful servants and select groups of women, the exchange of gossip is largely constructive and valuable, while for the transgressive sensational heroine, whose story is unwittingly traded, the ramifications of the gossip economy are just as damaging as her exclusion from patrilineal economic and legal systems. Thus, while the gossip economy certainly has the potential to empower women by allowing them to "attain (or retain) a social identity within the uncertainties of a capitalist economy," its instability mimics the market economy.[21] Wood's depiction of the circulation of gossip, then, emphasizes women's vulnerability even as it offers a way to challenge the forces that produce this vulnerability.

II. GOSSIP AS NARRATIVE STRATEGY

Wood asks the reader to sympathize with her misguided heroine. She explains that Charlotte "desperately intended to do right: but passions and prejudices are strong, unusually strong they were in her; and her mind was ill-regulated" (120). The *Saturday Review* critic notes his surprise that Wood "stands by her heroine" as she "speaks of her in terms of pity, and even modified approval."[22] Indeed, though Wood's narrator can be understood to be gossiping about Charlotte much like the women and servants in the novel, she does so with the different aim to "do her justice" (119). The narrator's voice, by competing with others in the novel, enters into and broadens their gossip economy. As this final section will show, gossip

---

[21] Deborah Wynne, "'See what a Big Wide Bed it is!': Mrs Henry Wood and the Philistine Imagination," in *Feminist Readings of Victorian Popular Texts: Divergent Femininities,* ed. Emma Liggins and Daniel Duffy (Aldershot: Ashgate, 2001), 89–107, 105.

[22] Review of *St. Martin's Eve, Saturday Review,* 31 March 1866, 387–88, 387.

becomes not only the currency of fictional characters but an overarching narrative device for Wood. Patricia Spacks argues that the activity of gossip is similar to the exchange between narrator and reader "since what reader and narrator share is a set of responses to the private doings of richly imagined individuals."[23] Similarities between reading novels and listening to gossip came to the fore with the rise of sensation fiction, a genre devoted to the exposure of personal secrets. In 1860 critic Francis Palgrave complained that novels were becoming indistinguishable from "living gossip": "People . . . go to books for something almost similar to what they find in social conversation. Reading tends to become only another kind of gossip."[24] The denigration of gossip and its comparison to high-selling popular fiction also has an economic element. Sensation fiction, as the term was understood in the 1860s, had nearly as much to do with popular success and cheap formats as with an identifiable style. In his 1863 review "Sensation Novels," H. L. Mansel complains, "A commercial atmosphere floats around works of this class, redolent of the manufactory and the shop."[25] Therefore, sensation fiction was dangerous to the reading public not only because it mimicked "living gossip" but because these novels did not hide their status as commodities.

Wood, however, challenged gossip's pejorative associations in crafting her narrative voice and, by doing so, also cannily addressed the problem of sensation's commodity status. Though her informal style left her open to attacks, it was part of a strategy that allowed Wood to cultivate her largely female audience and obscure her own financial interests by emphasizing the alternative value of the feminine gossip economy. In *St. Martin's Eve,* the narrator's frequent addresses to the reader, who is called "you," make the reader a recipient of gossip as much as an audience for literature, obligating the reader to take an active part in deciphering the narrative.[26]

---

[23] Patricia Spacks, *Gossip* (Chicago: University of Chicago Press, 1986), 22.

[24] Francis Palgrave, "On Readers in 1760 and 1860," *Macmillan's Magazine* 1 (1860): 487–89, 488.

[25] [H. L. Mansel], "Sensation Novels," *Quarterly Review,* April 1863, 481–514, 495–96. In *The Sensation Novel: From* The Woman in White *to* The Moonstone (Plymouth: Northcote House, 1994), Lyn Pykett notes that many "early commentators on the genre focused on it as a commodity in an increasingly commercialized literary marketplace" (8).

[26] Wood's narrator bears similarities to what Robyn Warhol has termed the "engaging narrator," a narrator who frequently addresses "you": "Writing to inspire belief in the situations their novels describe—and admittedly hoping to move actual readers to sympathize with real-life slaves, workers, or ordinary middle-class people—these novelists [Elizabeth Gaskell, Harriet Beecher Stowe, and George Eliot] used engaging narrators to encourage actual readers to identify with the 'you' in the texts" ("Toward a Theory of the Engaging Narrator: Earnest Interventions in Gaskell, Stowe, and Eliot," *PMLA* 101 [1986]: 811–18, 812). Warhol identifies in these authors a social element that is not central to Wood's novels, however.

Wood was criticized by contemporary reviewers for these chatty, personal addresses. In an 1863 review of Wood's *Verner's Pride,* a critic for *Littell's Living Age* complains, "An offensive seizing of the reader by the button for a jerk of personal address is part of the bad taste of the writer: We have such sentences as, 'The old study that you have seen before.' 'You have now seen him do so once again [etc., etc.].'"[27] Wood continued her gossipy tone in *St. Martin's Eve,* with statements such as "It was as well to mention this: you will see why, later" (32), and "*You* have met him before, reader, but Adeline had not" (183), and she even references her novel from the year before, *Mildred Arkell* (1865), when she says, "You have heard of these Carrs before, in a recent work" (198). The *Saturday Review* picked up on Wood's familiar style as well, noting that she takes the reader "in the most affable manner into her confidence, . . . telling him what is coming next, or wondering whether he will recognise so and so."[28] In these instances, Wood serves as a kind of "confidential" informant to her female readership, just as Honour does for Isaac.

In exchange for her stories, Wood not only receives material, financial benefits but demands an engaged readership. Kate Flint argues that while male sensation writers more often craft narrators that withhold information from the reader in attempts to stage suspense, female sensation novelists frequently "invite their readers to join in a process which involves the active construction of meaning, rather than its revelation."[29] In particular, Wood utilizes the positive aspects of gossip in her attempt to create a community of readers, who can engage with her characters' stories. She creates this community precisely through their shared possession of gossip: "Let *us* do her justice!" she exclaims when explaining Charlotte's motivations (119, my emphasis). Further, Wood implies through the fictional examples of characters such as Honour, Rose, and Charlotte that entering the gossip economy creates the potential for future exchanges, both symbolic and material. Her assumption that loyal readers have "heard of these Carrs before, in a recent work" makes sense in light of this communal construct (198); like Charlotte's mother, those readers might be expected to "give . . . an earldom" (or at least a few shillings) to hear more.[30]

---

[27] Review of *Verner's Pride, Littell's Living Age,* 18 April 1863, 99–103. Reprinted in *Varieties of Women's Sensation Fiction: 1855–1890,* 1: 63.

[28] Review of *St. Martin's Eve,* 388.

[29] Kate Flint, *The Woman Reader, 1837–1914* (Oxford: Clarendon Press, 1993), 292.

[30] *St. Martin's Eve* was first published as a three-volume novel. The standard price for each volume was ten shillings and sixpence (10/6d), or 31/6d for the entire set. This was beyond what most people could afford to spend on a novel, hence the monopoly of circulating libraries such as Charles Edward Mudie's. When Mudie set up shop in London, he charged only

Wood's supposed "bad taste" is due to her overt acknowledgment of fiction's close relationship to gossip, which was connected primarily to the talk of women and servants. Yet Wood's critical censure was paired with professional and financial success. While characters such as Honour and Rose use the gossip economy for symbolic and material economic benefits, they nonetheless remain under men's financial control, Honour as Isaac's servant and Rose as wife to Baron de la Chasse. As an author, however, Wood not only engaged with the gossip economy, trading and possessing other people's stories: she also profited from the market economy. In his biography of his mother, Charles Wood relates that Wood wrote short stories for ten years anonymously and without remuneration, until she finally "declared her unwillingness to continue these contributions month after month and year after year without acknowledgement."[31] As she came to insist on pay, however, she also cultivated a gossip style that implicitly separated her work from the marketplace, so that it appeared to be merely casual, unprofessional talk between women. Yet Wood's performance of gossip was strategic and came to bear on her position in the marketplace. Jennifer Phegley argues that Wood was a successful author, in part, because she cultivated a persona of herself as an amateur: she presented herself as a hobbyist and stressed her roles as a proper wife and mother, publishing under the name Mrs. Henry Wood.[32] Wood thus adopted a strategy that resulted in a paradoxical outcome: by playing the role of gossipy, feminine amateur, she actually achieved great financial, professional success. Her narrative voice calls attention to the exchanges of the gossip economy within the novel, suggests that this system can benefit women, and shows that she used this alternative economy to further her own success in the marketplace. Though the sensational heroine of *St. Martin's Eve* is denied the benefits of the gossip economy and the marketplace, the sensation novelist was privy to the satisfying exchanges of both.

---

one guinea for a year's subscription (Richard D. Altick, *The English Common Reader* [Chicago: University of Chicago Press, 1957], 295).

[31] Charles Wood, *Memorials of Mrs. Henry Wood* (London: Richard Bentley & Son, 1894), 253.

[32] Jennifer Phegley, "Domesticating the Sensation Novelist: Ellen Price Wood as Author and Editor of the *Argosy Magazine*," *Victorian Periodicals Review* 38.2 (2005): 180–98, 181.

CHAPTER 11

Charlotte Riddell

NOVELIST OF "THE CITY"

NANCY HENRY

> It would scarcely be too much to say that the hero of the story is the Bankruptcy Act of 1869, and the heroine, winding up an estate by liquidation.
>
> —Review of Charlotte Riddell's *Mortomley's Estate* (1874)[1]

Canonical works of Victorian literature are critical of greed, corruption, and dishonesty in the Victorian business and financial world. Exposing these ills of capitalism is a hallmark of Victorian realist novels in particular, so that even while they uphold a middle-class, Protestant work ethic, they maintain a tone of disapprobation when describing or referring to the mysterious workings of the credit economy generally and financial markets in particular. The last thing W. M. Thackeray, Charles Dickens, or Anthony Trollope, for example, intended their fiction to do was explain how aspects of financial markets or particular credit instruments functioned. These authors can seem uneasy in even appearing to possess such knowledge.

The distaste among literary authors for the unliterary world of "the City"—the square mile of London that was the financial heart of Great

---

[1] Review of *Mortomley's Estate*, *Saturday Review*, 10 October 1874, 481.

Britain and its empire—has a history that might be written in many ways. In *Genres of the Credit Economy* (2008), Mary Poovey argues that economic writing and literary writing were not originally distinct genres but rather became so in the nineteenth century through a strenuous effort on the part of poets, novelists, and critics to distinguish what they wrote from writing intended to convey information about the monetary system, such as financial journalism or works of economic theory.[2] This policing of literary boundaries is particularly evident in reviews of novels by the Irish immigrant to London Charlotte Eliza Lawson Cowan Riddell (1832–1906). Her work was popular from the 1860s to the 1880s, but her success faded in the 1890s, and she remains largely forgotten.[3]

Riddell not only asserts the fundamental honesty of businessmen and women but, in telling their stories, self-consciously resists some of the features that critics have traditionally valued as literary. Her novels are full of detailed commercial transactions, "City" slang, and even harangues by the narrator about specific financial legislation. She recognized the impact on individual lives of the Limited Liability and Joint Stock Companies Acts (1855–56) and the Bankruptcy and Debtors Acts (1869), probably because they affected her through her husband (an inventor and small businessman), who declared bankruptcy in 1871.[4] She also believed that the successful pursuit of business was incompatible with the type of

---

[2] Mary Poovey, *Genres of the Credit Economy: Mediating Value in Eighteenth- and Nineteenth-Century Britain* (Chicago: University of Chicago Press, 2008).

[3] Patricia Srebrnik has written particularly about Riddell's critical reception and the decline of her reputation. See Patricia Thomas Srebrnik, "Mrs. Riddell and the Reviewers: A Case Study in Victorian Popular Fiction," *Women's Studies* 23.1 (1994): 69–84. For other criticism on various aspects of Riddell's life and works, see John Reed, "A Friend to Mammon: Speculation in Victorian Literature," *Victorian Studies* 27 (1984): 179–202; Margaret Kelleher, "Charlotte Riddell's *A Struggle for Fame*: The Field of Women's Literary Production," *Colby Quarterly* 36.2 (June 2000): 116–31; Benjamin F. Fisher, "Mrs. J. H. Riddell and Late Victorian Literary Gothicism," in *In Memory of Richard B. Klein: Essays in Contemporary Philology*, Romance Monographs No. S-2 (Jackson: University of Mississippi Press, 2005); Linda H. Peterson, *Becoming a Woman of Letters: Myths of Authorship and Facts of the Victorian Market* (Princeton, NJ: Princeton University Press, 2009); Ranald C. Michie, *Guilty Money: The City of London in Victorian and Edwardian Culture, 1815–1914* (London: Pickering and Chatto, 2009); Tamara S. Wagner, *Financial Speculation in Victorian Fiction: Plotting Money and the Novel Genre, 1815–1901* (Columbus: The Ohio State University Press, 2010); Silvana Colella, "The Worth of Commerce: Charlotte Riddell's City Novels," *Rivista di Studi Vittoriani* 28–29 (2009–10): 25–44, and "'Glorious uncertainty': Business and Adultery in Charlotte Riddell's *Too Much Alone*," *Romanticism and Victorianism on the Net* 59–60 (2011).

[4] Riddell strove to free them from the nemesis of bankruptcy through her writing, an experience reflected in *Mortomley's Estate*. On bankruptcy in Victorian fiction, see Barbara Weiss, *The Hell of the English: Bankruptcy and the Victorian Novel* (Lewisburg, PA: Bucknell University Press, 1986).

CHAPTER 11. HENRY, "CHARLOTTE RIDDELL"

introspection that seemed to make fictional characters literary. To her, the honest, capitalist pursuit of wealth held unrecognized dramatic interest and demanded suitably realist narrative strategies. Despite the insights provided by her portraits of "City" life into the business subculture of Victorian London, a legacy of hostility to pro-capitalist writing—traceable to Victorian literary reviews—may account for the continued neglect of her financial novels.

Riddell's novels contain their share of romance and melodrama along with their evocative descriptions of the City, patient accounts of financial transactions, and occasionally passionate opinions about the shortcomings of both contemporary novelists and contemporary laws. While all realist novels incorporate multiple discourses, Riddell's City novels are unique hybrids of financial and literary writing. They intersect and overlap particularly with financial journalism, which was using different generic conventions to make arguments about representing financial life that were similar to Riddell's. Reviewers picked up on this hybridity by invoking financial journalism, unfavorably, to describe her novels. A reviewer of *The Senior Partner* (1882) observed that Riddell

> talks of bills, paper, and discount in a way which, for all we can see, would not discredit the City editor of *The Times* . . . we scarcely know whether, as a general rule, her novels should be reviewed in the columns that are set apart for literature, or whether they would not more fitly receive a notice side by side with the works on foreign exchanges or the currency.[5]

Another reviewer responded similarly when objecting to the appearance of the 1869 Bankruptcy Law in *Mortomley's Estate* (1874), observing,

> it is rather the services of an attorney than a literary critic that are required to draw up a brief statement or review of her case. . . . If ever the Merchant Shipping Act gets through, then we shall expect a romantic treatise on it equaling in length and in dullness *Mortomley's Estate*.[6]

Despite the sarcastic tone, the critique is serious in its implication that Riddell has violated genre boundaries, which it was the duty of literary critics (whose professional "services" are compared to those of a lawyer) to uphold. Such efforts to keep financial and literary works separate were not wholly

---

[5] Review of *The Senior Partner*, Saturday Review, 25 March 1882, 375.
[6] Review of *Mortomley's Estate*, Saturday Review, 10 October 1874, 481.

successful, and some critics applauded her innovations. Anne Thackeray (later Ritchie), for example, wrote in an 1865 review: "It seems strange as one thinks of it that before these books came out no one ever thought of writing about city life."[7]

Financial journalists had already recognized the gap in literary representations of the financial world and complained about the disproportionate attention paid to financial fraud and scandal in Victorian novels. In 1858 Walter Bagehot, whose *National Review* was in the forefront of magazines that combined articles on financial and literary topics, argued:

> The most remarkable deficiency in modern fiction is its omission of the business of life.... In most novels money *grows*. You have no idea of the toil, the patience, and the wearing anxiety by which men of action provide for the day, and lay up for the future, and support those that are given into their care.[8]

Riddell appeared on the scene in the 1850s as if to answer this call to represent "men of action." In doing so, she contributed to the ascendance of an inclusive realist aesthetic that makes business and finance central and essential to the nation's literature.

In her most successful novel, *George Geith of Fen Court* (1864), she sought to show "what trade really is; what an excitement, what a pain, what a struggle, and when honestly and honourably carried out, what a glory too" (97). In telling the story of a man who escapes a bad marriage by moving to London and becoming a City accountant and who then falls in love with the daughter of an aristocratic client who has lost all of his money by speculating in Welsh mines, she shows the potential of capitalism both to redeem and to ruin individuals. Her narrator argues that business was not interesting to outsiders "because business has never yet learnt to be self-conscious,—because it is in its very nature to work rather than to think, to push forward to the goal rather than to analyze the reasons which induce it to push forward at all" (98). City men seemed to lack the psychological complexity that, by the 1860s, might be assumed to make the characters in realist novels interesting. The narrator further contends that a tradesman "speaks of markets, of failures, of losses, or successes; but he cannot, or will not, reveal how these things affected his own feelings and thoughts" (98). This is one way that she resists literary conventions and the

---

[7] Anne Thackeray, "Heroines and their Grandmothers," *Cornhill Magazine,* May 1865, 634.
[8] Walter Bagehot, *The Collected Works of Walter Bagehot,* Vol. 2, ed. Norman St. John-Stevas. Cambridge, MA: Harvard University Press, 1965: 137.

CHAPTER 11. HENRY, "CHARLOTTE RIDDELL"

Romantic legacy of interiority that we now call psychological realism. Her narrator complains directly about other novelists:

> The woes of governesses are drugs in the markets. The trials of sensitive men who cannot make sixpence a year, have been repeated till even young ladies are weary of making heroes of them. . . . It is only trade, only that which is the backbone of England, only that which furnishes heiresses for younger sons; . . . which can find no writer worthy of it. (144–45)

She sought to become a writer worthy of trade and all the aspects of credit and capital that rested on that "backbone of England."

Like Bagehot, Riddell viewed men of business as men of action and turned lack of introspection into a virtue. She seemed to see her role as speaking for men, complicating the intersections of business and gender both within her novels and in the history of their reception. She brought to her representations the sensibility of a woman who was more aware of the gendered nature of the business and financial world than male journalists. Further, in her fiction she could test boundaries by imagining the consequences of a woman pursuing a business career.

I. WOMEN AND GENDER

> "She had sense enough to know it is impossible for any one to be man and woman too."
>
> —Charlotte Riddell, *Austin Friars* (1870)[9]

It is important to remember that Riddell was popular. Patricia Srebrnik calls her "one of the best-known and most widely discussed novelists of the time" (70), and Margaret Kelleher documents the relatively successful sales of her novels. In 1931 the critic S. M. Ellis devoted a chapter of his book *Wilkie Collins, Le Fanu and Others* to her, reflecting on her popularity and seeking an explanation for it.[10] He observed that she was equipped specially to represent the "hectic excitements of business affairs, stocks and shares, and Company promoting" by her "personal liking for men and a sympathetic understanding of the masculine mind" (279). Riddell herself

---

[9] Charlotte Riddell, *Austin Friars* (London: Hutchinson and Co., 1870), 52.
[10] S. M. Ellis, *Wilkie Collins, Le Fanu and Others* (Freeport, NY: Books for Libraries Press, 1968).

explained in an 1890 interview in the *Pall Mall Gazette:* "I understand men well, I have much in sympathy with them, and I always find them easier to describe than women."[11] This male-identification complicates Riddell's position within Victorian literary and financial cultures. It reveals her distinctive self-consciousness about gender roles, which she defied, seemingly not out of political conviction, but rather because of a personal inclination and sympathy. She surprised critics by understanding men and by knowing and writing about finance, a typically masculine form of knowledge.

In *Austin Friars* (1870), her heroine Yorke Friars contemplates running her own business. The narrator comments:

> She had sense enough to know it is impossible for any one to be man and woman too; that is to say, she understood if a woman strayed either by choice or necessity into a man's position, she could not expect to be treated while there with that considerate tenderness which is due to those who keep themselves fenced in by every social propriety and protection. (52)

Like a dog or sheep, a woman "strays" into a "man's position." It is the social gender role, not the sex of the person, that matters most, and there is bitterness in the notion that "considerate tenderness" is "due" only to those who "keep themselves fenced in." Her novels protest the defeminizing effect that entering the financial sphere had on social perceptions of women.

Riddell did not choose to keep herself fenced in, and she used a variety of strategies to succeed in the literary marketplace, including writing about the trials of a female author trying to make it in the London literary world as a subplot in *George Geith,* and later as the primary plot in *A Struggle for Fame* (1883).[12] Early in her career, she published under pseudonyms, including six novels as F. G. Trafford. She also used other gender-ambiguous names such as T. C. Newby, R. V. Sparling, and Rainey Hawthorn.[13] A reviewer of *City and Suburb* (1861) wrote that the novel included material that "seems to belong exclusively to men, with business details, a dabbling with practical scenes, railways, inventions, patents, and so forth, all treated in a masculine tone" (356). The spotting of apparent contradictions between the author's knowledge of City matters and other aspects of her writing was common before *George Geith* established her authorial identity and her

---

[11] Raymond Blathwayt, "Lady Novelists: A Chat with Mrs. J. H. Riddell," *Pall Mall Gazette,* 18 February 1890, 3.

[12] *A Struggle for Fame* also portrays a female author taken by critics to be a man. See Peterson, *Becoming a Woman of Letters,* 151.

[13] Srebrnik, 74.

literary fame. Reviewers of *Too Much Alone* (1860) and *City and Suburb* in the early 1860s were writing in the wake of the revelation that "George Eliot" was Marian Evans, the woman who lived with the married George Henry Lewes and called herself Mrs. Lewes. As a writer in London, Riddell, as well as her critics, would have been familiar with the controversy over the authorship of *Scenes of Clerical Life* (1858) and *Adam Bede* (1859) that was unfolding throughout 1859 and that ultimately "outed" Marian Evans as George Eliot. The case of George Eliot, following on the earlier example of Charlotte Brontë, led critics to discuss the gendered nature of writing. It was a question of the moment whether one could tell a female from a male author through voice, implied experience, and subject matter. We do not know why Riddell used pseudonyms, but we can speculate that it was at least partly an attempt to have her work taken seriously.

Even after she began publishing under the name Mrs. J. H. Riddell, questions of gender persisted in ways that seem unique to her fiction because of its financial content. Reviewing *The Race for Wealth* (1866) in the *Westminster Review,* J. R. Wise ventured the observation that, "Next to George Eliot, though at a very long distance, we are inclined to put Mrs. Trafford, as we suppose we must call her, for a certain masculine power."[14] A reviewer of *Austin Friars* commented grudgingly that the "facility with which she handles commercial slang is remarkable in a lady."[15] (748). Commercial experience, language, and knowledge all seemed to be gendered male to Riddell's reviewers, and she consistently frustrated their expectations. A reviewer in *Harper's Magazine* wrote of *A Life's Assize* (1871): "Though written by a lady (Mrs J. H. Riddell), it is very far from being a lady's novel—is, in fact, peculiarly not a lady's novel."[16]

Further overturning expectations of ladies' novels, Riddell's works are striking for the passion they bring to financial matters. In *The Race for Wealth,* the narrator asserts: "No person who has not studied the statistics of companies can have the faintest idea of the deluge which came upon the earth for its wickedness when once Parliament opened the sluice-gates by doing away with Unlimited Responsibility" (139–40). One must study the "statistics" in order to know what a "deluge" came upon the earth for its "wickedness" because of a specific act of Parliament. Along these lines, Riddell criticized writers who "jeer at business and treat with contempt that which is holy in God's sight," seeing business instead as holy and its representation as an act of faith (*George Geith,* 145).

---

[14] Review of *The Race for Wealth, Westminster Review,* 1 October 1866, 526.
[15] Review of *Austin Friars, Saturday Review,* 4 June 1870, 758.
[16] Review of *A Life's Assize, Harper's Magazine,* June 1871, 139.

This unusual mixing of the factual and mythic registers lends emotion to her financial novels that was noticed by critics, as when John Ashcraft Noble, reviewing *Mitre Court* (1885) in the *Academy,* referred to her "fearful and wonderful knowledge of matters financial."[17] Years after the initial legislation was passed, she was still denouncing limited liability, which had led businessmen to take irresponsible risks and resulted in so many company failures.[18] In *The Senior Partner,* she wrote that "while one section of society was blessing the Act, another was anathematizing the day they trusted their good money to its tender mercies" (434). Her invectives led a reviewer to observe that limited liability "fills her mind in much the same way as the Pope of Rome used to fill the minds of anxious Protestants."[19] It is sometimes unclear whether reviewers objected more to her masculine knowledge of financial language and facts or to the emotional (therefore feminine) awe with which financial matters affected her. But even if her reviewers and her heroines thought it impossible for anyone to be "man and woman too," Riddell's writing draws simultaneously on her knowledge of feeling and finance to resist these limitations.

II. AUSTIN FRIARS

> "Has it never struck you as being a little singular that there should be an Austin Friars a place and an Austin Friars a man?"
>
> —Charlotte Riddell, *Austin Friars* (1870), 361

The title *Austin Friars* would seem to refer to the name of that novel's protagonist, Austin Friars. But Austin Friars is no hero. He is a social-climbing bounder, petty swindler, and forger. So it is tempting to think that the title refers to the courtyard in the City of London where he was left on a doorstep and after which he was named—Austin Friars being a shortened name for the Friars of the order of Augustine which once inhabited the space. The unusual blending of names between place and person may be an ironic twist on the aristocratic naming of a character after his "seat," the theme of the fallen aristocracy being central to many of Riddell's novels.

---

[17] James Ashcroft Noble, Review of *Mitre Court, The Academy,* 5 December 1885, 371–72.

[18] On limited liability, see Donna Loftus, "Limited Liability, Market Democracy, and the Social Organization of Production in Mid-Nineteenth Century Britain," in *Victorian Investments: New Perspectives on Finance and Culture,* ed. Nancy Henry and Cannon Schmitt (Bloomington: Indiana University Press, 2009), 79–97.

[19] Review of *The Senior Partner, Saturday Review,* 25 March 1882, 375.

CHAPTER 11. HENRY, "CHARLOTTE RIDDELL"

To complicate matters further, the main City location in the novel is not Austin Friars but Scott's Yard, of which the narrator says on the first page: "Concerning who Scott may have been, and why he was considered worthy of having a yard named after him, not merely general but local history is silent" (1). And so Riddell plays with names, origins, and identities (as she did with her pseudonyms), destabilizing them in a way that is consistent with her project of representing the real social changes in Great Britain as they are reflected in that part of London where a family name means less than one's ability to succeed in business. Upon his engagement, Austin is disillusioned by learning that the man he thought was his father, the wealthy businessman Mr. Collis, is in fact merely his mother's half-brother and that his real father was a servant. He therefore cannot expect to inherit the money he counted on, having no legal claim to it. Collis, who does not like Austin, somewhat ironically reassures him about Londoners: "Provided a man be wealthy, I do not imagine they care particularly who his father may have been, or whether indeed he ever had one" (73).

As if to reinforce the importance of place and experience over name and birth, Riddell begins *Austin Friars* by linking her own novels through continuity of place, asking her readers "who have walked with me ere now over so many and many a mile of the city pavements, to forget about the Cannon Street Terminus, and go back with me in spirit to the time when Scott's Yard was as quiet as Laurence Pountney Lane and Fen Court still are" (2). Ellis notes that Riddell once lived in Scott's Court (destroyed by the construction of the Cannon Street Station in 1866), so that in addition to referring to her own past works, she incorporates a biographical dimension in her invocation of City places.[20] This emphasis on place in an age of displacement and migration reinforces the argument made in all her City novels that the geographical center of Britain's financial empire is worthy of treatment in fiction.

The real hero of the novel is Austin's mistress, Yorke Friars, who, like George Geith, has escaped from marriage, privilege, and the country by taking on a new identity in the City. The portrait of her relationship with Austin is daring for its sexual frankness. Yorke lives with Austin in a house in Scott's Yard. She is the silent partner in the (unspecified) business to which he gives his name and which his actions and decisions have made unprofitable. She masquerades as the widow of his (fictional) brother; hence she has assumed the name Friars. They are lovers who cannot marry because Yorke's older, wealthy husband, Mr. Forde, from whom she ran

---

[20] Ellis, 274.

away on her wedding day, is still alive, though he knows nothing of her whereabouts or her incognito.

When the novel opens, we find Yorke a doting mistress who learns that Austin has been secretly wooing the daughter of a wealthy but honest City man, Alexander Monteith, and has proposed to the young heiress, Mary Monteith, in order to advance himself and become the father's business partner. Though Austin proposes that they continue as lovers, arguing that his advancement will benefit them both, Yorke determines to leave him and to continue running their small business. Justifying her decision to remain a businesswoman, Yorke asks: "What is to prevent the business being carried on by Y. Friars as well as it was by A. Friars?" (44). As an author who employed pseudonyms and ultimately adopted her husband's initials as part of her authorial identity, Riddell implicitly compares writing novels to running a business, recalling her assertion in *City and Suburb* that "the grand difference between the author and the shop-keeper, is but the power of expression" (3). Austin falsely told Yorke that he was related to the "Hertfordshire Friars," and she only belatedly learns that Austin Friars, like Oliver Twist, is a fictional name bestowed on a foundling. She, however, keeps the name "Mrs. Friars" in preference to her maiden name (Haddon) or married name (Forde). The name Friars adds another layer to the complexities of Yorke's identity. Mrs. Friars is a purely fictional identity meant to cover an adulterous relationship. "Friars" is doubly outside the law, being a name arbitrarily given to Austin and inaccessible to Yorke because she could not marry him. The gender ambiguity of the name "Yorke," furthermore, allows her to turn Yorke Friars (or Y. Friars) into a professional identity associated with her business.

With the help of Austin's former clerk, Luke Ross (who is also in love with her), Yorke carries on the business. When she demands that Austin return her initial £1,000 investment in the business, she sets up a complex chain of events involving bills, discounts, and dishonored assurances that are described in the sort of detail that earned the amazement of critics. Austin's bad behavior runs counter to what Riddell views as the more usual, honest business practices in the City. In Austin she creates a villainous financial swindler comparable to characters such as George Vavasor in Trollope's *Can You Forgive Her* (1864–65) or Ferdinand Lopez in *The Prime Minister* (1876).[21] Significantly, even before he becomes corrupt, Austin is a bad businessman whose initial partnership in business with

---

[21] On the home-grown, English financial swindler in Victorian fiction, see Wagner, *Financial Speculation in Victorian Fiction*.

CHAPTER 11. HENRY, "CHARLOTTE RIDDELL"

Yorke left her to do most of the serious work. He is contrasted both to her and to the three honest businessmen, Luke Ross, Mr. Monteith, and Mr. Collis, who ultimately save Austin from himself and from prosecution for his misdeeds when they collaborate to help him leave the country.

In *Austin Friars,* as she had in all her previous City novels, Riddell enhances her story by insisting on the inextricability of everyday financial details from other aspects of common life. In a chapter called "Those Little Bills," Riddell writes:

> This story does not profess to be other than a record of the common everyday life, wherein, let the tragedy of a man's existence be piled ever so high one hour, he has the next to come down to the ordinary considerations . . . has to devote himself the moment after leaving [his lover] to the arrangement of that little bill due to-morrow . . . in short to thoughts the reverse of sentimental, having relation merely to pounds, shillings, and pence, and all the other prosaic matters which, with love, hate, death, joy, sorrow, meeting, parting, quarrelling, reconciling, go to make up the sum total of our experience in this work-a-day world. (202)

We feel for Riddell's quiet hero, Luke Ross, who takes on Yorke's cares as she battles with the consequences of Austin's transgressions and repeated calls on her to honor their love by helping him out of financial difficulties. Riddell is unflinching in her acknowledgment that Luke, born into vulgar, lower-middle-class respectability and burdened by a family of shallow, carping women, never had a higher ideal to work toward. His attempts to succeed financially are repeatedly frustrated by economic circumstances beyond his control, but he is ennobled by his love for Yorke (who still loves and enables the worthless Austin).

Again, Riddell mixes the details of everyday financial matters with passion. She sees the inevitable swings of economic circumstance as part of the "love, hate, death, joy, sorrow, meeting, parting, quarrelling, reconciling, [which] go to make up the sum total of our experience in this work-a-day world"—the reality of common businessmen and women. In addition to a romance plot that is inevitably tied to its financial plot, *Austin Friars* is notable for the extreme similes Riddell employs to describe economic depression as affecting the whole of society: "Like the wind, these times of universal depression come as they list. . . . Where the money goes, or why it should be so difficult to procure, is a mystery even to the elders in Israel" (205). She uses metaphors of natural disaster and epidemics to describe financial downturns: "Like the cause of influenza, there are numberless conjectures concerning [the origins of economic depression]; but the only fact which can be positively stated is, that the pecuniary depletion is felt by every class in the community; that the epidemic being, no respecter of persons, affects millionaires as well as struggling young beginners" (205). It is not the swindles of a great financier that account for economic misfortune but rather a force that Riddell was able to conceptualize and compare to natural phenomena; even with her financial knowledge of facts and statistics, "the economy" remained a mystery, requiring emotionally charged references to nature, God, and the supernatural.

Even with this sense of the economy as a force of nature that buffets the honest as well as the dishonest capitalist, the narrator of *Austin Friars* rewards virtue in business with a miraculous turn that defies the realistic account that has preceded it. Yorke's elderly husband, Mr. Forde, conveniently dies, and she determines to marry her long-suffering admirer, Luke. But in another complicated legal twist of plot, she requires permission from the executors of Mr. Forde's estate to do so. After fearing she will have to give up Forde Hall and its fortune, she is in the end allowed to keep both Luke and the money. It is a circuitous route for Yorke as the daughter of a tenant farmer who escapes to the City, lives as a mistress and businesswoman, takes up with a lowly clerk, and ultimately returns to the country as a happily married, wealthy landowner.

Even in the occasional fairy-tale ending, Riddell's novels are distinctive for insisting that the business sphere is essential not only to the economic life of England and its empire, but also to a geographically situated subculture that demands a particular kind of realistic representation. Her plots reinforce her explicit aesthetic statements, in which she takes on her fellow realists to argue for the honesty of businessmen and complains that "the majority of writers who have undertaken to portray business know nothing on earth about it" (*Austin Friars,* 235). "A business life," Riddell writes, "is one which exposes those engaged in it to temptations greater than humanity can withstand": "herein, I take it, may be found the cause of that instinctive distaste for trade of any kind which those whose position enables them to stand aside and watch . . . feel for those engaged in commercial pursuits" (310). Riddell identifies intensely with the temptation to corruption experienced by the average businessman in times of economic crisis and wants readers who may be prejudiced against commercial society to feel the same. Her heroes and heroines rise above petty temptations and instead carry on honest business even in the face of an unpredictable economy. In contrast to those who "stand aside and watch," they are

CHAPTER 11. HENRY, "CHARLOTTE RIDDELL"

men (and women) of action who do rather than reflect, and Riddell is their chronicler.

Like her contemporary critics, we still do not know exactly how Riddell acquired her "fearful and wonderful knowledge of matters financial." We know only that her husband was a man of business, that she lived for a time in "the City," and that she had an affinity for businessmen. From her novels, we know that she viewed business as a social leveler, and in realistically presenting its detailed workings and inherent drama to readers, she was educating them and also performing what she saw as an almost sacred duty—contributing to discourses of both art and business. As Srebrnik argues, her novels appealed to women by "providing non-working wives with detailed information concerning the 'public' lives of their businessmen husbands."[22] Though Riddell's knowledge was seen as unfeminine, her novels helped to transform that perception.

We have been unable to place Riddell's portraits of business life on our critical map because we reproduce the nineteenth-century expectation that literature will criticize the financial sphere, not praise and explain it. Perhaps the time is right to recover Riddell's contributions to British literature by recognizing the centrality of business and financial life to our overall understanding of Victorian culture and to question the assumed separation of financial and literary spheres in Victorian writing. Riddell's position as a woman writing about finance more authoritatively than her male contemporaries might make her an example of how masculine and feminine spheres of influence were not as separate as they have seemed. Her novels represent a commingling of financial and fictional discourses that was resisted by critics and other novelists. She sought to extend the acceptable subject matter for realist fiction and to show the effects of seemingly abstract financial legislation on the everyday lives of common people. She was attacked in print, but she was also praised and credited with advancing by expanding the genre of the novel. Her obituary in the *Times* was laudatory about her accomplishments, reflecting: "In the 'sixties' it was the fashion, in English novels and plays, to look down on men engaged in trade. Mrs. Riddell's chief object seems to have been to prove that a man did not lose caste by engaging in business in the City. The point has long since been conceded in English society."[23] In her interview with the *Pall Mall Gazette,* she recalled that despite being "sharply criticized," her City matters were "always right" (3).

---

[22] Srebrnik, 76.
[23] "Mrs. J. H. Riddell," Obituary, *Times,* 26 September 1906, 8.

CHAPTER 12

A "Formidable" Business

BRITISH WOMEN TRAVELERS
IN THE COLONIAL MEDICAL MARKET

NARIN HASSAN

*A*mong its advice for proper clothing, meals, house furnishings, and the management of servants, the 1864 domestic guide *The Englishwoman in India: Containing Information for the use of Ladies Proceeding to, or Residing in, the East Indies* emphasizes the importance of a portable medical chest for successful travel. Suggesting that "for traveling and distant stations" ladies prepare "a small, well-made medicine chest" stocked with necessary drugs and objects, it proceeds to detail all the ingredients necessary for medical mixtures and poultices.[1] Written by an anonymous "lady resident" as "a compendium of all the information actually necessary for domestic comfort," the guide engages with the language and rhetoric that would shape the field of Victorian tropical medicine (viii). The text refers to the potential dangers of a tropical environment to European bodies, noting, for example, that "camphor and camphorated spirits of wine are supposed to be inimical to certain unpleasant insects" and

---

[1] Anonymous, *The Englishwoman in India: Containing Information for the use of Ladies Proceeding to, or Residing in, The East Indies on the Subjects of their Outfit, Furniture, Housekeeping, The Rearing of Children, Duties and Wages of Servants, Management of The Stables, and Arrangements for Travelling to which are added Receipts for Indian Cookery, by a Lady Resident* (London: Smith, Elder & Co., 1864), 32.

advising that travelers "take a couple of jars of chloride of lime and several packets of Allnutts fumigating paper" on their sea voyages (7). A number of mid-nineteenth-century texts focused on illness in foreign regions and advised women in particular with tips to prepare for and maintain the health of their families overseas. While a number of popular health guides were published in this period—many by medical doctors, such as Edward Tilt and William Moore—*The Englishwoman* exemplifies how women contributed to and also benefitted from discourses surrounding health and travel.[2] The text reflects the increased immersion of Englishwomen within colonial spaces and signals how women's domestic roles converged with the discourses and practices of Western medicine. Medical knowledge for and by women also provided them with economic opportunities: women travelers participated in native trade by doctoring, and such encounters supported the publication and circulation of their narrative accounts in literary markets.

While much groundbreaking critical work has engaged with the woman traveler, her privileged access to private spaces such as harems, and her relationship to colonial expansion,[3] few scholars have considered gender and travel in relation to the economics of Victorian medical culture and colonialism.[4] This essay examines how British women narrated their experiences abroad in relation to an emerging market of colonial medicine that they helped to establish. I suggest that the new discourses of "family medicine" and, more specifically, a medical kit allowed women to act as figures of Western medical knowledge, shaping both the figure of the mem-

---

[2] See, for example, Edward John Tilt, *Health in India for British Women, and on the Prevention of Disease in Tropical Climates* (London: J & A Churchill, 1875); W. J. Moore, *A Manual of Family Medicine for India* (London: J & A Churchill, 1877); and J. T. Gracey, *Medical Work in Foreign Lands* (Dansville, NY: A. O. Bunnell, 1881).

[3] Maria Frawley, *A Wider Range: Travel Writing by Women in Victorian England* (London and Toronto: Associated University Presses, 1994); Sara Mills, *Discourses of Difference: An Analysis of Women's Travel Writing and Colonialism* (New York: Routledge, 1992); Susan Morgan, *Place Matters: Gendered Geography in Victorian Women's Travel Books about Southeast Asia* (New Brunswick, NJ: Rutgers University Press, 1996); Simon Gikandi, *Maps of Englishness: Writing Identity in the Culture of Colonialism* (New York: Columbia University Press, 1996); Billie Melman, *Women's Orients: Englishwomen and the Middle East, 1718–1918—Sexuality, Religion and Work* (Ann Arbor: University of Michigan Press, 1992); and Antoinette Burton, *Burdens of History: British Feminists, Indian Women and Imperial Culture, 1865–1915* (Chapel Hill: University of North Carolina Press, 1994).

[4] See Anna Harriette Leonowens, *Life and Travel in India: Being Recollections of a Journey before the Days of Railroads* (Philadelphia: Porter and Coates, 1884) and *The Romance of the Harem* (Charlottesville: University Press of Virginia, 1991); and Maneesha Lal, "The Politics of Gender and Medicine in Colonial India: The Countess of Dufferin's Fund, 1885–1888," *Bulletin of the History of Medicine* 68 (1994): 29–66.

sahib and the lady doctor abroad while exposing new markets for medical care. Thus, in the colonies of India and the Middle East, material objects such as medical guides and toolboxes professionalized the role of the British woman traveler—allowing her to manage her own health and domestic practices while carving out a new role as female "doctor" to natives. Doctoring allowed women to participate in and build medical markets overseas while distributing common tinctures and remedies brought from Britain to the colonies. As forms of "portable property," to use John Plotz's term, pillboxes and medical chests were physical belongings that "gained their power in motion," as did the women who traveled and made use of them abroad.[5] Plotz describes the value of portable objects as cultural agents, emphasizing their outward flow from England. In this essay, I suggest that women's medical chests and the remedies they contained functioned as more circular forms of "portable property": they produced new and powerful roles for women as agents of modern medical knowledge and encouraged economic exchanges with natives overseas, eventually also shifting perceptions of female influence (medical and colonial) at home. The mobility of the women writers I discuss coupled with the portability of medical objects and supplies that accompanied their journeys produced opportunities for women to gain literary and medical authority and to engage with native economic systems.

This essay argues that women travelers extended their domestic duties and basic medical knowledge to produce alternative economies, describing their domestic environments as "shops" or marketplaces to tend to native patients, and distributing medicines and pills in exchange for native goods. Isabel Burton and Lucie Duff Gordon characterize their interactions with natives as building alternative forms of exchange, which granted them fame, greater mobility, and respect from their readers. In the case of Duff Gordon, amateur doctoring in Egypt also allowed her to gain recognition from the medical establishment at home. Their narratives illustrate how forms of bartering and medical charity allowed women to gain influence within colonial spaces, even without Western forms of payment. Despite the real limits to their medical authority and knowledge, these female travelers emphasize the active labor they perform in the colonies, ascribe the term "doctoring" to their experiences and the title "doctress" to themselves, and describe building "practices" and marketplaces of their own while establishing reputations as successful healers.

---

[5] John Plotz, *Portable Property: Victorian Culture on the Move* (Princeton, NJ: Princeton University Press, 2008), xv.

CHAPTER 12. HASSAN, "A 'FORMIDABLE' BUSINESS"

On 14 April 1864, in a detailed description of a disease outbreak in Luxor, Lucie Duff Gordon documents her response to the diseased surroundings as follows:

> Luckily I am very well, for I am worked hard, as a strange epidemic has broken out, and I am the *hakeemeh* (doctress) of Luxor. The *hakeem* Pasha from Cairo came up and frightened the people, telling them it was catching, and Yussuf forgot his religion so far as to beg me not to be all day in the people's huts; but Omar and I despised the danger, I feeling sure it was not infectious, and Omar saying *Min Allah*.
>
> The people get stoppage of the bowels and die in eight days unless they are physicked; all who have sent for me *in time* have recovered. Thank God that I can help the poor souls. It is harvest, and the hard work, the spell of intense heat, and the green corn, beans etc., which they eat, brings on the sickness. Then the Copts are fasting from all animal food, and full of green beans and salad, and green corn. The 'lavement machine' [enema] I brought was an inspiration. (155)[6]

This passage, from Duff Gordon's *Letters from Egypt* (1865), reveals her newly discovered role as a healer within the community and contrasts her response to the outbreak with that of native men. Representing herself as a bold and daring "hakeemeh," or lady doctress, Duff Gordon also claims that close encounters with natives allow her to read their symptoms and gain their trust. Despite her lack of medical training, she insists that the native Egyptians relied on her and recovered as a result of her timely assistance. She does not define herself as a nurse or simply a helpmate, but as the female doctor of the community. Her conviction that she herself is not susceptible to the epidemic disease and her assurance that it is "not infectious" give her the authoritative position of a physician who can recognize and curtail possible self-contagion. She confirms her own distance from the natives in terms of domestic practices; by assigning the cause of the disease to the crop harvest of beans and other greens, Duff Gordon connects the disease directly to the foreign land and the eating habits of the natives. Finally, her mention of the "lavement machine" as an "inspiration" directly invokes the connection between Western medicine and emerging technologies at the same time as it highlights her entrepreneurial and innovative spirit.

---

[6] Lady Duff Gordon, *Letters from Egypt*, ed. Gordon Waterfield (New York: Praeger, 1969); See also Katherine Frank, *Lucie Duff Gordon: A Passage to Egypt* (London and New York: Tauris Parke, 2007).

PART IV. WOMEN'S BUSINESS

Duff Gordon's description of her lavement machine as an instrument of healing provides an image of penetration and exploration that evokes the traditional motifs of male-dominated European travel. As Anne McClintock and others have shown, traditionally colonized lands were represented as female spaces open for penetration by male explorers.[7] Duff Gordon may be seen as inverting this image—here it is the female traveler accessing the private worlds of Egypt—and adopting the stance of European healer. Surprisingly, Duff Gordon does not seem uncomfortable sharing this penetrative tool. Instead, her fascination with the effects of this cleansing machine as a medical device takes precedence, since it functions to elevate her as a healer within this community and, in turn, allows her to gain greater access to native homes and patients. As an instrument of medical knowledge, the "machine" further underscores how a material object, transported through travel, can produce, for Duff Gordon, a new identity as useful, colonial "doctress."

This is a profitable identity. After visiting many homes with her self-ascribed knowledge, she writes two months later that "the epidemic here is all but over; but my medical fame has spread so, that the poor souls come twenty miles (from Koos) for physic" (178).[8] Describing the success of her doctoring business, she writes, "I am very popular here, and the only Hakeem. I have effected some brilliant cures, and get lots of presents" (214). In a later letter, she notes: "the Hakeem business goes on at a great rate . . . a whole gypsy camp are great customers—the poor souls will bring all manner of gifts" (234). These claims emphasize Duff Gordon's growing clientele and reveal her diverse economic transactions. Her "business" secures her fame and popularity, which results in a broader reach to native communities, and her medical efforts are reciprocated with gifts that are tokens of her power and her ability to provide remedies. Being a "hakeemeh" also allows Duff Gordon to witness concerns far beyond physical illness, and she describes how natives enter her "shop" for a range of services:

> My fame as a Hakeemeh has become far too great, and on market days I have to shut up shop. Yesterday, a very handsome woman came for medicine to make her beautiful, as her husband had married another who teased her, and he rather neglected her. And a man offered me a camel load of

---

[7] Anne McClintock, *Imperial Leather: Race, Gender, and Sexuality in the Imperial Context* (New York: Routledge, 1995), 3, 22.

[8] Lucie Duff Gordon, *Letters from Egypt,* ed. Sarah Searight (London: Virago Press, 1983).

CHAPTER 12. HASSAN, "A 'FORMIDABLE' BUSINESS"

wheat if I could read something over him and his wife to make them have children. (275–76)

Duff Gordon entices her readers with gossip about various characters and illnesses in town, contributing to the financial success of her widely distributed narrative, which sold out in its first run with Macmillan & Co. and was reissued twice in the same year. More importantly, she reveals the success of her "shop" where she distributes medicines. While Duff Gordon does not describe any monetary income gained from these transactions, she expresses the possibility of an alternative economy based on bartering and gift exchange. In addition to acquiring local goods, Duff Gordon's trading of services for "a camel load of wheat" suggests her ability to immerse herself within the local culture and participate in native traditions and rituals of exchange. As the quotation above demonstrates, Duff Gordon's "shop" is itself a marketplace that attracts natives to services beyond medical care—she represents herself as simultaneously a magical healer, beautician, fertility doctor, and advisor, and in this way we can read her "practice" as one that offers diverse services and goods to build and benefit from a broad clientele. Duff Gordon creates a one-stop, flexible trading station where she can manage a wide range of medical exchanges and establish herself as a useful member of the local community and economy.

While Duff Gordon does not consistently record the payments she receives, she claims that "my doctoring business has become quite formidable. I should like to sell my practice to any 'rising young surgeon.' It brings in a very fair income of vegetables, eggs, pigeons, turkeys etc." (272). Along with referencing such opportunities for barter, Duff Gordon encourages native trust in European processes of medicine and suggests to her readers that Western doctors are necessary, welcome, and well paid. She writes, "None of them will any longer consult an Arab *hakeem* if they can get a European to physic them" (107). As further proof she mentions, "The mark of confidence is that they now bring the sick children which was never known before, I believe in these parts, I am sure it would pay a European doctor to set up here" (277). In these ways, Duff Gordon's text suggests that women can, through their informal transactions, drive an economic and imperial engine forward, encouraging the expansion of Western medicine and testing new markets for professional physicians. Despite the nontraditional medicine she offered, the likely exaggeration of her abilities, and the gossipy tone of her letters, Duff Gordon did gain some respect from the English medical community, which was itself extending the reach of Western medicine into colonial realms. An 1865 article in the *Lancet* devoted to "Lady Duff Gordon on the Climate of Egypt" celebrates her efforts and notes: "Besides the general lesson of sound-mindedness" taught by her letters, "they contain also much of painful interest on the condition of the people immediately prior to the outbreak of cholera."[9] Thus the article suggests the value of travel writing to promote understandings of cultural difference and to influence the expanding practice of medicine itself. Further, by arguing that "it would best profit the sick traveling in search of health to imitate [Duff Gordon]," the *Lancet* helps promote her medical reputation and her literary career (269).

Published a few years after Duff Gordon's *Letters from Egypt*, Isabel Burton's *The Inner Life of Syria, Palestine and the Holy Land* (1875) traces her travels in the Middle East with her husband Richard Burton; the memoir provides representations of native scenes and landscapes, but also establishes Isabel Burton as an active female medical guide and healer. Like Duff Gordon, she describes herself as a well-prepared traveler who brings domestic and medical tools into the territories she explores. She appears particularly knowledgeable about the gadgetry and ingredients of a successful, mobile pillbox that functions as an important extension of "home." Burton's organization of portable tinctures and tablets reflects the new science of domestic management that was guided by such Victorian domestic manuals as Isabella Beeton's regimented *Book of Household Management* (1861). In a description that functions as both a guide for travel and an assertion of her pragmatism, Burton writes:

> Travellers often suffer from dysentery and fever, but if they would only travel with necessary drugs, and take a day's rest when attacked, they would neither die nor carry away with them the remnants of a complaint that lasts them for a year, or for a life. I always carry a little leather medicine chest, about the size of a respectable brick; it contains antibilious pills, calomel, and all needful for bilious attacks, diarrhoea and dysentery; burnt alum and kohl, and several other things for the eyes; quinine and Warburg's drops for fever; opium and many other simple remedies.[10]

Although Burton emphasizes the usefulness of these medical items for her own well-being, she also suggests that with these concoctions she can aid

---

[9] "Lady Duff Gordon on the Climate of Egypt," *Lancet*, 2 September 1865, 269–70.

[10] Isabel Burton, *The Inner Life of Syria, Palestine and the Holy Land* (London: Henry S. King & Co., 1875), 117.

her fellow travelers and locals: "None of our camp were ill for more than a day, unless from wounds. My cotton wool, lint, spermaceti, and strapping all travel in an old canister, and do not overload the baggage animals" (117). Like Duff Gordon, who highlights the importance of all the "common drugs—Epsom salts, senna, aloes, rhubarb, quassia" (257) which she must order from England, Burton illuminates the value of her pillbox—and the English commerce that supplies it—for successful medical work in the colonies.

The contents of these pillboxes carried by Duff Gordon and Burton were referred to in medical manuals of the period as well as the *Englishwoman* guide discussed earlier. Moore's *Family Medicine for India* included an encyclopedic list of common drugs that could be administered by what he termed "unprofessional" readers. The descriptions of his "Indian medicines" (drugs that would be commonly available in Indian bazaars) list the origin of the drug in native locations. While Burton and Duff Gordon describe such drugs as part of their English medical chest—for Burton, medicines should be "packed in tins" and shipped from England—the drugs themselves were often derived from indigenous substances and medical practices. Duff Gordon and Burton thus participate in a cultural and commercial exchange that demonstrates the global movement of plants and drugs as material objects that originate in the tropics and are then marketed as products of English medical progress. Their application of such tinctures and pills, like Duff Gordon's use of her lavement machine, exposes the importance of commercial objects and goods to the civilizing process. In their reading of colonial encounter, Comaroff and Comaroff write, "Abroad and at home, civilizing goods ushered in new orders of relations—both symbolic and substantial—that bound local consumers to an expanding world order."[11] The purchase, distribution, and consumption of medical goods outlined by these travel writers show how women travelers supported an expanding global medical "market" among natives and colonial settlers as well as with readers back home.

These women writers negotiate their roles within both domestic and public spheres, sometimes proudly establishing their medical tasks as "work" and other times carefully reminding readers that they are simply extending the domestic duties expected of them. Burton describes her medical work as a largely natural, effortless occupation. She emphasizes the fact that she is an amateur, and yet suggests that her efforts are more

---

[11] Jean Comaroff and John Comaroff, *Ethnography and the Historical Imagination* (Boulder, CO: Westview Press, 1992), 41.

effective than practices by native doctors. In *The Inner Life of Syria,* she writes:

> People say that it is a very risky thing for amateurs to practice medicine; but I found that with some natural instinct about medicine, and a few good books, by dint of daily experience, by never using any but the simplest remedies, and not those unless I was quite sure of the nature of the illness, that I managed to do a great deal of good. I found that native doctors killed numbers, whereas I not only did not kill but cured.... Our garden presented the strangest scene in the afternoon—fever patients making wry faces over quinine wine, squalling babies guggling oil, paralytic and rheumatic Bedawin being shampooed and gouty old women having joints painted with iodine.... Whoever wants to be charitable here must keep up a chemist's shop in the house, well stocked with English drugs, packed in tins to prevent the sea and climate affecting them; and whoever wishes to succeed must multiply an English dose by four. (311–12)

Burton's home clinic is a site where readers are exposed to the ailments of her patients as well as to her own medical "instinct" and ability. Through depictions of disease, Burton posits herself as a domesticated Englishwoman who manages medicine within her home and immerses herself in the care of natives with a "scientific" as well as charitable approach to doctoring. Burton establishes her amateur doctoring as a service that attracts a range of native patients, and while she emphasizes the altruistic nature of her work, this is certainly a successful venture: Burton gains renown and up to fifty patients a day. Her text, like Duff Gordon's, suggests that vast populations in colonies are open to and in need of medical care and can be the source of new and profitable opportunities for women. Her vivid account of patients producing a "strange scene" in her garden also provides exotic narrative content that would attract an active readership. Her description echoes medical and literary accounts that imagined the native body as essentially different from the European and contributes to medical claims that began to assert the dangers of native doctors and midwives, who, according to Burton, "killed numbers." As both these travel narratives reveal, the process of doctoring was assisted by domestic objects (such as medical toolboxes) that were marketed to and by British women.

It is not just in the performance of medical tasks but also in the communication of them through writing that these women benefit from colonial exchanges; the intimate transactions between women and native subjects provide the narrative for their texts, which in turn feed a curious literary market. Women's travel narratives became increasingly popular in the nineteenth century, as women could provide more intimate and direct accounts of the manners and customs of natives, particularly of veiled and secluded native women. Doctoring, and the access to native bodies and ailments that it offered, afforded fresh narrative material for readers and demonstrated women's abilities to participate in colonial economies. Duff Gordon's commercially and critically successful *Letters* received glowing reviews from *Fraser's Magazine* and the *Westminster Review,* and both highlighted the importance of her doctoring.[12] Although initially her husband's adventures and narratives overshadowed Isabel Burton's fame, Mary S. Lovell notes that her "best-selling" *Inner Life of Syria* launched her own successful literary career.[13]

Both Duff Gordon and Burton carefully negotiate the economic stakes of their work. They highlight their entrepreneurial roles as "doctors" at the same time as they emphasize their healing as a natural, domestic, female alternative to Western male doctors and native healers; indeed, journals even emphasized their "unselfish benevolence."[14] Such narrative descriptions of female doctoring as flexible, innovative, and open to alternative forms of economic exchange offered an important model for professional women who sought medical practice. While women struggled to gain admission to medical schools and build practices within England, the colonies provided an alternative space for women to gain clinical experience. For example, Edith Pechey, a pioneering "lady doctor" who gained admission to Edinburgh University's medical school in 1869, built a practice in India and was able to demand fees equivalent to those of many of her male peers; like Mary Scharlieb, who trained in medicine in Madras and London, she found that sojourns abroad provided a more liberating and rewarding professional experience than those provided at home. Pechey and Scharlieb were involved with the first women's hospitals in India—Scharlieb founded the Royal Victoria Hospital for Caste and Gosha Women in Madras, and

---

[12] See, for instance, "*Letters from Egypt, 1863–65*" [Review], *Fraser's Magazine for Town and Country* 72 (November 1865): 580–88, and "*Letters from Egypt, 1863–65* by Lady Duff Gordon" [Review], *Westminster Review* 122 (October 1865): 108–19.

[13] Mary S. Lovell, *A Rage to Live: A Biography of Richard and Isabel Burton* (New York: Norton, 1998), 769, 583.

[14] Both reviews emphasize Duff Gordon's unselfish, charitable, and useful work. *Fraser's* notes "Lady Gordon's unselfish benevolence" (588), and the *Westminster Review* concludes that "she won the love of all with whom she came into contact, doctoring their sick . . . " (108). In a recent biography of Duff Gordon, Katherine Park notes the critical and commercial success of her letters (301). The *Dictionary of National Biography* (1890), vol. 22, also notes that her letters were circulated widely (221–22). Leslie Stephen and Sidney Lee, *Dictionary of National Biography* (London: Smith, Elder, and Co, 1890).

Pechey worked at the Cama Hospital in Bombay. Thus both women built successful medical practices overseas. Mary Scharlieb also produced a number of popular health guides and domestic manuals as well as a published memoir.[15] While women were often restricted from the field of medicine at home, the profession and its rewards were relatively open for them abroad.

These medical women navigated new economic exchanges in their professional practice in much the same way that Duff Gordon and Burton narrated the profitability of their travels. Indeed, *Reminiscences,* Scharlieb's memoir of her work with patients in India, evokes images similar to those described by Burton and Duff Gordon when she records her work with patients in India:

> I was told that a man from the country wanted to see me. Seated in my consulting room I found a strong, middle-aged farmer from the Nellore district. I asked him what he wanted, and he said that he had two teeth that gave him great pain and required removal. I advised him to go to the hospital because I was not a dentist, nor did I accept men patients. He was both sorrowful and indignant. He urged that he had walked seventy miles to see me, that he had brought me a beautiful valuable Nellore cow and also two jars of honey. (113)

Here, patients seek out the female doctor and offer her items considered highly valuable within a native context in exchange for medical advice or services. Noting that she eventually gave in to "the good man's pleading," Scharlieb emphasizes the value of her efforts and its rewards: "It was quite true he had brought me both the cow and the honey, as fine a fee as could be desired!" (114). In the narration of such experiences, Scharlieb, like the other women considered here, emphasizes how her doctoring practice secures her a broad range of patients and ailments and adjusts flexibly within a native economy based on barter.

As a field, medicine was itself redefined and professionalized in the nineteenth century. In a rare reading of the economics of nineteenth-century medicine, Anne Digby notes that the early and middle decades of the nineteenth century were marked by an oversupply of doctors and medical

---

[15] Scharlieb published a number of successful texts including *A Woman's Words to Women on the Care of Their Health in England and India* (London: Swan Sonnenschein & Co. Ltd., 1895), which addresses both English and Indian women, and her memoir *Reminiscences* (London: Williams and Norgate, 1924), which recounts her travels overseas as well as her efforts to pursue medicine and build a practice.

unemployment within Britain.[16] Further, doctors had to negotiate being entrepreneurial while simultaneously projecting a caring and empathetic approach to their patients; thus medicine was a respectable, but not necessarily profitable, profession. However, the demand for private physicians in growing colonies made travel more lucrative for doctors who could not make a viable living at home.[17] Douglas Haynes's discussion of imperial medicine offers a useful reading of the relationship of medical men to the vastly expanding British Empire, but travel, and the medical opportunities it offered, clearly appealed to women as well. Widely circulating medical reference books and guides addressed women readers and allowed them greater access to medical ideas and norms, and the colonies were a source of professional and financial opportunity for women. Stories of doctoring within women's travel narratives reveal the power of medicine as a "tool of empire," to use Daniel Headrick's term,[18] but they also represent the domestication of that empire and the extension of domestic economies from Britain to its colonies. Women overseas made use of both basic domestic and professional medical knowledge, and their transactions promoted the expansion of Western medicine as an entrepreneurial enterprise both in colonies and at home. Indeed, by the end of the nineteenth century, a number of trained medical women built successful medical practices overseas, and considered medical work not only remunerative but a powerful means of reforming native health as well as cultural practices.[19]

The manuals and medical chests that women carried to the colonies professionalized their roles as travelers and doctors overseas as they participated in the development of alternative medical markets and established a normative model of the healthy body that was shared between colonies and the metropolitan center. While considerations of the material objects and economic thrusts of empire often focus on what came back—the products, commodities, and objects that entered Victorian homes through the global circulation of peoples and things—the medical chests and remedies

---

[16] Anne Digby, *Making a Medical Living: Doctors and Patients in the English Market for Medicine, 1720–1911* (Cambridge: Cambridge University Press, 1994), 137–40.

[17] Douglas Haynes, *Imperial Medicine: Patrick Manson and the Conquest of Tropical Disease, 1844–1923* (Philadelphia: University of Pennsylvania Press, 2001), 129.

[18] See *Tools of Empire: Technology and European Imperialism in the Nineteenth Century* (Oxford: Oxford University Press, 1981).

[19] A number of texts trace the broad influence of women doctors in colonies, and reveal how women could support both medical and cultural reform. See, for example, Margaret Balfour and Ruth Young, *The Work of Medical Women in India* (London: Oxford University Press, 1929); and Mary Frances Billington (with an Introduction by the Marchioness of Dufferin and Ava), *Woman in India* (London: Chapman and Hall, 1895).

that traveled from the metropole to imperial spaces, and the amateur and then professional female doctors who went with them, were also powerful in shaping the economics of travel and colonial medicine. Women travelers created their own unique workshops of medical exchange that allowed them to fashion profitable new identities for themselves, whether in the shops and clinics they created abroad, or on the literary stage at home.

Afterword—and Forward

ECONOMIC WOMEN IN THEIR TIME, OUR TIME, AND THE FUTURE

REGENIA GAGNIER

The theme of this volume, as stated by the editors in their introduction, recalls Adam Smith's Invisible Hand, that "self-interested gain and mutual cooperation could be compatible; even as [women] pursued their own livelihoods, they also provided models for other women" (26). The volume begins with Economic Man as isolated individual Robinson Crusoe. In showing women's place in economic life and theory, it illuminates forms of collectivity and intersubjectivity—the family, paternalism, philanthropy, caring, writing—familiar to women while retaining a focus on economic individualism. The volume has certain unsentimental optics through which it views the nineteenth century: economic standing was more effective than feminine cultural capital in allowing women to intervene as agents of change in their communities (Gleadle); women's wealth could allow them to transcend gender, or at least to destabilize gender relations (Godfrey); Florence Nightingale could be both maternal caretaker (lady with the lamp) and public administrator wielding statistics in transforming the health system, Harriet Martineau could contribute to a war economy, and both were visible in the public domain (Poovey). The essays show that women's economy is both micro—individual relationships, choices, and behaviors—and macro—functioning within global trade in people, goods, and finance. In methodological terms, it shows that there are no contradictions between markets and the humanities, between economics and decision-making in the novel (Bigelow), and between finance and fiction (Henry). Literature represents everyday economic life between the genders, and this life is refracted through discourses of technology, machinery, and economic operations. Employing more recent distinctions between high and popular literatures, popular literature especially concerns itself with the technology and machineries of modernity, whether the systematic intelligence of business, law, and government, or of finance and science.

If most of these essays show the tunefulness of current scholarship with market society, some of them show urgent social issues in their nineteenth-century beginnings: modern anorexia as a social condition, the ascetic or self-sacrificing body versus the consuming body (Gleadle, Blumberg); the role of gossip as information (MacDonald), and the volatility of information in economic panics; the unsustainability of mass consumer culture (Kreisel). The institution of the family here appears fascinatingly contemporary: women extricating themselves from abusive marriages (Rutterford); men as calculating and as consumerist as women in deciding whether to marry, liking their bachelor life of "lavender kid gloves, patent-leather shoes, and silk stockings" while longing for a simpler, less consumerist, less competitive culture abroad; women appearing contrary to the mythic woman-as-consumer, rather as economical and ingenious household managers (Rappaport). Abroad, women professionals found a market in colonial medicine (Hassan), whereas today, Britain recruits doctors and nurses from abroad to sustain its aging population.

The families here are concerned with accounting as well as philanthropy, "values"—as ideological memes—as well as ethics. In Thorne-Murphy's account of the Anti-Corn Law League, free-market women in the charity bazaar "could transform debatable policy proposals into religious and moral imperatives that allowed no legitimate counter-argument." In showing nineteenth-century British women as practical, economical, ideological, and mostly as individuals rather than as classes or movements, we see Economic Woman equal to Economic Man. To this extent, this is a collection for our time. Here, class is often treated less as an economic relation, identity, or culture, as in earlier treatments, than as a visible manifestation of taste, like a brand.

The women here are mostly bourgeois, professional, and individual: Katherine Plymley, Harriet Martineau, George Eliot, Florence Nightingale, Emily Westmeath, Ellen Wood, Charlotte Riddell, Lucie Duff

Gordon, and Isabel Burton. A lesser-known one that many readers will nonetheless remember is young Jane Plymley, starving herself to death to protest the dearth of 1800–1801. The volume opens avenues for further investigation of poor and working women and their corresponding forms of collectivity, and of more immigrant women and theirs. Yet there is doubtless much evidence to support the continuities between then and now, and, as the editors suggest, much inspiration here in women's ingenuity, entrepreneurialism, and sheer industriousness, which latter never ceases to awe even those of us who have studied the period for decades.

We are well ensconced in a neoliberal world with nineteenth-century roots. At the 2012 U.S. Democratic National Convention in Charlotte, North Carolina, all references were to an interpellated "middle class": the Democratic Party was the party of the middle class, or of those who aspired to be middle-class. The essays in this volume suggest a prehistory of this universality of middle-class-ness in their emphases on individual activity as inspiration for other individuals, individuals trading their goods and services on the market, the individual as the unit of analysis, and the economy as the salient niche of identity-formation. Yet while a focus on narratives of individuals can often obscure institutional political, legal, and financial structures of power and indeed can often exclude the less advantaged, these essays rather show the women embedded in diverse communities that may contribute to those structures of power. The Victorians—for although the volume ranges across the full nineteenth century, most of this collection is about the Victorians—were still strange and diverse, in their daily activities, in their religion that drew them toward collectivities as well as hailed them as individuals, and in the variety of their economic situations. The manor house here has the role of the plantation in postcolonial studies, the microcosm of a world of coherent but unequal relations, often dependent on external markets, socially an enclosed emanation of a fantasy (in Edouard Glissant's term).[1] The bazaar functions as a small economy, like a farmer's market or souk, but produces ideology supporting the largest abstraction of them all, The (Free) Market. The courts, the marriage market, the City of London, and the empire are present here but fully imbricated in the economic lives of women. When neoclassical tools of analysis such as consumption patterns, methodological individualism, and formalism take precedence in this volume over social classes and relations such as those between land/rent/landowners, labor/wages/

---

[1] Edouard Glissant, *Poetics of Relation,* trans. Betsy Wing (Ann Arbor: University of Michigan Press, 1997), 67.

workers, and capital/profit/entrepreneurs, we see the place of women in specifically bourgeois economic relations. We see Economic Woman equal to Economic Man as we know him.

Yet many Victorians, especially those toward the end of the century when productive capacity had raised many above scarcity, had concerns beyond the market. They were concerned with reconciling freedom and equality. True freedom would begin with providing for needs equally, so that individuals could then develop according to their individual tastes and capacities. In another book on economic women in the nineteenth century, also representative of its time, *Eve and the New Jerusalem* (1983), the socialist feminist Barbara Taylor quoted an Owenite Socialist plan for their communities of 2,000 persons, in which all property was in common; marriage, contraception, and divorce were available on demand; and child care was socialized. In the plan, all work would be streamed by age rather than gender, that is, by the productive and accumulative energies, experience, and knowledge of the communards. Housework would be performed by children of eleven years or younger. Between twelve and twenty-one, communards would produce the wealth; from twenty-two to twenty-five, young adults would preserve and distribute it; from twenty-five to thirty-five, they would teach the young; from thirty-five on, mature adults would shoulder the responsibility of government; and at forty-five, they would be freed for artistic or intellectual pursuits, travel, or leisure as they liked, at each stage women performing exactly the same tasks as men.[2]

This Owenite vision has charmed me for much of my lifetime. This is probably because it sees human contributions to social life as a life cycle or ecology, rather than as competitive individualism and ceaseless productivity. It joins other great economic visions of the period that rejected economic reductionism in human possibility. In the nineteenth century, the century known for economic liberalization, they were nonetheless seldom confined to free markets. Marx and Engels observed that the original, unequal division of labor was in sexual reproduction and child-rearing (*The German Ideology*, 1846; *The Origin of the Family, Private Property, and the State*, 1884). Perceiving that liberal equality in market society consisted in being equally regarded as a self-sufficient monad, they speculated that once the narrow horizon of bourgeois rights had been transcended, the good, or just, society would give to each according to need and take from each according to ability (*Critique of the Gotha Programme*, 1875). Oscar Wilde, whose views were doubtless shaped by his sexuality, refined this by pointing out that we could not identify real individuals until all society

---

[2] Barbara Taylor, *Eve and the New Jerusalem* (New York: Pantheon, 1983), 52.

started from an equal base, achieved in the first instance through socialist redistribution. Only when we all started from a level playing field could individuals develop according to their diverse needs, tastes, and abilities ("Soul of Man under Socialism," 1891). Trained from infancy in the political economic traditions of Adam Smith and David Ricardo, John Stuart Mill was a firm believer in competition as the way to elicit optimal capacity, as in athletic games. In *On Liberty* (1859) Mill defended competition in the marketplace of ideas as the only way truth could prevail, and in *The Subjection of Women* (1869) he argued strenuously for women's full participation in the marketplace as a prerequisite for women's full subjecthood and social optimality. Yet he thought that capitalist monopolies and government support of inherited wealth and the status quo often prevented competition. And so, toward the end of his life, he defended market socialism, in which firms of workers would compete to sell the best product, distributing the rewards of their labor and abstinence, thus fulfilling the promise that capitalism had failed to fulfill, compensation equal to one's contribution.

Each of these visions was characteristic of the compromises between the leading ideologies of their time: liberal individualism and social duty. They had a wider frame than economics—the study of choice among scarcity—in which to define human possibility, not by its relationship to scarcity (Economic Man, economics) but to creativity, taste and preference, and personality. The contributors to this volume are less interested than I am in socialism, but they are attuned to the forms of social duty characteristic of economic liberalization: professional responsibility of doctors and writers, moral economies of religion and sustainability, charity organizations and philanthropy.

We might conclude with women's relation to economic progress itself, which in nineteenth-century Britain referred to growth in scientific knowledge, technology, and wealth. The conditions of economic progress duly impressed the world, not only throughout Europe, but even from the Meiji Restoration in midcentury Japan and the May Fourth and New Culture Movements in early twentieth-century China. Yet these and other movements were also interested in humanistic progress, or progress in moral, social, or political affairs. In his now-classic neoliberal manifesto "The End of History?" (1989), Francis Fukuyama thought that economic progress would inevitably lead to political progress. He also thought that there was an inevitable trajectory from the satisfaction of basic needs to tastes to high mass consumption.[3] The question remains whether economic progress has

---

[3] Francis Fukuyama, "The End of History?" *National Interest,* Summer 1989, 3–35 and *The*

led to moral and political progress. Or whether we are any nearer to reconciling freedom and equality. If ethics, as essays in this volume frequently point out, means our responsibility toward others, are we any closer to a moral economy? Or is Fukuyama's neoliberal inevitable progress as utopian as the Owenites'?

Today, the World Bank estimates that 1.5 billion people are living in absolute poverty. Absolute poverty is defined as the absence of enough resources (such as money) to secure basic life necessities. Absolute poverty means severe deprivation of basic human needs, including food, safe drinking water, sanitation facilities, health, shelter, education, and information. Many of these living in absolute poverty are women.[4] The Market is global; wealth and even provision are highly localized and unequal.

A report commissioned by the International Trade Union Confederation in 2008 shows that, based on their survey of sixty-three countries, there is a significant gender pay gap of sixteen percent. With the gender pay gap globally ranging from thirteen to forty percent, with an average of sixteen percent worldwide, women are today often educated as highly as men, or to a higher level, but "higher education of women does not necessarily lead to a smaller pay gap; in some cases the gap actually increases with the level of education obtained." The report also argues that this global gender pay gap is not due to lack of training or expertise on the part of women, since "the pay gap in the European Union member states increases with age, years of service and education."[5] Even with a woman Director of the International Monetary Fund, Christine Lagarde, and leader of the European Union, Angela Merkel, Economic Women still have some way to go to equal Economic Man, even if that is the highest that we can currently imagine humankind.

End of History and the Last Man (New York: Avon, 1992).

[4] "World Bank Sees Progress Against Extreme Poverty, But Flags Vulnerabilities," World Bank, 29 February 2012, http://www.worldbank.org/en/news/2012/02/29/world-bank-sees-progress-against-extreme-poverty-but-flags-vulnerabilities. "1.5 Billion People Living in Absolute Poverty Makes Its Eradication Humankind's Most Significant Challenge, Second Committee Told," General Assembly of the United Nations GA/EF/3313 Department of Public Information News and Media Division, New York Sixty-Sixth General Assembly Second Committee 13th & 14th Meetings (AM & PM), http://www.un.org/News/Press/docs/2011/gaef3313.doc.htm.

[5] Catherine Chubb, Simone Melis, Louisa Potter, and Raymond Storry, *The Global Gender Pay Gap*, International Trade Union Confederation, February 2008, "Gender Pay Gap Stuck at 16% Worldwide: New ITUC Report," ITUC Report (February 2008), http://www.ituc-csi.org/gender-pay-gap-stuck-at-16.html?lang=en.

CONTRIBUTORS

GORDON BIGELOW, T. K. Young Associate Professor of English at Rhodes College, is the co-editor (with John O. Jordan) of *Approaches to Teaching Dickens's* Bleak House (Modern Language Association, 2009) and the author of *Fiction, Famine, and the Rise of Economics in Victorian Britain and Ireland* (Cambridge University Press, 2003).

ILANA M. BLUMBERG is Associate Professor of Humanities at James Madison College of Michigan State University. She is the author of *Houses of Study: A Jewish Woman among Books* (University of Nebraska Press, 2007) and *Victorian Sacrifice: Ethics and Economics in Mid-Century Novels* (The Ohio State University Press, 2013), as well as numerous journal articles on related subjects.

LANA L. DALLEY is Associate Professor of English at California State University, Fullerton. She has published articles on women and political economy in *Victorian Literature and Culture*, *Victorian Poetry*, *Victorians Institute Journal*, and *Harriet Martineau: Authorship, Society, and Empire* (Manchester University Press, 2010). She is currently completing a book manuscript on mothering and economics in nineteenth-century literature and culture.

REGENIA GAGNIER is Professor of English at the University of Exeter, Editor-in-Chief of *Literature Compass* and its *Global Circulation Project*, and Senior Research Fellow in the ESRC Centre for Genomics in Society (Egenis). Her books include *Idylls of the Marketplace: Oscar Wilde and the Victorian Public* (Stanford University Press, 1986); *Subjectivities: A History of Self-Representation in Britain 1832–1920* (Oxford University Press, 1991); *The Insatiability of Human Wants: Economics and Aesthetics in Market Society* (University of Chicago Press, 2000); and *Individualism, Decadence and Globalization: On the Relationship of Part to Whole 1859–1920* (Palgrave Macmillan 2010). Her co-edited books include *The Politics of Gender in Anthony Trollope's Novels: New Readings for the Twenty-First Century* (Ashgate, 2009) and *The Palgrave Sourcebook on Victorian Literature* (2012). From 2009 through 2012 she was President of the British Association for Victorian Studies. Her current research is on the global circulation of the literatures of liberalization.

CONTRIBUTORS

KATHRYN GLEADLE is Tutor and Fellow in History at Mansfield College, University of Oxford. Her books include *Borderline Citizens: Women, Gender and Political Culture in Britain, 1815–1867* (Oxford University Press, 2009) and *Women in British Politics, 1760–1860: The Power of the Petticoat* (Palgrave Macmillan, 2000).

ESTHER GODFREY is Assistant Professor of English at the University of South Carolina Upstate. She is the author of *The January–May Marriage in Nineteenth-Century British Literature* (Palgrave Macmillan, 2009) and "Jane Eyre, from Governess to Girl Bride" in *Studies in English Literature 1500–1900* (2005).

NARIN HASSAN is Associate Professor in the School of Literature, Media, and Communication at The Georgia Institute of Technology. She is the author of *Diagnosing Empire: Women, Medical Knowledge, and Colonial Mobility* (Ashgate, 2011) and co-editor (with Tamara Silvia Wagner) of *Consuming Culture: Narratives of Consumption in the Long Nineteenth Century* (Lexington Books, 2007). Her work has appeared in *Mosaic*, *Nineteenth-Century Gender Studies*, and *Women's Studies Quarterly*.

NANCY HENRY is Professor of English at the University of Tennessee. She is the author of *The Life of George Eliot: A Critical Biography* (Blackwell, 2012), *The Cambridge Introduction to George Eliot* (Cambridge University Press, 2008), and *George Eliot and the British Empire* (Cambridge University Press, 2002). She is the co-editor (with Cannon Schmitt) of *Victorian Investments: New Perspectives on Finance and Culture* (Indiana University Press, 2009).

DEANNA K. KREISEL is Associate Professor of English at the University of British Columbia. Her book *Economic Woman: Demand, Gender, and Narrative Closure in Eliot and Hardy* was published by the University of Toronto Press (2012); she has published parts of this work in *Novel* and *English Literary History*.

TARA MacDONALD is an Assistant Professor of English at the University of Amsterdam. Her current research on Victorian sensation fiction has been published in *Critical Survey* (2011) and *The Cambridge Companion to Sensation Fiction* (2013), and she has co-edited, with Anne-Marie Beller, a special issue of *Women's Writing* titled "Beyond Braddon: Re-Assessing Female Sensationalists" (2013). In addition, she recently completed a monograph on the New Man in the late-Victorian novel and has published articles and book chapters on Victorian masculinity.

MARY POOVEY is Samuel Rudin University Professor in the Humanities and Professor of English at New York University. Her books include *Genres of the Credit Economy: Mediating Value in Eighteenth- and Nineteenth-Century Britain* (University of Chicago Press, 2008) and *A History of the Modern Fact* (University of Chicago Press, 1998).

ERIKA RAPPAPORT is Associate Professor of History at the University of California, Santa Barbara. Her publications include *Shopping for Pleasure: Women in the Making of London's West End* (Princeton University Press, 2000) and numerous articles on gender and consumption in Britain and its empire. She is currently editing a volume entitled *Consuming Behaviors: Identity, Politics and Pleasure in Twentieth-Century*

CONTRIBUTORS

Britain and is completing *An Acquired Taste: Tea, Empire and the Creation of a Global Consumer Culture*.

JILL RAPPOPORT is Associate Professor of English at the University of Kentucky and author of *Giving Women: Alliance and Exchange in Victorian Culture* (Oxford University Press, 2012). Her articles on women and gift economies in nineteenth-century literature appear in *Nineteenth-Century Literature, Victorian Literature and Culture,* and *Studies in English Literature 1500–1900*.

JANETTE RUTTERFORD is Professor of Financial Management at The Open University Business School. Her research interests are the history of investment, women investors, equity valuation, and pension fund management. Her most recent books include *Introduction to Stock Exchange Investment* (Palgrave, 3rd edition, 2007). She is the co-editor of *Women and Their Money 1700–1950: Essays on Women and Finance* (Routledge, 2009) and of *Men, Women, and Money: Perspectives on Gender, Wealth and Investment* (Oxford University Press, 2011).

LESLEE THORNE-MURPHY is Associate Professor of English at Brigham Young University. Her interests include nineteenth-century prose fiction, women's literature, and book history. Her articles on Charlotte M. Yonge, Elizabeth Barrett Browning, and Victorian short fiction have appeared in *Book History, Journal of Victorian Culture, Women's Writing,* and *Studies in English Literature 1500–1900*.

INDEX

Page numbers in *italics* refer to figures.

abolition, role of free trade in, 55, 55n36
adultery, 8, 62, 69–71, 129–30, 132, 169n17, 171, 175, 201–4
adulthood, marriage as criteria for, 145n7
alienation of women, in marriage, 66, 164–65
alimony, in Westmeath divorce, 135–37
"angel in the house," 119, 155, 166
anorexia nervosa, 35–38, 220, 221
Anti-Corn Law League bazaar (1845), 6–7, 41–59
army hospitals, Nightingale's campaign to improve, 78–87
Army Medical Statistics (Royal Commission), 78–79
Austen, Jane, *Sense and Sensibility,* 162, 163
"average man," Quetelet on, 91–92

bachelors: consumerism of, 14–15, 144–45, 155–58; criteria for adulthood of, 145n7; prostitution and, 150, 151
Bagehot, Walter, 196, 197
Bankruptcy Act of 1869, 194, 195
Barings Bank, 137–38
Bates, Joshua, 137–40, 141
bazaars, 43–44, 51, 58–59. *See also* Anti-Corn Law League bazaar

Beeton, Isabella, *Book of Household Management,* 212
Bentham, Jeremy, 98
birth control, infanticide as method of, 56–57
Blackwood, John, 74
blood, economic meanings of, 11, 120. *See also* Stoker, Bram
bodies of women: blushes in *Dracula* (Stoker), 116–17, 118; fasting by Plymley (Jane), 6, 30, 35–40; lactation in *Dracula* (Stoker), 11, 119–21; in *Romola* (Eliot), 8, 62, 70; in *St. Martin's Eve* (Wood), 183–84, 188
Booker, Beryl Lee, 144
bourgeois households: commodification of, 151; domesticity in, 149, 151, 154–55; domestic work in, 145, 149; gossip by women of, 187–89; rise of consumerism in, 103, 146
Braddon, Mary Elizabeth, 182n13
bread: in *Daily Telegraph* letters, 149; in gentry's response to food shortages, 33–34; regulation during food shortages, 26
breast milk: in *Dracula* (Stoker), 11, 119–21; economic meanings of, 11, 120
Brontë, Charlotte, 199; *Jane Eyre,* 171n21
Burckhardt, Jacob, *The Civilization of the Renaissance in Italy,* 64n7, 68, 68n11
Burke, Edmund, 31

INDEX

Burton, Isabel: commercial success of, 215; *The Inner Life of Syria, Palestine and the Holy Land,* 212–14, 215; medical practice of, 18, 208, 212–16

Burton, Richard, 212, 215

business practices, 16–18; information exchange in, 16–17; literary writings on, 17, 193–97, 205 (*See also* Riddell, Charlotte); as one of many arenas for female economic activity, 4; of women, 17–18, 197, 198, 201–4

Butler, Joseph, *Analogy of Religion,* 35

capitalism: anxiety about sustainability of, 118–19, 122–23; connection between vampirism and, 114–15, 122; gender roles complicated by, 170n18; literary writings on, 17, 193–97, 205 (*See also* Riddell, Charlotte); neoliberalism and, 223–24; self-sustaining economic activity in, 120–21

Carlyle, Thomas, 94

Caton, Eliza, 137–42, 138n46, 139n49

CD. *See* Contagious Diseases

census of 1851, 16, 94, 146–47

charitable work, 4–7; by Anti-Corn Law League, motivations for, 6–7, 48–50, 58–59; engagement in moral economy and, 28; medical practices in colonies as, 214; Plymley (Katherine) and, 5–6, 30, 31–32; in *Romola* (Eliot), 69–70

children: consumerism of, role of families in, 151–53; consumption of, in *Dracula* (Stoker), 121–22; feeding of, in *Romola* (Eliot), 8, 62, 69–70; as form of conspicuous consumption, 157–58; inheritance by, in primogeniture, 12, 128n2, 183; killing of, 52, 56–58, 183, 185–86; as legal property of fathers, 127n2, 131

China, economic progress in, 223

circulation: of gossip, 17, 179–82, 184–89; of medical information and supplies in colonies, 208, 210, 211–14, 217; of publications, 17, 67–68, 71–74, 190, 191n30; of women, 65–66

City, the (London): definition of, 193–94; Riddell's novels on, 194–205

civilizing process, medicine in, 213

Clarkson, Thomas, 28, 37

class. *See* social class

Cobden, Richard, 55n36

collecting, egoism in, 64

Collins, Wilkie, *The Woman in White,* 13, 162–75; coverture in, 167–71; disempowerment of men in, 13, 166–67, 171, 174; economic agency of women in, 13, 165–71, 175; legal reforms influencing, 169–70; marriage settlement in, 165–66, 166n9, 168; masculinity in, 163, 165, 170, 172–75; men marrying for money in, 164–71; social class in, 165, 171–74

colonies: *Dawn Island* (Martineau) on free trade in, 52–58; emigration to, as solution to costs of marriage, 158–61; medicine in (*See* medical practices); single women in, 158–59

commodification: of gossip, 184, 187; of the middle class, 151; of sensation novels, 190, 190n25; of women, 66, 149, 151

common law: on marriage, 15, 127n2, 131n12, 167, 168, 170; on primogeniture, 12

competition, Mill on necessity of, 223

conduct books, 2, 164

conjugal rights, 127, 131, 167n12, 170

consumerism, 13–15, 103, 143, 144–46, 151–53, 155–58, 161, 180

consumption, 11, 38, 99, 110, 111–12, 113, 157–58, 180. *See also* Stoker, Bram

Contagious Diseases (CD) Acts, 150, 151

coverture, 12, 12n17; definition of, 133, 167, 167n10; marriage settlements as alternative to, 166n9; in Westmeath marriage and divorce, 133–41; in *The Woman in White* (Collins), 167–71

INDEX

Crimean War: Martineau on, 85; Nightingale's experience in, 10, 78

Daily Telegraph (newspaper) letters, 13–15, 143–61. *See also* consumerism
Darwin, Charles, 158
Debtors Act of 1869, 194
debts: and gender, 14–15; in marriage, liability for, 127n2, 136; in *Romola* (Eliot), 66, 67, 69; in *The Woman in White* (Collins), 166
Defoe, Daniel, *Robinson Crusoe,* 1–2, 219
demand: insufficient, anxiety about effects of, 111, 112, 113; theory of value, 11, 50n22, 111, 123
Dickens, Charles, 193; on self-sustaining economic activity, 120–21; women in works of, 2
disease, in colonies, 209–10. *See also* Nightingale, Florence; hospitals
division of labor, gendered, origins of, 1, 222
divorce, 15, 127, 128, 128n3, 130, 133, 136, 142, 147, 169, 169n17. *See also* alimony, in Westmeath divorce; Westmeath, Emily
Divorce Act of 1857. *See* Matrimonial Causes Act of 1857
doctoring by women. *See* medical practices
doctress, use of term, 208, 209
domesticity: bourgeois, 149, 151, 154–55; in colonies, 57–58, 159–60; in *Dawn Island* (Martineau), 57–58; literature limiting women to sphere of, 2
domestic manuals: on household management, 212; for women travelers in colonies, 206–7, 213
domestic work. *See* labor, domestic
dowries, 66, 133, 141
dual-income families, 155n59
Duff Gordon, Lucie: commercial success of, 215, 215n14; *Letters from Egypt,* 209–12, 215; medical practice of, 18, 208–16

ecclesiastical courts, divorce in, 128n3, 131, 136
Economic Man, 1–5, 219, 220, 222, 224
economics: household management in, replacement of, 2, 9, 26; professionalization of, 117;female theorists of, rarity of, 9; writing on, boundaries between literary writing and, 193–97, 205. *See also* neoclassical economics
Economic Woman, 1–4, 18, 219, 220, 224
economy: alternative forms of, 16–17, 61, 180, 181, 208, 211, 215, 217–18; downturn in, 27–40, 203–4; emergence of modern concept of, 26–27; fear of stagnation in, 111, 112, 113, 122; as force of nature, in Riddell's novels, 203–4; relationships between household management and, 5, 26; and sacrifice, in *Romola* (Eliot), 7–8, 61–62, 68–74. *See also* free trade; moral economy; political economy
Edgeworth, Francis Ysidro, 106n25
Edgeworth, Maria, 106n25
Eliot, George, 60–74, 97–109; *Adam Bede,* 199; "Brother Jacob," 60; commercial success of, 60, 72, 74; control over works of, 73–74; *Daniel Deronda,* 105–7; *Middlemarch,* 10–11, 14, 97–109, 144n3; misers and thieves in works of, 60; neoclassical economics and, 10–11, 99–101, 100nn9–10, 108–9; *Principles of Political Economy* (Mill) read by, 99; revelations about gender of, 198–99; *Romola,* 7–8, 60–74, 98–99; royalties earned by, 60, 73–74; sacrificial exchange by, 61, 69, 73–74; *Scenes of Clerical Life,* 199; *Silas Marner,* 60, 72
elites. *See* gentry class
Ellis, Sarah Stickney, 2, 164
Ellis, William, 52n31
emigration: and medical practices, 18, 206–7, 208–16; as solution to costs of marriage, 143–44, 145, 158–61
Engels, Friedrich, 170n18, 222

231

INDEX

equality: gender, 169, 220–24; social, 222–23
equity law, 127n2, 131, 131n12, 170
ethical exchange, 4–8. *See also* moral economy; sacrifice
exchange, value in, vs. value in use, 97–98
Ezekiel, book of, 70n13

family, 12–15, 111–12, 151–53, 157–58, 174–75. See also *Daily Telegraph* letters
Faraday, Michael, 108
Farr, William, 78
Fawcett, Millicent Garrett, 9
financial journalism, 195–96
First Annual Statistical Report on the Health of the Army (Royal Commission), 79
food: campaign for free trade in, 43; in *Dracula* (Stoker), 122; gossip compared to, 180; in origins of women's economic activities, 8; in poor relief, 32; prices of, 26–28, 29, 31, 32; in *Romola* (Eliot), 8, 62, 70; shortages of, 5–6, 26–40
France, British wars with, economic effects of, 29–30, 29n15
free trade, 6–7, 41–59. *See also* Anti-Corn Law League

Galton, Francis, 87, 95, 95n32, 96
gemstones. *See* jewels
gender equality, 169, 220–24
gender roles: in capitalism, complication of, 170n18; in investing by Westmeath (Emily), 15, 135, 137–42; in Plymley family during food shortages, 30, 32, 33, 34, 35, 37–40; Riddell's defiance of, 197–99
genre: economic vs. literary writing, 193–96, 205; handbill vs. manuscript, 71–72; of Martineau vs. Nightingale, 82–83, 84–86; psychological realism, 196–97; realist novel, 193, 195–96,

205; sensation novel, 180–82, 190, 190n25, 191; travel narrative, 18, 208–16
gentry class, 5–6, 25–40
Gissing, George, 147; *The Odd Women,* 163
Gore, Catherine, 179–80, 179n1
gossip, 16–17, 179–92. *See also* Wood, Ellen
grain. *See* food
Great Exhibition of 1851, 41n1, 150
Greg, William Rathbone, "Why Are Women Redundant?," 147, 147n12
Gregory, John, *A Father's Legacy to His Daughters,* 38
Guerry, A. M., 89

Hall, Samuel Carter, 48n14
heredity: habits of, in *Middlemarch* (Eliot), 103; insanity and, 187–89; statistical approach to, 95, 95n32
heterosexuality, compulsory, in marriage, 163–64
hoarding: economic stagnation caused by, 111, 112; in *Romola* (Eliot), 62–65
Homestead Act, U. S., 159n84
Homo Economicus. *See* Economic Man
hospitals: colonial, 215, 216; military, Nightingale's campaign to improve, 78–87
household management: in economics, replacement of, 2, 9, 26; manuals on, 212; Owenite, 222; relationships between national economy and, 5, 26; women and, 145, 149. See also *œconomy*
housekeeping. *See* labor, domestic

identity: gender, fluidity of, 163–64; national, after emigration, 160; social class in, 5–6, 28–29
illiteracy: decline of, 71–72; historical meaning of, 71n14
immigration. *See* emigration
income gap, 224

232

indexes of vampirism, in *Dracula* (Stoker), 116–17, 116n14, 118
India, colonial, 1857 uprising in, 79
individualism, 1–2, 83, 84–86, 91–92, 219, 221–22
infanticide, 52, 56–58, 56n37
insanity, in *St. Martin's Eve* (Wood), 183, 188–89, 188n19
International Trade Union Confederation, 224
intersubjectivity, 11, 108, 219
introspection: in *Middlemarch* (Eliot), 102–4; in Riddell's novels, lack of, 194–95, 197
investments, of Westmeath (Emily), 15, 135, 137–42
Invisible Hand, 219

Japan, economic progress in, 223
Jevons, William Stanley, 10–11, 95, 95n32, 99, 100–101, 100n9, 102, 104, 105, 106n25, 107–8, 117
jewels, value of, 97–99, 98n2, 99n5, 105
Joint Stock Companies Act of 1856, 194
jointure, 128n2, 133–34

"keeping-while-giving," 74, 74n20, 186
Keynes, John Maynard, 138
Kingsley, Charles, 172n23
knowledge: in business practices of women, 16; in economic vs. literary writing, 194–95; Eliot's conception of, 64–65, 70, 72, 103; gossip as circulation of, 180–81; ingestion and absorption of, 70, 70n13; medical, 208, 214–16; statistical presentation of, 10, 83, 87–94

labor: Anti-Corn Law League bazaar on value of women's, 7, 50; *Dawn Island* (Martineau) on value of women's, 50–58; domestic, 14, 57–58, 145, 149, 153–55; gendered division of, origins of, 1, 222; reproductive, value of, free trade and, 56–58; theory of value, 49, 49n22, 112
lactation. *See* breast milk
lavement machine, 209–10
laws, economic: divorce, 15, 127, 128, 128n3, 142, 147, 169; equity, 127n2, 131, 131n12; and family finances, 12, 13, 15; on food shortages, 26; limitations of benefits to men, 13; poor, evolution of, 4–5, 27, 31n22; in Riddell's novels, 194, 195, 199–200. *See also specific laws*
Lewes, Agnes, 74
Lewes, George Henry (G. H.), 72, 74, 100, 199
Lewes, Thornton, 72, 74
libraries: circulating, 191n30; Medici, 67, 68. *See also* Eliot, George
Limited Liability Act of 1855, 194, 199–200
Linton, Eliza Lynn, "Girl of the Period," 152–53
literacy, rise of, 71–72, 71n14
lower middle class: fear of poverty, 148n16, 149–50; satire on, 147–48, 148n17; voting rights for, 150. See also *Daily Telegraph* letters.

Malthus, Thomas, 27, 56, 57, 158
Marcet, Jane, 9
marginal-utility school: definition of, 117; in *Dracula* (Stoker), 117–18; and market economy, 100–102, 104; rise of, 95, 99, 111, 112, 114, 117
marital status: in census of 1851, 146–47, 149; and women's property, 133–39, 166–71
market economy: and bazaars, 48–50, 58–59; Eliot's critique of, 61, 104; vs. gossip economy, 181, 182; and marginal-utility school, 100–102, 104
market socialism, 223
marriage: common law on, 15, 127n2, 131n12, 167, 168, 170; compulsory heterosexuality in, 163–64; consumerism in context of, 13–15; as criteria

for adulthood, 145n7; delayed, consequences of, 146, 150–51, 156–57, 173n24; economic stability vs. autonomy in, 15, 162; emigration as solution to costs of, 143–44, 145, 158–61; family finances in, 12–15; insanity as disqualifier for, 188, 188n19; settlements, 127n2, 156–66, 166n9, 168; as socially sanctioned prostitution, 163; weakening of patriarchal authority in, 147; women in, 12n17, 13, 14, 39, 66, 127, 127n2, 129, 129n6, 130, 133–41, 135n29, 142, 144, 158–60, 163, 164–71, 175. *See also* alimony, in Westmeath divorce; *Daily Telegraph* letters; divorce

Married Women's Property Act of 1856, failure of, 169–70

Married Women's Property Acts of 1870 and 1882, 12n17, 127, 128, 142, 169n16

Marshall, Alfred, 95

Martineau, Harriet, 50–59; abolitionism of, 55; *Dawn Island*, 7, 45, 50–59, 53; "Demerara," 55; *England and Her Soldiers*, 10, 78, 79, 83–87, 89n14; *Illustrations of Political Economy*, 10, 51, 57n42, 84, 85; "Independent Industry for Women," 168; needlework of, 45, 51, 58–59; as popularizer of economics, 9

Marx, Karl: on Economic Man, 1, 4; on gendered division of labor, 1, 222; on vampirism and capitalism, connection between, 114–15, 122

masculinity: and consumerism, 14–15, 152–53; economic agency of wealthy women and, 163, 165, 170, 172–75; physicality in, 172n23

mathematics: establishment of political economy as form of, 9, 77, 95; statistics as form of, 90–91

Matrimonial Causes Act of 1857, 15, 127, 128, 128n3, 142, 169–70

matter, laws of, 101

mean distribution, 92

medical practices: manuals on, 213; professionalization of, 216–17; of women in colonies, 17–18, 206–18

men: in Anti-Corn Law League bazaar, 45–46; consumerism of, vs. women, 14–15, 152–53; in cooking and consumption, 33–34; dependence on women for financial stability, 13, 163–71; in divorce, responsibilities of, 15; in gossip economy, 181, 187–88; Riddell's depictions of, 197–98; sensation novels by, 191; threats to economic power of, 13, 166–67, 171, 174

Menger, Carl, 117

middle class: commodification of, 151; consumerism and, 13–15, 103, 143, 145–46; domestic work by, thriftiness in, 14, 145, 149, 153–55; dual-income families in, 155n59; gossip by women of, 187–89; satire on, 147–48, 148n17; servants used by, 154–55. See also *Daily Telegraph* letters

Mill, Harriet Taylor, "Enfranchisement of Women," 169

Mill, John Stuart: on fixed laws in political economy, 100–101; Jevons's critique of, 100–101, 100n9; *On Liberty*, 223; *Principles of Political Economy*, 9, 99, 158; on social class relations, 94; *The Subjection of Women*, 223; on theories of value, 98, 99, 105; women in works of, 9

modern girls, *Daily Telegraph* letters on, 152–53

Moore, William, 207; *Family Medicine for India*, 213

moral economy, 4–8, 25–40

More, Hannah, *The Riot*, 29

mortality: in army, Nightingale on, 78–83, 88–91; in *Dawn Island* (Martineau), 52, 56–57

motherhood: *Daily Telegraph* letters on, 153–61; in *Dracula* (Stoker), 119–21; in *St. Martin's Eve* (Wood), 185–86; value of, free trade and, 56–58; in Westmeath marriage, 129–32

Mudie, Charles Edward, 191n30

narrative strategies: of Riddell, 193–96, 198–200, 204–5; of Wood, gossip as, 181, 182, 189–92, 190n26
needlework, 7, 45, 50, 51, 58–59
neoclassical economics: consumption in, 11; links between Eliot and, 10–11, 99–101, 100nn9–10, 108–9; on poverty and wealth as measures of human souls, 108. See also Jevons, William Stanley
neoliberalism, 221, 223–24
New Poor Law of 1834, 4–5, 31n22
Nicholl, Sir John, 129n6, 132
Nightingale, Florence, 10, 77–96; campaign to improve military hospitals, 78–87; *A Contribution to the Sanitary History of the British Army*, 78, 88–89, 88n13; and *England and Her Soldiers* (Martineau), 10, 78, 79, 83–87; "In Memoriam," 91, 93–94; *Mortality of the British Army*, 78, 88; *Notes on Hospitals*, 79; *Notes on Matters Affecting the Health of the British Army*, 78–83, *80, 81,* 82n6, 90, 92; Quetelet's influence on, 88, 91–94; religious views of, 10, 93–94, 96; statistics used by, 10, 83, 87–94; understanding of mathematics, 90–91; on "vulgar public," 83, 83n8, 88, 88n11; wealth of, 87
Norton, Caroline, *English Laws for Women in the Nineteenth Century,* 169
Nugent, Emily. See Westmeath, Emily Nugent, Marchioness of
Nugent, George. See Westmeath, George Nugent, Marquis of
Nugent, Rosa, 130, 131

œconomy, 4, 9, 26, 38. See also household management
Owenism, 222

pain, in *Middlemarch* (Eliot), 104–7
Paley, William, *Principles of Moral and Political Philosophy,* 35

paraphernalia, 135n29
Parliament: divorce by private act of, 128n3, 169, 169n17; response to food shortages by, 33. See also specific laws
paternalism, in moral economy, 5–6, 26
patriarchal authority, in marriage, weakening of, 147
pay gap, 224
Pechey, Edith, 215–16
Peel, Robert, 55n36
pension, of Westmeath (Emily), 135, 137
philanthropy. See charitable work
Phillips, Catharine, *Considerations on the Causes of the High Price of Grain,* 29
Physiocracy, 120, 120n22
pin money, 129, 129n6, 130, 133, 135
Pitt, William, 29–30
Playfair, William, 89
pleasure, 98, 104–7, 144–45, 155–56
Plymley, Jane, 28, 35–40; death of, 30, 36; efforts in response to food shortages, 6, 30, 35–40; health problems of, 35, 36; Quaker influence on, 35n46
Plymley, Joseph: on cause of food shortages, 32; children of, 28, 39; efforts in response to food shortages, 6, 33–34; Katherine's accounts of opinions of, 29–30; public and private virtues of, 37; second wife of, 39
Plymley, Katherine, 5–6, 28–40; on cause of food shortages, 32; commitment to poor relief, 31–32; on dietary changes by gentry, 33–35; on grain price-fixing, 32; on Jane's dietary asceticism, 6, 30, 35–39; on Joseph's opinions, 29–30; motivations for charitable work of, 5–6, 30; political views of, 28–30; religious views of, 34–35; social class in identity of, 5–6, 28–29
polar-area diagrams, 88–91; in *A Contribution to the Sanitary History of the British Army* (Nightingale), 88–89, 88n13; in *England and Her Soldiers* (Martineau), 79, 89n14; invention of, 89; Nightingale's opinion of, 88; in *Notes on Matters Affecting the Health*

of the British Army (Nightingale), 79, 80, 81, 82, 90

political economy, 8–12; class relations addressed in, 94–95; in *Daily Telegraph* debate, 148, 157–58; fixed laws in, debate over existence of, 100–101; invisibility of women in theory of, 9; vs. moral economy, ideals of, 4–5, 26; persistence of moral economy in, 4–5, 27, 39; on poor relief, 27, 31; rise of, 4–5, 8–9, 26–27; as science, 9, 77, 95; secularization of, 94–96; value in use vs. exchange in, 98; women's contributions to development of, 9–10

political progress, linked to economic progress, 223–24

portable property, medical chests as, 208

poverty: absolute, 224; evolution of poor laws, 4–5, 27, 31n22; food riots and, 26–28, 29; free trade as form of aid, 6–7, 49; lower-middle-class fear of, 148n16, 149–50; married women as paupers, 142; as measure of human souls, 108; persistence of moral economy in, 27; political vs. moral economy on aid, 27, 31

prices, artificially inflated, at Anti-Corn Law League bazaar, 6, 44–45, 49–50. *See also* food

primogeniture, 12, 128n2, 183

print culture: business practices of women in expansion of, 16; gossip in, 189–92; handbills vs. manuscripts in, 71–72

private sphere: literature limiting women to, 2; women's opportunities for virtue in, 37–38; women travelers' access to, 207, 210

professionalization: of economics, 117; of medicine, 216–17; of women travelers, 208, 217; of women writers, 3, 9, 17, 73, 202

property ownership by women, 147, 168–70; common law on, 127n2, 167; Married Women's Property Acts on, 12n17, 127, 128, 142, 169n16

prostitution: debate over regulation of, 151; and delayed marriage, *Daily Telegraph* letters on, 150, 151; marriage as socially sanctioned, 163

pseudonyms, male, of women writers, 198–99, 202

public sphere: business practices in, 193–95, 204–5; debate over consumerism in, 143, 150; women's entry into, 2n4; women's opportunities for virtue in, 37–38. *See also Daily Telegraph* letters

Quetelet, Adolphe, 88, 89, 91–94, 91n19, 93nn23–24

Reform Act of 1867, 150

regression analysis, 95, 95n32

religious views: in census of 1851, 94; in *Daily Telegraph* debate, 148; of Nightingale, 10, 93–94, 96; of Plymley (Jane), 35n46; of Plymley (Katherine), 34–35

Ricardo, David, 50n22

Riddell, Charlotte (Mrs. J. H.), 17, 193–205; *Austin Friars,* 198, 199, 200–204; businessmen in works of, 194, 196–97; businesswomen in works of, 194, 197, 198, 202–3, 204; *City and Suburb,* 198, 202; commercial success of, 197; decline in popularity of, 194, 195; financial journalism and, 195–96; financial problems in family of, 194; *George Geith of Fen Court,* 196–97, 198; laws in works of, 194, 195, 199–200; *A Life's Assize,* 199; *Mitre Court,* 200; *Mortomley's Estate,* 193, 195; obituary of, 205; pseudonyms of, 198, 199, 202; *The Race for Wealth,* 199; reviews of novels of, 193, 194, 195, 196, 197, 198, 199, 200; *The Senior Partner,* 195, 200; *A Struggle for Fame,* 198, 198n12; *Too Much Alone,* 199

Ritchie, Anne Thackeray, 196

royalties, book, 60, 73–74
Ruskin, John: "The Ethics of the Dust," 111–12, 114–15; on insufficient demand, 111, 112, 113; *Munera Pulveris,* 112, 114; on pursuit of knowledge, 64–65; on self-sustaining economic activity, 120–21; on vampires, 114–15

sacrifice: definition of, 61–62; by Eliot as writer, 61, 69, 73–74; as female form of exchange, 61; human, in *Dawn Island* (Martineau), 52, 56–58, 56n37; in *Middlemarch* (Eliot), 107; in *Romola* (Eliot), 7–8, 61–62, 68–74; surplus of value as end of, 62
Scharlieb, Mary, 215–16, 216n15
scientific method, in economics, 99, 101, 102
secularization, of political economy, 94–96
self-help, rise of, 4, 6
self-interest: of Economic Woman, 2, 18, 219; Jevons on, 104, 107–8; in *Romola* (Eliot), 61–64, 73
self-sacrifice. *See* sacrifice
sensation novels, 162–75, 179–92; financial insecurity in, 180; gossip in, 181–82, 188; market for, 190, 190n25; by men vs. women, 191
servants: gossip by, 17, 181, 184–87; middle-class families' use of, 154–55
Shaw, George Bernard, *Mrs. Warren's Profession,* 163
Simmel, Georg, 61–62
single men. *See* bachelors
single women: in colonies, 158–59; vs. married women, consumerism of, 14, 144; as redundant females, 146–47
slavery. *See* abolition
Smith, Adam: on Invisible Hand, 219; on labor theory of value, 49, 49–50n22; and poor relief, 31; on value of jewels, 97–98, 98n2; *Wealth of Nations,* 97–98

Smith, Barbara Leigh, *A Brief Summary in Plain English of the Most Important Laws of England Concerning Women,* 167n10, 169
social class: economic options limited by, 16; in Plymley's (Katherine) identity, 5–6, 28–29; political economy on questions of, 94–95; in *The Woman in White* (Collins), 165, 171–74. *See also Daily Telegraph* letters; *specific classes*
socialism: market, 223; Owenite, 222
social sciences, use of statistics in, 87–88
statistics: applied, 95–96; as form of mathematics, 90–91; Nightingale's use of, 10, 83, 87–94; origins of use in social sciences, 87–88; pie charts in, 89, 90; religion linked to, 10, 93–94, 96; in university curricula, 95–96, 96n33
Stephenson, J., 53
Stoker, Bram, *Dracula,* 11–12, 110–23; anxiety about consumption in, 113–23; breast milk in, 11, 119–21; conspicuous consumption in, 110; extravagant consumption in, 113–19; indexes of vampirism in, 116–17, 116n14, 118; marginal-utility theory in, 117–18; paradox of female demand in, 110–13
subjectivist theory of value. *See* Jevons, William Stanley
sugar: boycott on, 34n37, 36; tariffs on, 55n36
sustainability: of capitalism, anxiety about, 118–19, 122–23; in ideal of self-sustaining economic activity, 120–21
Sutherland, John, 78
sympathy: Eliot on need for education in, 60, 65; in *Romola* (Eliot), 65, 68–73; in *St. Martin's Eve* (Wood), 183, 189

taxes: Plymley (Katherine) on rise in, 30, 31; during wars with France,

29–30n15, 30. *See also* Anti-Corn Law League bazaar
Tilt, Edward, 207
travelers, women, 18, 206–18. *See also* medical practices.
Trollope, Anthony, 193; *Can You Forgive Her?*, 202; *The Prime Minister,* 202

use vs. exchange, value in, 97–98
utilitarianism, Eliot on, 61, 67, 67n10, 70

value: exchange of, in sacrifice, 61–62; of gossip, 181, 182; of medical supplies, 208; theories of, 7, 9–11, 49, 49–50n22, 50–59, 97–99, 102, 104, 105, 111, 112, 123
vampirism, connection between capitalism and, 114–15, 122. *See also* Stoker, Bram
Veblen, Thorstein, 99
virtue, public vs. private, Plymley family views on, 35, 37–38
voting rights: *Daily Telegraph* letters on, 150, 150n35; expansion of, 150

Walras, Léon, 117
wars, with France, economic effects of, 29–30, 29–30n15
wealth: appearance of, during food shortages, 31; as measure of human souls, 108; of Nightingale, 87; women's, 13, 15, 163–71, 175. *See also* Westmeath, Emily
Wedgwood, Josiah, 28
Wellington, Duke of, 132, 135, 136–37, 136n34, 138
Westmeath, Emily Nugent, Marchioness of, 15, 127–42; alimony owed to, 135–37; alternative sources of income for, 15, 135–42; articles of separation of, 130, 130n10, 132, 132n16, 135; children of, 129, 130–31; coverture and, 133–41; cruelty in marriage of, 131–33; legal costs to, 133, 133n20; in litigation over divorce, 131–33; marriage of, 129–31; married name used by, 140n53; pamphlets produced by, 129n6, 137; pin money of, 129, 130, 133, 135; premarital contract of, 133–35; youth of, 128–29
Westmeath, George Nugent, Marquis of, 129–42; alimony owed by, 135–37; articles of separation of, 130, 130n10, 132, 132n16, 135; children of, 129–31, 130n8, 132; cruelty in marriage of, 131–33; extramarital affairs of, 129–30, 132; Irish estates of, 130, 133–34; legal costs to, 133; in litigation over divorce, 131–33; marriage of, 129–31; pamphlets produced by, 129n6
Wilberforce, William, 28, 37
Wilde, Oscar, 222–23
Wilson, George, 43n6
Wood, Ellen, 179–92; in *Argosy* (magazine), 180; commercial success of, 180–81, 192; conventional reputation of, 180, 180n6; *Danesbury House,* 180; *East Lynne,* 181–82; financial problems in family of, 180; gossip as narrative strategy of, 181, 182, 189–92, 190n26; *Mildred Arkell,* 191; *St. Martin's Eve,* 16–17, 179–92, 191n30; *Verner's Pride,* 191
working class: gossip in, 17; women as primary breadwinners in, 170n18. *See also* servants
World Bank, 224
writers, women: businesswomen compared to, 202; commercial success of, 3, 9, 17, 180–81, 182, 191–92, 208, 214–15, 216–18; and competition with men, 175; on economic theory, 9; as Economic Woman, 3; male pseudonyms of, 198–99; Riddell's depiction of, 198, 198n12, 200. *See also specific writers*

Young, Arthur, 31

www.ingramcontent.com/pod-product-compliance
Lightning Source LLC
Chambersburg PA
CBHW020123240426
43673CB00038B/570